RECLAIMING THE DON

An Environmental History of Toronto's Don River Valley

A small river in a big city, the Don is often overlooked when it comes to explaining Toronto's growth. With *Reclaiming the Don*, Jennifer L. Bonnell unearths the missing story of the relationship between river, valley, and city from the establishment of the town of York in the 1790s to the construction of the Don Valley Parkway in the 1960s. Demonstrating how mosquito-ridden lowlands, frequent floods, and over-burdened municipal waterways shaped the city's development, *Reclaiming the Don* illuminates the impact of the valley as a physical and conceptual place on Toronto's development.

Bonnell explains how for more than two centuries the Don has served as a source of raw materials, a sink for wastes, and a place of refuge for people pushed to the edges of society, as well as the site of numerous improvement schemes that have attempted to harness the river and its valley to build a prosperous metropolis. Exploring the interrelationship between urban residents and their natural environments, she shows how successive generations of Toronto residents have imagined the Don as an opportunity, a refuge, and an eyesore. Combining extensive research with in-depth analysis, *Reclaiming the Don* will be a must-read for anyone interested in the history of Toronto's development.

JENNIFER L. BONNELL is an assistant professor in the Department of History at McMaster University.

Reclaiming the Don

*An Environmental History
of Toronto's Don River Valley*

JENNIFER L. BONNELL

UNIVERSITY OF TORONTO PRESS
Toronto Buffalo London

© University of Toronto Press 2014
Toronto Buffalo London
www.utppublishing.com
Printed in the U.S.A.

ISBN 978-1-4426-4384-0 (cloth)
ISBN 978-1-4426-1225-9 (paper)

Printed on acid-free paper with vegetable-based inks.

Library and Archives Canada Cataloguing in Publication

Bonnell, Jennifer, 1971–, author
Reclaiming the Don : an environmental history of Toronto's Don River Valley /
Jennifer L. Bonnell.

Includes bibliographical references and index.
ISBN 978-1-4426-4384-0 (bound)   ISBN 978-1-4426-1225-9 (pbk.)

1. Don River Valley (Ont.) – Environmental conditions – History.   I. Title.

FC3097.56.B65 2014   971.3'541   C2014-903352-4

Significant portions of chapter 5 were published in the *Canadian Historical Review* as
"An Intimate Understanding of Place: Charles Sauriol and Toronto's Don River Valley,
1927–1989" 92, no. 4 (December 2011). Portions of chapter 4 were published in *Reshaping
Toronto's Waterfront*, ed. Gene Desfor and Jennefer Laidley (University of Toronto Press,
2011).

University of Toronto Press acknowledges the financial assistance to its publishing
program of the Canada Council for the Arts and the Ontario Arts Council, an agency of
the Government of Ontario.

 Canada Council   Conseil des Arts
for the Arts   du Canada

 ONTARIO ARTS COUNCIL
CONSEIL DES ARTS DE L'ONTARIO
an Ontario government agency
un organisme du gouvernement de l'Ontario

University of Toronto Press acknowledges the financial support of the Government of
Canada through the Canada Book Fund for its publishing activities.

This book has been published with the help of a grant from the Canadian Federation
for the Humanities and Social Sciences, through the Awards to Scholarly Publications
Program, using funds provided by the Social Sciences and Humanities Research
Council.

To Scott, Will, and Maya –
my home and my heart

Contents

Colour plates follow page 138

List of Illustrations

Maps

Illustrations

Colour plates (following page 138)

Acknowledgments

Many people helped to bring this book into being. Thanks first to the dedicated citizen activists, local historians, and "lost rivers" enthusiasts who have worked to imagine a different future for the Don River Valley and to bring public awareness to its past, especially John Wilson and Helen Mills. Their enthusiasm for my research and their love for the valley assured me that I was doing something worthwhile.

Many others provided assistance and information. Thanks to staff at the City of Toronto Archives, especially John Huzil and Lawrence Lee, whose knowledge of the city helped to build my understanding. Michael Moir, Archivist at York University's Clara Thomas Archives and Special Collections, shared his detailed knowledge of the Toronto waterfront. Jeff Hubbell at the Toronto Port Authority Archives and Sean Smith at the Archives of Ontario provided kind assistance and support. I am very grateful for the financial support provided by the University of Toronto, Ontario Graduate Scholarship program, the Canadian Federation for University Women, and the Social Sciences and Humanities Research Council of Canada (SSHRC) during the research and writing of this book.

Ruth Sandwell helped me to see the possibilities of a place like the Don. Through her I encountered the field of environmental history and many of its practitioners across Canada and beyond. Her warmth, professionalism, and dedication to her work as a historian continue to inspire my teaching and research. Bill Turkel's interest in the project from an early stage and his unconventional approach to academic endeavours nurtured the development of this book and helped to shape its guiding arguments. And for her keen critical eye and her constructive comments on earlier drafts of this work, I would like to thank Cecilia Morgan.

Early on in my research, I found myself at the Toronto Reference Library, printing and taping together a mosaic of fire insurance plans in an attempt to make sense of what was a dynamic and confusing historical landscape. Generous and patient assistance from University of Toronto GIS and Map Librarian Marcel Fortin opened up a world of possibilities in using Geographic Information Systems (GIS) to achieve the same ends. With financial support from the Network in Canadian History and Environment (NiCHE) and skilled assistance from University of Toronto Geography student Jordan Hale, we produced the Don Valley Historical Mapping Project, an online database of geo-spatial information on the environmental and industrial history of the Don watershed. The project greatly facilitated my ability to interpret the historical geography of the area. It remains a resource for a broader community of researchers seeking geographic information on the Don Valley and Toronto's east end.

It has been a pleasure to work with the scholarly publications staff at the University of Toronto Press. Len Husband's enthusiasm for the manuscript from the beginning and his relaxed and capable approach helped to demystify the world of academic publishing. Frances Mundy guided the book through its production, and Jim Leahy's sharp eye as copy editor improved its consistency and flow. Thanks to Rajiv Rawat for his creativity and persistence in producing the book's four custom maps. Insightful comments from H. Viv Nelles and Steve Penfold helped me to see the valley for the river and convinced me of the merits of incorporating a highway history. Steve read the entire manuscript a second time and guided its final evolution, for which I am in his debt. Thorough and thoughtful assessments provided by two anonymous reviewers also greatly improved this book.

A number of other people deserve mention here. Gene Desfor supported this project in multiple ways, funding archival image purchases from his SSHRC collaborative research grant on urban waterfronts, commenting on chapter drafts, and sharing his deep knowledge and passion for the history of Toronto's waterfront. Wendy Wickwire's passionate advocacy for her students is renowned; I am grateful to have been one of them. I would like to thank Larry MacDonald, who many years ago sparked my interest in history. Thanks also to Adele Freeman, Amy Thurston, and Ken Dion of the Toronto and Region Conservation Authority for their assistance at various points in my research. To Kristin Lindell, Erika Cordes, Cecilia Brumér, and Anya Kater, thanks for many years of friendship and encouragement. And for Friday dinners and the respite of a playdate, thanks to Judith Bowden and Jeff Cummings.

Support from a dynamic and growing community of environmental historians in the Toronto area nurtured the development of this book at various stages. Thanks especially to Ben Bradley, Jim Clifford, and Jay Young, who commented on earlier drafts of this work and helped me to draw out its major conclusions. Collegial support was also found at the meetings of the Toronto and Area Environmental History Reading Group and the Changing Urban Waterfronts group. For revelry, gossip, and encouragement, thanks to the women of the Toronto Area Women's Canadian History Group. Among them, special thanks to Alison Norman, for her friendship and her no-nonsense approach to pregnancy, motherhood, and academic life.

The Department of History at the University of Guelph gave me a warm welcome and the opportunity to build my skills as a historian. A heartfelt thanks especially to Stuart McCook, Peter Goddard, Cathy Wilson, and Catherine Carstairs, who welcomed me as a colleague and helped to make my stay such a pleasant and productive one. Generous support from the L.R. Wilson Institute for Canadian History at McMaster University contributed to the book's rich visual presentation. My students continue to challenge and inspire me, and remind me that I'm on the right path.

Writing this book has reminded me of the vital supports of family. Support from Betty and Morley Singer gave me the opportunity to pursue a career in history. Gail Singer provided humour, good company, and memorable meals throughout the project. My mother, Pam Bonnell, gave her support to all of us – in the garden, in the kitchen, and over the phone. Melissa and Mark Collins believed in me. My father Rick Bonnell and his partner Leslie Whyte were always there to cheer my achievements and bolster my resolve. Will and Maya brought joy and welcome distraction in many late afternoons at the playground and never failed to remind me where my priorities lay. To Scott go my greatest thanks, for his love and unwavering support throughout the writing of this book.

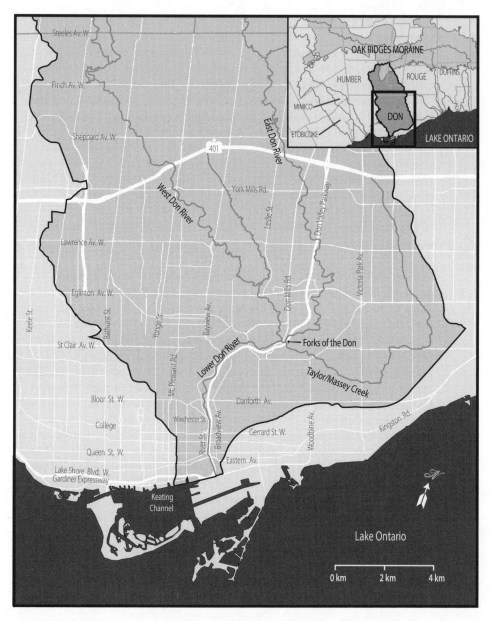

Map 1 The Don River Watershed. (Map composed by Rajiv Rawat using boundary data courtesy of the Toronto and Region Conservation Authority.)

Introduction

On 31 July 1958, Princess Margaret visited Toronto as one of many stops on an official tour of Canada. Her visit sparked weeks of wrangling by civic politicians about the proposed route of her tour through the city and the duration of her exposure to various publics. In her highly choreographed visit, the princess was to arrive at Malton Airport (today's Pearson International Airport) late on the evening of 30 July and meet briefly with dignitaries before travelling by special train into the city. She would "spend the night aboard the train in a quiet spot in the Don valley between Rosedale and Don stations." At noon the following day, her train would pull up at a siding at Riverdale Park, where she would greet the public and assembled schoolchildren from a footbridge over the Don River before carrying on to City Hall.[1]

Among the concerns of local residents and politicians alike was just what Toronto she would see from her rail car, and what impression of the city she would carry away following her brief visit. Responding to City Council's last-minute frenzy of tidying in preparation for the royal visit, a *Toronto Daily Star* editorial admonished:

> The mayor and other officials of Toronto have good cause to be ashamed of the filthy condition of that section of the Don river along which Princess Margaret will be driven to Riverdale park. With belated zeal they have rushed a crew of laborers armed with rakes and pikes and disinfectants to tidy the ground and sweeten the atmosphere that Her Highness may not learn how Toronto has befouled one of its beauty spots.

The editors went on to compare the city's efforts to that of "courtiers waving handkerchiefs dipped in perfume before the nostrils of the king of France as he drove through the tenements of Paris, that his majesty's nostrils might not be offended by the odor from the open drains."[2] Satirically titled "Our Perfumed Don," the editorial made no further reference to perfume, noting only the city's efforts to disinfect the rank waters of the river by scattering chloride of lime along its banks.

Like a game of telephone, however, the elements of the story became confused through many retellings in the years following the princess's visit. Rather than being about a quick (and surely futile) effort to "cleanse" the river with disinfectant, the story became even more absurd still, with city workers pouring perfume into the river to please the princess as she waved from the footbridge. The Royal Commission on the Future of the Toronto Waterfront repeated this version of the story in 1992, noting that "the City had perfume poured into the Don, to mask its stench."[3] A different version of the story had appeared ten years earlier, when *Toronto Star* writer Jack Brehl commented in a review of local conservationist and writer Charles Sauriol's 1981 book, *Remembering the Don*, that the "stream itself got so turgid and polluted that a few years ago it had to be perfumed to keep from offending the sensibilities of the Queen as she walked across a footbridge."[4] Shortly after Brehl's comment was printed, Sauriol received a letter from Dorothy B. Lewis of the York Pioneer and Historical Society. Lewis described a vivid dream or memory she had about the river and asked Sauriol to verify if the events had indeed happened:

> When the present Queen Mother and George VI visited Toronto in 1939, the school children were gathered in the amphitheatre of Riverdale Park, on the east side of the Don, south of the Viaduct. Here they were greeted by Their Majestys [*sic*]. Then the cavalcade drove to the foot bridge over the Don, leading to the Zoo. Here they dismounted and walked over the bridge. As we all know, the Don does not always smell like a rose. This disturbed the city council. It is my "memory" that they poured gallons of scented water up-stream, arranging that this would be flowing under the bridge at the appointed time.[5]

Ms Lewis apparently scanned newspaper accounts of the visit for references to perfume, with no success (indeed the 1939 accounts of the event in the Toronto papers make no mention of perfume). No record exists of Sauriol's response, but it seems most likely that Lewis, and Brehl, confused the 1939 royal visit with Princess Margaret's 1958 visit to the same location.[6]

The story of the princess's visit and its subsequent transmutations highlights three central themes in the history of the relationship between the river, the valley, and the city. First, it emphasizes the nature of this relationship as mutually constitutive. Just as the river and its valley shaped the city, city processes transformed the river valley, producing the conditions that threatened to offend the princess. And for the princess, impressions of the river and its valley would shape her impression of the city as a whole. Tied up in this is the nature of Toronto in this period as an aspirational city, a place where appearances mattered. For Toronto residents, and for appraising foreign eyes, it was not to be seen as a place that befouled its beauty spots.

The choice of the Lower Don River Valley as the location to show off the city not only to the outside world, but also to its own residents, illustrates these tensions between material conditions and their appearances, the city and its disagreeable edges. On a footbridge overlooking the grassy amphitheatre of Riverdale Park, with the Don running beneath her, Princess Margaret would kick off her official visit to the city of Toronto. Presumably this choice was not a casual one: Mayor Phillips and his advisers saw in the sweeping panorama of Riverdale Park, with its easy proximity to rail and its ample space for crowds, a fitting place to present the city to the princess, and the princess to the city. The landscape of the Lower Don would represent Toronto to the world, while reflecting back to Toronto residents who they were and how far they had come. Pleasing photo opportunities would be produced for the newspapers and the evening television news, media that happily excised the river's gag-inducing stench. Accounts of the event suggest that the city's superficial efforts were successful: like the roughly 2,000 Torontonians who gathered to greet the princess as she stepped from her train, reporters seemed willing to accept the ruse of a clean river in order to focus their attention on the princess herself, who, "radiant in blue," stepped slowly across the "red-carpeted footbridge across the freshly-cleaned Don river ... waving and smiling at children."[7]

Second, the story of the city's preparations for the royal visit points to the place of pollution in the modern city, both in the sense of its physical location at the margins of the metropolis, and its location in public perception as either an indication, or a repudiation, of a city's modern status. While most nineteenth- and twentieth-century Torontonians were prepared to accept pollution as an unfortunate by-product of prosperity, a smaller number used it as evidence of how far the city still had to go to define itself as a modern metropolis. Linked to this is the significance of notions of improvement in the larger story of the river, the valley, and the city, and the historical tendency of civic authorities to respond only in times of crisis, and even then to adopt solutions that failed to address the root of the problem. In trying to make a grossly polluted urban waterway presentable for a moment in time – the princess's walk across the footbridge – city officials applied a band-aid solution to a real and serious problem. The Lower Don River in 1958 was very likely more polluted than it had been at any other point in its history: rapid urban development and a legacy of inadequate sewage infrastructure in the postwar years had turned the Don and other Toronto-area rivers into little more than open sewers, receivers of partially treated efflu-ents from a series of overburdened upstream treatment plants. Just eight years before the princess's visit, in 1950, a provincial conservation report had identified the Don as Ontario's most polluted waterway.[8] That city officials waited until the day before the princess's arrival to clean up the offending stream is also emblematic of what constituted, in 1958, well over a century of unrealized intentions. Reaching back to the early 1830s, a long line of studies and plans commissioned for the river and the Toronto harbour at its mouth had met with apathetic or otherwise ineffectual responses by governing authorities. This legacy of mounting pollution and inadequate response created the river that threatened to embarrass Toronto in front of the world in July 1958. The stench of the river alone made the past undeniably present.

Finally, the story of the visit points to the interconnections between place and public memory. Returning to Dorothy Lewis and her efforts to decipher the story of the perfumed river as memory or dream, actual event or subconscious fabrication, we encounter an example of the ways that memory shapes our understanding of past events, and the ways that landscape works to incite and affect such memories. A history enthusiast herself, Lewis's review of newspaper accounts for references to perfume mirrors my own efforts to comb the records for traces of perfume and princesses, and, in the book more generally, to piece together a coherent narrative of events through a multiplicity of sources, some trustworthy, some not. The incident, and its reverbera-tions in individual and collective memory, serves as a useful illustration of the ways in which we make sense of the past.

This book explores the history of Toronto's Don River Valley and the relationship between the river, the valley, and the city that developed alongside and around it. Spanning over 200 years, from the establish-ment of the town of York in the 1790s to the present, it investigates the changing uses and conceptions of the river valley over time, and the ways the river valley, in turn, shaped the evolving city. This small urban river, I find, played a surprisingly large role in the city's development, alternately enabling and constraining its growth as a provider of raw materials and a destroyer of property, lives, and livelihoods; as a receiver of wastes and a source of disease; as a corridor for movement along the valley bottom; and as a formidable barrier to circulation across the tablelands. It also claimed an important place in the history of ideas about the city and its future, its landscapes conceived by different groups in different periods as verdant wilderness, picturesque countryside, polluted periphery, predestined industrial district, restorative retreat, vital refuge, dangerous underworld. Over the course of the river's relationship with the city, a series of improvement schemes, from major channel realignment to highway construction and parkland acquisition, have mobilized these competing ideas, harnessing the river and its valley as a transformative force in building a prosperous and productive future metropolis. The relative success of these plans, and the effects they had upon valley ecologies, upon individual lives, and upon the life of the city, are explored in this book in order to better understand the history of relationships between urban residents and the natural environments upon which they depend.

From its headwaters in the Oak Ridges Moraine, a vast, glacially formed landscape of rolling hills and porous gravels north of the city, to its outfall thirty-eight kilometres south, in Toronto harbour, the Don drains a watershed of approximately 360 square kilometres. The river system includes two main branches: the East and West Don, which join to form a single stream, the Lower Don River, at the forks about seven kilometres north of Lake Ontario. A major tributary of the river, Taylor-Massey Creek, also joins the main stream at the confluence (see map 1). Other significant tributaries include German Mills Creek, which runs through the municipalities of Richmond Hill and Markham in the northeast section of the watershed, and Wilket Creek, which runs from Bayview Avenue and York Mills Road southeast to join the West Don near Eglinton Avenue. Like the other six watersheds in the Toronto Area,[9] each of which originates along the southern margin of the Oak Ridges Moraine and follows a similar southeasterly direction to Lake Ontario, the Don's wide valleys and deep signature ravines are the result of glacial action during the last ice age and drainage patterns that developed after the glaciers receded.

Today's Don River winds through one of the most urbanized watersheds in Canada. While much of the valley bottom lands have been protected as parkland, close to 90 per cent of the lands within the river's catchment area have been developed for residential, commercial, or industrial uses. The watershed is home to almost 1.2 million people. Urbanization has wrought both obvious and more subtle effects upon the ecology of the watershed. Over the past 200 years, almost all of the significant wetlands within the watershed have been drained or filled to support urban development. The six tributaries of the lower river have mostly disappeared, buried by fill or encased within sewage infrastructure.[10] Agricultural and later industrial and residential development on the tablelands above the valley has compacted soils, removed tree cover, and altered the hydrology of the river system, contributing to flash floods and sending higher quantities of sediment-laden runoff into the river channel. Sewage treatment plants have deposited their effluents, at one time only minimally treated, into the river, and storm sewers have added oil, herbicides, and road salt from area roads to the cocktail, making conditions for aquatic life extremely toxic. The river's only major dam, constructed on the west branch of the river in 1973 to protect the floodplain development of Hogg's Hollow, reduces flow levels downstream. Only the headwaters of the East Don, north of Toronto in the municipality of Vaughan, remain relatively undeveloped. The last rural landscape within the watershed, this area lies within the Oak Ridges Moraine, an important source of groundwater for the region. In 2005, it received protection from urban development as part of the Ontario Greenbelt Plan.

From the beginning of European resettlement activities in the Toronto area, the Don River Valley was entwined in important ways with imagined futures for the evolving city. This notion of imagined futures is a central theme of this book. It describes the practice of re-envisioning the landscape of a particular territory or district to accord with the economic and political realities, and the technological capabilities, of a particular time and place. Sometimes realized and more often abandoned, the plans and schemes that imagine the future for a particular place have much to tell us about relationships between humans and nature in different periods. In their tendency to crystallize prevailing attitudes towards the natural world, together with the language and character of contemporary social and economic aspirations, they make compelling documents for historical analysis.

In this book, imagined futures range in form from personal aspirations and projects effected upon the landscape of the river valley – the selection of an appropriate site for a grist mill and the investments and aspirations caught up in its construction – to much grander and more costly state initiatives to transform an area for the purposes of expanding industrial production, creating transportation efficiencies, or rationalizing unpredictable environments. The Don Improvement Project of the 1880s is illustrative of the latter. Wrapped up in the idea of imagined futures is the rhetoric of improvement that characterized approaches to land use in nineteenth- and twentieth-century capitalist economies. Land clearing, wetland drainage, and river canalization were understood in this period as improvements to a wild nature that was fundamentally deficient, disorderly, and unpredictable. Through human labour, a chaotic wilderness could be transformed into a productive and orderly garden.[11] By mobilizing a rhetoric of improvement, nineteenth- and early-twentieth-century imagined futures had the capacity to dramatically alter local environments; they also had the effect of displacing or replacing earlier visions or realities.

Imagined futures for the Don River Valley as an agent of growth and revitalization for the city as a whole created the landscape we live with today. From colonial visions of agricultural resettlement, to late-nineteenth-century perceptions of the Lower Don as a "space apart" for industrial production and waste assimilation, to mid-twentieth-century visions for the valley as a corridor for automobility and suburban growth, changing ideas about the function of this space at the city's edge and its role in the development of the metropolis transformed valley landscapes.

As much as these visions for the valley emerged as the most successful – or at least most apparent – in their respective periods, other imagined futures coincided with and pushed against them. Aboriginal uses of the river valley persisted for a number of years after the establishment of York in the 1790s; claims on the land and its future continue to challenge European appropriations in the early twenty-first century. The history of the conservation movement surrounding the valley is another example. From the 1940s until the present, a growing number of individuals and organizations have attempted to forward a different vision for the river valley and its role in the city, one that positions the valley corridor as an urban wilderness and a restorative retreat for harried urban minds and bodies. This alternative imagined future has claimed some successes in the protection of valley lands for parks purposes, the restoration of several wetland habitats throughout the watershed, and, most recently, the securing of state funds to redesign the mouth of the river as part of a larger revitalization plan for the Toronto waterfront. This book explores the development (and occasional implementation) of these imagined futures for the Don River Valley, the ways they intersected, and the effects they had upon the evolving city.

Unlike other sites of urban nature – the city park, the residential garden, the waterfront, the wilds of the backstreet alley – rivers have been uniquely cast as facilitators of human labour and, as such, as bearers of possibilities. As both picturesque landscapes and energy-producing currents, rivers have been connected to a legacy of imagined futures for the city writ large. Pittsburgh's relationship with the Allegheny, Monongahela, and Ohio Rivers; New Orleans's tangled and tragic history with the Mississippi; Vancouver's unusual relationship with the Fraser; and Calgary's and Montreal's relationships with the Bow and the St Lawrence, respectively, have all been the subject of urban river histories in recent years.[12] While the Don shares some similarities with these rivers – it, too, was mobilized as a driver of industry, a conduit for waste, and a site of recreation – its lack of power and its small size make it a river more of local than regional or national significance. A small urban waterway in a region dominated by the Great Lakes, its short and shallow course links neighbourhoods and districts rather than major centres.

And yet, size matters in this story as much as it does in the history of the Mississippi or the St Lawrence. The Don's unimpressive character and relative lack of power-generating potential influenced both how the river was altered and what kinds of interests held a stake in its development. Unsuitable as a source for irrigation or hydroelectricity projects, the Don was historically valued primarily as a sink for wastes and a site for industrial development. In this way it is more like the Cuyahoga, the Chicago, and a number of other small branching rivers with heavily urbanized catchment areas in the lower Great Lakes region. Horribly polluted by the final decades of the nineteenth century, the river's condition was generally accepted as the price of prosperity and the cost of keeping other parts of the city habitable.

Comparisons with Toronto's other main river valley, the Humber, provide a useful counterpoint in understanding why the river developed as it did. More than double the length of the Don, and draining a watershed almost three times the size, the Humber River's southeasterly course formed the dividing line between the Township of York and the Township of Etobicoke, some eight kilometres west of the historic city centre. For much of its human history, its course comprised the main leg of the Toronto Carrying Place – the preferred corridor for movement between Lake Ontario and Lake Simcoe, and from there to the upper Great Lakes. Prior to 1700, Iroquoian groups established agricultural village sites along the river that were considerably larger and longer-occupied than those along the Don. More significant than the Don in the years prior to European resettlement, the Humber receded in importance after the founding of York at the eastern end of Toronto harbour in 1793. With its outfall in Lake Ontario rather than the protected waters of Toronto Bay, the Humber offered a less defensible location for the future settlement. Lieutenant-Governor John Graves Simcoe's choice of a location near the mouth of the Don for his town plot set the two river valleys on different historical trajectories, influencing the kinds of development they attracted and the divergent land uses that persist. Although both rivers supported milling operations and later small milling communities, the Humber never attracted the intense industrial development that the Don did. Separated from the city centre by a considerable distance – from the harbour and from important rail intersections – it was never as closely tied to the city's development. Today, most of the river corridor from the northern city limits to the lakeshore is designated as parkland. Never subject to straightening for rail or expressway development, the river maintains much of its historic course, and the wetlands near the river mouth remain largely intact. In the upper watershed, rural uses still predominate.[13] The Don, in short, was Toronto's river; the Humber was a river one encountered on the road to Hamilton.

This history of the 200-year relationship between a small urban river, its valley, and what is today Canada's largest city revolves around the idea of the river, the valley, and the city as mutually constitutive – each shaping the development of the other. As the city grew, it radically altered the physical and ecological composition of the river valley, denuding slopes, polluting waterways, filling wetlands, and levelling hills. Just as the city transformed the valley, the valley presented certain possibilities and foreclosed others as the city expanded. From the mosquito-infested marsh at its mouth to the occasionally devastating floods it wrought upon valley landowners, to the large quantities of silt and debris it washed into Toronto harbour, the river was an active participant in the city's development.

The valley's geography, with its steep ravine walls and wide plateaux, was even more influential, at once a formidable barrier to the eastward expansion of the city and an enabling corridor for transportation and urban growth. Until the completion of the Prince Edward

(Bloor Street) Viaduct in 1918, no bridges existed across the wide valley expanse north of Gerrard Street, and travellers were forced to travel south to Winchester Street or north to Pottery Road to access communities east of the river. Those bridges that did exist were precarious structures prone to washout during seasonal floods, further constraining access for landholders and industrialists east of the Don. As much as the lower valley posed a barrier to east–west communication, it invited movement north–south. Rail development happened first, in association with the Don River Improvement Plan of the 1880s and 90s. Seventy years later, the Don Valley Parkway took the valley's corridor function to its full potential, carving six lanes of highway from the Gardiner Expressway near the lakeshore to Highway 401 north of the city. Reconfigured as a metropolitan corridor, the valley facilitated suburban development along its length, stimulating the growth of the city.

The river valley has also served as a different kind of corridor, laying a swathe of green space through the heart of the city. Through the nineteenth century, its steep, corrugated ravines resisted agricultural and residential development, surviving as pockets of woodland within an increasingly deforested landscape. Parkway construction in the mid-twentieth century capitalized on valley woodlands as an aesthetically pleasing backdrop to the curving ribbon of road, and a site for roadside parkland and recreational areas. In the aftermath of Hurricane Hazel in 1954, valley parklands served a secondary function as development-free drainage corridors. For 1940s-era conservationists and twenty-first-century urban explorers, valley green spaces provided, and continue to provide, a welcome respite from the monotony of the urban grid, a place to restore body and mind within easy distance of the city core. Corridors of movement for urban wildlife, producers of oxygen and sinks for carbon, these green spaces also serve important ecological functions. Once feared as a harbour for gangsters and social deviants, today's valley lands are appreciated for their role in "wilding the city." The valley is, however, as it always has been, an ambiguous space, subject to multiple uses and divergent ideas about its future: busy recreational trails expose the ramshackle tents of the homeless; the burble of a blackbird at a restored wetland site challenges the hum of traffic on the parkway; at the river's edge, hardy riparian grasses push through the metal grid of a discarded shopping cart.

Over the course of this study, a pattern emerges in the relationship between the river, the valley, and the evolving city. Valley landscapes shift from a central position in the geography and material life of the early settlement, to a polluted and reviled periphery in the latter half of the nineteenth century. Not until the mid-twentieth century, when the valley was reconfigured as a transportation corridor, and conservationists worked to erode persistent perceptions of the river as a blighted and neglected place, was the valley "re-centred" again as a significant landscape in the city's development.

This shift from centre to periphery and back to centre had dramatic implications· for both the ecology of valley landscapes and the perceptions they produced among Torontonians. By the 1880s, the lower river valley was widely considered – at least by those who viewed it from a comfortable distance – as a diseased and dangerous place, a fitting repository for the waste products of an industrializing, urbanizing society. It was a place to be avoided, denigrated, cast from the mind, and with it, the sewage, the offal, and the effluents; the impoverished, the homeless, and the insane – the externalities of the process of city-building. By continuing to serve the vital function of absorbing and removing urban wastes, the river valley allowed, in a way, for this blindness among elite residents to the ecological and social consequences of their actions. A century later, changes in transportation and manufacturing technology saw the relocation or closure of many industries along the waterfront and the river corridor, leaving contaminated brownfields in their place. More people than ever before traversed valley landscapes along the route of the Don Valley Parkway, and valley ravines were reimagined as iconic Toronto landscapes by a new generation of Canadian writers and artists. The rise of the environmental movement contributed to changing public perceptions of the valley as a degraded but ultimately salvageable natural system, and fuelled efforts to recast the Don as Toronto's urban wilderness.

In a place subject to such dramatic change over time, memory is a slippery thing. As historian Joy Parr has shown in the context of twentieth-century megaprojects, the loss or radical transformation of familiar environments has a disorienting effect upon those who knew them best.[14] For many places in the valley, the rich visual and documentary record is all that remains of historic landforms and landscapes. Memories of Sugar Loaf Hill, levelled in the late 1950s during the construction of the Bayview Avenue Extension, must be conjured from photographs or narrative accounts rather than from a physical place. This sense of the human experience of changing landscapes, and the role of memory in shaping that experience, runs throughout the book, from responses to major developments such as the 1880s Don River

Improvement or the 1960s Don Valley Parkway, to efforts to reconfigure the Lower Donlands for the twenty-first century. In each of these cases, the collective memory of the river valley influenced the degree of public support that projects enjoyed, the expectations they generated, and the sense of loss they produced among those whose lives and livelihoods were closely linked to valley landscapes. In the words of French historian Pierre Nora, such developments tend to produce "sites of memory," *lieux de mémoire* – photographs, accounts, heritage sites that function as a kind of pale echo of the everyday lived experience of historical places lost to rapid and destabilizing stage.[15] This book is one of those sites.

This history of a river valley and its relationship with the evolving city is also a history of the dynamic urban fringe. In thinking about the Don and the changing uses and perceptions that it attracted over time, the concept of "borderland" is helpful. The term refers not only to an area "near the edge," but also to a place where things overlap, an indeterminate area between two conditions or categories that is difficult to define because it contains the features of both. Landscape historian John Stilgoe used the term to describe "a zone between rural space and urban residential rings" – a mixed-use landscape of working farms, remnant woodlands, and elite country estates at the periphery of the nineteenth-century city.[16] For Stilgoe, the lands that formed "the country" or "borderland" in nineteenth-century terms became the sprawling suburbs of the postwar years. In the mid-nineteenth century, the lower Don especially fit this description of not quite rural and not quite urban – a place in-between. The ambiguity of this space and its proximity to the city centre made it attractive for particular uses: as a dumping ground, a transportation corridor, and a refuge for marginalized populations. As industrialization and improvement schemes transformed the lands of the lower valley in the late nineteenth and early twentieth centuries, this borderland space shifted further north, to the largely rural lands of the upper valleys.

The term "borderland" also has significance for historians as a middle ground between designated territories, a geography of accommodation and negotiation.[17] This connotation is also appropriate in accommodating the function of the valley not only as a zone of transition between urban and rural land uses, but also as a kind of middle ground where the hallmarks of industrial capitalism – brick factories and railway lines – existed alongside indicators of older ways of getting by: the small farm, the gang hideout, the hobo shack. Within the context of the larger city, the valley offered an ambiguous space – what Catalan architect and historian Ignasi de Solà-Morales has called a *terrain vague* – where old and new political economies overlapped. At once neglected and obsolete, available and rich with possibility, places like the Don River Valley, Solà-Morales argued, have historically held an evocative potential within the context of the larger city.[18]

"Nature" in this study is understood not as a pristine entity acted upon, defiled, or improved by humans, but rather a hybrid entity difficult to separate from the built environment that envelops it and for which it forms a constitutive part. A polluted urban waterway encased in concrete and hemmed in by rail and expressway corridors is still at one level a "natural" river, compelled to flow by hydrological cycles beyond human control. Ecological processes intertwine with political, economic, and technological forces in constructing the urban environment. As Matthew Gandy observes in his work on infrastructure development in New York City, nature is built into the fabric of the city not only as a material element of urban form, but also as a commodity vital to the imperatives of modern capitalism. Urban landscapes and urban infrastructure – what Gandy calls "metropolitan natures" – are produced, therefore, not only through networks that bring together raw materials from far-off places, but also through the ideologies that support city life.[19] Attempting to differentiate what is natural from what is constructed becomes in this context a fruitless and meaningless task.

Our story begins with the establishment of the town of the York (now Toronto) west of the river mouth in 1793. Chapter 1 explores colonial uses and conceptions of the river and its valley and their relationship to the early development of the town of York. It traces the place of the river valley in Lieutenant-Governor John Graves Simcoe's vision for the future settlement, as a provider of lumber, clay, and other raw materials, and as a public commons housing the parliament and other government buildings. The role of valley geographies in destabilizing Simcoe's vision, and reorienting the development of the settlement, marks the beginning of a gradual shift in the function of the lower river valley from a central provider in the lives of early Toronto residents to a polluted and vilified space at the urban periphery by the latter half of the nineteenth century. The industrialization of the Lower Don River in the late nineteenth century is the subject of chapter 2. The focus here is on the years between 1850 and 1890, when the lower river first emerged as a site for noxious industries and sewage pollution became increasingly apparent. Here I examine the factors that attracted industry to the lower valley, the effects of industrial activities upon the lower river and the marsh at its mouth, and the perceptions of place that facilitated the use of the valley as a corridor for wastes. A conflict that erupted in the 1890s over the Gooderham and Worts cattle byres, and their role in befouling Ashbridge's Bay marsh at the mouth of the river, sheds light on the place of the river in civic debates about pollution and public health, and the class dynamics that infused these debates. By the end of the century, the Lower Don Valley had emerged as a space "set apart" for the purposes of industrial production and waste assimilation to service the expanding city.

Chapter 3 documents a series of initiatives between 1870 and 1930 to "improve" the Don in the name of industry, transportation, and public health, centring on the ambitious Don Improvement Plan of the 1880s. The central question explored here is why Toronto chose to invest so heavily in the development of a minor river close to the city centre, at a time when other North American centres were reducing their dependence on rivers as drivers of industry. In the Don Improvement Project we see the first attempt by civic authorities to capitalize upon the function of the valley as a "natural" corridor for transportation. Originally intended to produce a navigable ship channel up the Don, the project in its final manifestation facilitated movement along the river corridor not by ship but by rail. Here another imagined future for the Lower Don went awry, as visions of a productive and sanitary lower river succumbed to conflicting institutional priorities, insufficient funds, and a general failure to comprehend the complexities of environmental conditions on the ground. The legacy of the project for the river's ecology and the character of the city's eastern waterfront reverberates throughout the chapters that follow.

Chapter 4 explores further the nature of the area's undesirability and the implications it had for people who called the valley home, temporarily or for longer periods of time, in the late nineteenth and early twentieth centuries. The ways in which the Don was conceived as a semi-rural space at once isolated and proximate, restorative and befouled, had implications for the kinds of uses to which it was put and the opportunities it allowed for those living on the edges of society. In ways reflective of the valley's function as a dumping ground for material wastes, it emerges through the historical record as a repository for human undesirables as well. Four case studies illustrate the valley's role as both a harbour, and a holding ground, for Toronto's social outcasts. The first plumbs the rationales employed in the establishment of a cluster of reformatory institutions constructed in the lower valley in the 1860s, each of which positioned the lower valley north of Gerrard as a restorative landscape. The second follows the trial of members of the valley's Brooks Bush Gang for the murder of a local MPP in 1859, gleaning from the trial record insights into the experience of "living rough" in the lower valley in the mid-nineteenth century. The final two case studies jump ahead to the early twentieth century, when two groups of "undesirables" received significant coverage in Toronto newspapers: small Roma family groups who set up camp in the upper valley in the 1910s and 20s; and the large numbers of unemployed men who formed a "hobo jungle" on the flats of the river in 1930 and 1931. In each of these cases, the river valley provided refuge – and in some instances, limited subsistence – for people on the margins. Social divisions, as cultural geographer Rob Shields has observed, had spatial expression.[20]

Chapter 5 investigates citizen efforts to protect the river valley from the 1940s to the 1980s. This chapter takes a biographical approach, tracing the evolution of the conservation movement surrounding the Don through the life experiences of Don Valley cottager and conservation champion Charles Sauriol. Changes in the approaches to protecting urban nature, I argue, are reflected in Sauriol's personal experience – the strategies he employed, the language he used, and the losses he suffered as a result of urban planning policies. A different kind of imagined future, Sauriol's vision for the valley as a protected green space within the city achieved some purchase when civic authorities gave new urgency to floodplain protection following Toronto's "storm of the century" in 1954. His disappointments struck close to home: the construction of the Don Valley Parkway (DVP) through the valley in the early 1960s resulted in the expropriation of a portion of his valley holdings and the bulldozing of his family's beloved cottage retreat. Chapter 6 examines the history of the parkway project and its repercussions for the valley and for the city as a whole. The unique municipal circumstances that compelled its construction, and the role, once again, of individual actors in seeing it through, are explored here through the character of influential Metro Toronto Chair Frederick Gardiner. The grand fulfilment of half a century of visions for a transportation corridor through the valley, the DVP used valley lands to transform the city, opening the rural lands northeast of the centre to residential development. Completed in 1966, the parkway repositioned the valley from the edge of the old city to the centre of a rapidly growing metropolitan region. Once an enabler of growth in the fledgling town of York, the river valley by mid-twentieth century drove the city's suburban expansion, shaping the city as Torontonians know it today.

Chapter 7 brings the narrative into the twenty-first century with an examination of the proposed Lower Don Lands project, a tri-government initiative to transform the existing mouth of the Don River into a cleaner and "more natural" river outlet to Lake Ontario. This chapter looks at the ways the past informs current plans for the mouth of the Don with reference to three overlapping sites of memory: (1) the physical realities of the site and the ways they place demands upon the present; (2) references within the planning documents to past landscapes and planning processes; and (3) processes and methods informed by past experience. It compares the current plans for the river mouth with the 1880s Don Improvement Plan, with particular attention to the political and economic contexts within which they were created and the territories they sought to transform. Despite their differences, the plans are united in their basic strategy to rework the Lower Don Lands for the purposes of capital accumulation. Just as industrial capital reshaped the Lower Don Lands in the late nineteenth century as a landscape of production, the twenty-first-century plan reconfigures urban nature once again to produce an imagined landscape of consumption.

Each of these stories describes different kinds of efforts, in different periods, to reclaim this river valley at the city's edge and to harness its promise as a transformative force for the evolving city. From the colonial reclamation and resettlement of valley lands, to the physical reclamation of valley lands for transportation and industrial purposes in the late nineteenth century, to efforts by conservationists to reclaim the valley corridor as an urban wilderness, the river valley provided the physical and imaginative impetus to make and remake the city at key points in its history. My own efforts to invest this small urban river valley with the significance it deserves in the broader story of Toronto's development mark a final kind of reclamation, one that aims to shed light on spaces at the urban periphery and their role in the process of city building.

RECLAIMING THE DON

An Environmental History of Toronto's
Don River Valley

1 The Colonial River

"This Evening," Elizabeth Simcoe wrote in her diary for 11 August 1793, "we went to see a Creek which is to be called the River Don. It falls in to the Bay near the Peninsula. After we entered we rowed some distance among Low lands covered with Rushes, abounding with wild ducks & swamp black birds with red wings. About a mile beyond the Bay the banks became high & wooded, as the River contracts its width."[1] On a return trip the following month, she described the difficulty of travelling along the river in its wild state: "We rowed 6 miles up the Donn [sic] to Coons, a farm under a hill covered with Pine," she wrote. "We found the River very shallow in many parts & obstructed by fallen Trees. One of them lay so high above the water that the boat passed under[,] the Rowers stooping their heads."[2] Simcoe's observations focus us on two narrative threads in the early history of the river: efforts to understand the geography of the river, and the imaginative power of the colonial gaze.

From the earliest European resettlement activities in the area, the Don River Valley has played an important role in imagined futures for the developing city. Efforts to stimulate the growth and prosperity of the settlement saw the extraction of valley resources such as clay, timber, and fish, and the harnessing of valley waters to power mills, supply ice, and sluice pollutants. In the colonial period, these imagined futures took on a specific character conducive to contemporary imperatives of claiming and remaking New World spaces in Europe's image – transforming an unfamiliar, chaotic wilderness into a predictable, ordered garden. Colonial ideas, and the practices that flowed from them, contributed to material change for the river and its valley. Imagining and then building the colonial urban centre involved displacing and replacing indigenous nature and indigenous peoples in both material and symbolic ways, from representations of New World landscapes as *terra nullius* or vacant land, to land-surrender agreements and the removal of Aboriginal people to reservations; from representations of indigenous nature as wild and unruly, to material efforts to "improve" it through land clearances and the establishment of farms and gardens. This chapter explores these colonial uses and conceptions of the river and its valley and their relationship to the early development of the town of York.

A Landscape of Possibility

The earliest detailed maps of Toronto Bay portray a circular water body almost completely enclosed by a sandy peninsula stretching from the east end of the bay into a wide, hooked sandbar at its western entrance. Joseph Bouchette's 1797 survey sets out the harbour landforms that would persist into the middle of the next century: the wide peninsula or spit running east-west across the lakefront, narrowing in the east to enclose an extensive lagoon known as Ashbridge's Bay Marsh; the thin sandbar extending south from the lakeshore, separating the marsh from the bay; and the distinctive form of the Don River, meandering first west across the top of the marsh and then south to enter the bay about halfway down the length of the north-south sandbar (see figure 1.1). Formed through a combination of deposition from an ancient predecessor of the Don, and ongoing accumulation of sands and gravels by lake currents from the east, the peninsula is a product of both the river and the lake. The marsh, too, owed its existence to the interactions of lake and river forces: sand-bearing lake currents produced the peninsula separating the marsh from the lake, and sediment deposits from the Don, contained behind the peninsula, contributed to the shallow wetland conditions of the marsh.[3]

Similar processes were at work in shaping the river valley itself. At the end of the last ice age 11,000 to 13,000 years ago, retreating ice fronts left rivers of meltwater in their wake. The Don River originated from a long glacial deposit north of Toronto known as the Oak Ridges Moraine. Its east and west branches originally flowed south as two separate rivers, cutting deep ravines through the soft alluvial plain of sand, gravel, and clay tills before depositing into the glacial Lake Iroquois. Much of downtown Toronto is built on the floor of this ancient lake; its former shoreline forms the prominent ridge stretching across the city south

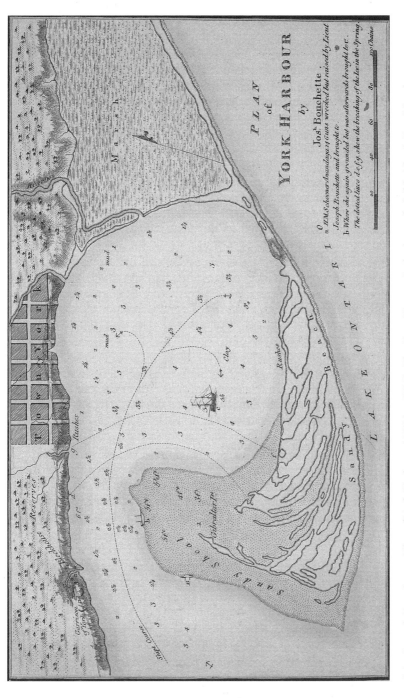

1.1 Joseph Bouchette, *Plan of York Harbour*, 1815 (ca 1797). The Don River winds through Ashbridge's Bay Marsh to enter the harbour in the top right. A sketch of Simcoe's town plot appears to the west of the mouth of the Don.* (Toronto Public Library, T1815/fold)

* The lower reaches of Taddle Creek forms its eastern boundary.

of St Clair Avenue and east to the Scarborough Bluffs. A large hooked sandbar, much like the one that sheltered Toronto harbour in the late eighteenth and nineteenth centuries, formed at the point where the rivers entered the lake – the result of the combined forces of sediment-bearing river waters, wave action, and westward shoreline currents. Gradually, sands, silts, and clays accumulated behind the bar, creating a protected lagoon that now underlies the valley north of the Forks.

About 9,000 years ago, the ice front retreated north of the St Lawrence Valley, freeing a passageway at the east end of the Lake Ontario basin. Lake Iroquois drained to the east and the water level in the basin fell to about sea level. As water levels dropped, the two main branches of the Don River joined at the sandbar on the old Lake Iroquois shoreline, together with a third stream, today's Taylor-Massey Creek. United as one, the new Lower Don River flowed first west and then south across the old lakebed before meandering back and forth along the valley bottom to its outlet in the newly formed Lake Ontario. Long depressed under the weight of up to two kilometres of ice, the block of the earth's crust underlying most of Quebec and northeastern Ontario slowly rebounded to its present level (it continues to rise, but at a much slower rate). As the elevation of the outlet to the St Lawrence increased, the level of Lake Ontario rose, pushing water into the lower reaches of Toronto's ravines. In the Don watershed, sediment washed down from the upper valley accumulated in the water-filled reaches of the lower valley, eventually creating the distinctive plateau that defines the lower river from Bloor Street Viaduct to the lake. At the point where the river entered Lake Ontario, the process of building a sandbar and backshore lagoon was repeated, forming the sandy peninsula (today's Toronto Islands) and the protected lagoon of Ashbridge's Bay Marsh.[4]

Native inhabitants of the area, French-Canadian voyageurs, and early European settlers would have experienced the river as a dense network of branching tributaries and wetlands stretching from the Oak Ridges Moraine near today's Richmond Hill thirty-eight kilometres south to its marshy meeting with Lake Ontario. Draining an area approximately 360 square kilometres in size, the river drew its water sources both from the underground aquifers of glacial water in its headwaters and from the annual rainfall and snowmelt that seeped through the soils of the region's forests.

Scanning the waterfront on a reconnaissance expedition in the spring of 1793, Upper Canada's first Lieutenant-Governor John Graves Simcoe saw in the sheltered curve of the east end of Toronto Bay and its tributary streams a landscape of possibility. He noted the harbour's natural defensibility and its potential to supply the future settlement with lumber. "At the Bottom of the Harbour," he reported to acting colonial administrator Alured Clarke in May 1793, "there is a Situation admirably adapted for a Naval Arsenal and Dock Yard, and there flows into the Harbour a River the Banks of which are covered with excellent Timber."[5] Satisfied with his assessment of the area's potential, Simcoe had his surveyor lay out a plot for the future town of York west of the mouth of the Don, at the base of today's Parliament Street. He reserved a large area for military purposes at the west end of the harbour, and at the east end, between the town site and the Don River, set aside 400 acres for future government buildings. Four years later, the capital's first parliament buildings stood just west of the "Government Park" on the eastern lakeshore (see figure 1.2).[6]

The features that attracted Simcoe, of course, nestled within a larger set of considerations which positioned the area as a suitable site for settlement. Proximity to the Carrying Place trail along the Humber River to Lake Simcoe and the Great Lakes beyond was one of these. As J.M.S. Careless concluded, Toronto's location had "specific significance ... as a junction point of land and water routes that transected the Great Lakes region"; its "accessible lake harbour, low, easily traversed shoreline, and gate position on a passage through the midst of southern Ontario" distinguished it from other potential sites.[7] Political circumstances also played a role. The decision to locate the capital at Toronto was a defensive one, based on concerns of an American invasion given the larger hostilities between Britain and France that erupted in the spring of 1793. Faced with the threat of imminent attack, Simcoe decided to establish a naval base at Toronto and to relocate the capital from its exposed position at Newark to the comparatively greater security of Toronto. His decision would ultimately transform a relatively insignificant outpost into the political and economic engine of the region.

In Simcoe's appraisal of Toronto Bay we can locate what art historian Albert Boime has described as the "magisterial gaze" – a perspective common to North American landscape painting in this period wherein the viewer assumes a kind of "imaginative control" over the land, taking a reading of the reality before him that is "profoundly personal and ideological at the same time."[8] Looking out over the eastern bayfront and the mouth of the Don River, Simcoe imagined an urban-agricultural society in Britain's image. His colonial gaze projected onto the landscape before him the imperatives of imperial resettlement: to

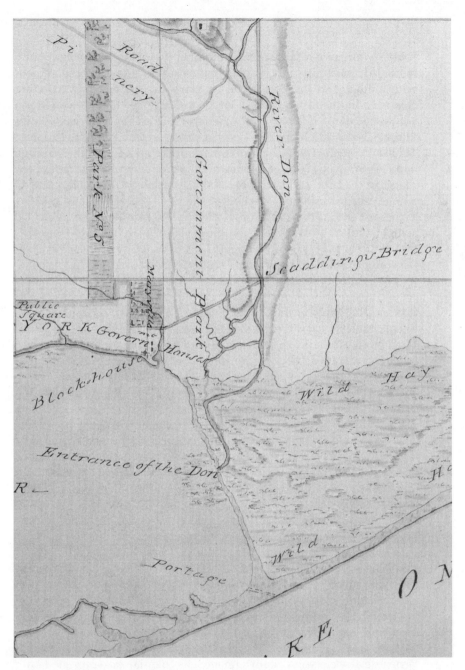

1.2   The Town of York and Government Park Reserve, 1802. The Government Park reserve runs along the west side of the river and the "Governmt House" [*sic*], or parliament buildings, is indicated northwest of the river mouth. Ashbridge's Bay Marsh appears southeast of the river mouth. (Detail from William Chewett, *Plan of 916 ¼ Acres, in the Township of York in Upper Canada*, 1802, Toronto Public Library, MS1889.1.6)

replace existing forests and wetlands with orderly farms and gardens, and to displace and ultimately replace existing "primitive" peoples with more "civilized" European settlers. Carolyn Merchant describes this as a process of "reinventing Eden," wherein acts of improvement become the mechanism through which to recover a fallen world. This secular narrative of transformation, she argues, guided and legitimized the settlement of the Americas.[9] Recovering Eden from nature involved reshaping the earth and manipulating its resources, and for this, the Don River Valley provided rich terrain for the imagination. It served in Simcoe's vision as a seat of political power, a conduit for transportation, a generator of water power, and a supplier of raw materials with which to forge the future capital at York.

Early colonial assessments of the river valley also evaluated its potential as a corridor for travel and transportation of goods. Although the river itself was only navigable for two to three miles north of the lakeshore, the valley formed part of an ancient Aboriginal trail network linking Lake Ontario with Lake Simcoe and the upper Great Lakes – an alternative to the more frequently travelled Carrying Place trail along the Humber River. In October 1793 Simcoe set out on foot with a small party of men from Holland Landing, immediately south of Lake Simcoe, to locate what was reputed to be a more direct southerly route to York. "Known only to a few Indian Hunters," the portage route proved difficult to follow, and Simcoe and his men lost their way repeatedly before relying on a compass to complete the journey.[10] Following heights of land and transecting the river valleys, their route offered an arduous but direct passage between York and the gateway to the Upper Lakes. Triumphant, Simcoe sent a surveying party to run lines for a roadway along the route the following spring. The long, straight path of Yonge Street – Toronto's central artery – was cut several months later, and east-west lots were laid along the length of the roadway through the watershed north of today's Eglinton Avenue.[11]

Underlying Simcoe's vision for future settlement was an understanding of the land as vacant. Asserting "imaginative control" over a space involves seeing what one wants to see, and descriptions of Toronto Bay in this period emphasized its status as an unoccupied wilderness. Joseph Bouchette recalled the "untamed aspect" of the country during his first survey of York harbour in 1793:

Dense and trackless forests lined the margin of the lake, and reflected their inverted images in its glassy surface. The wandering savage had constructed his ephemeral habitation beneath their luxuriant foliage – the group then consisting of two families of Mississaugas – and the bay and neighbouring marshes were the hitherto uninvaded haunts of immense coveys of wild fowl.[12]

As Victoria Freeman has observed, Bouchette takes these to be the only inhabitants of the place, rather than, as was more likely, a satellite family group established at the site for seasonal hunting and fishing.[13] And as Colin Coates has shown for colonial Montreal, writers and artists made Canadian landscapes knowable to distant metropolitan audiences by "using conventions and tropes that were rooted in distant, European aesthetics."[14] Such conventions involved the exclusion of the Aboriginal presence from the landscape. Suggestions of an essentially unoccupied, "hitherto uninvaded" landscape lent support to European territorial claims. Silent, mysterious, and ephemeral, the area's first inhabitants "left no trace" of their passing: by failing, in the terms of Lockean logic, to use the land to its full capacity, they had no legitimate claim to the lands they occupied.[15] And without the investment of human labour to transform the land, its potential remained untapped, wasted. "Primeval" landscapes and first peoples, then, were united in the colonial imagination in a romantic space "before time" – a hazy and unremarkable existence before the European instigation of a more disciplined and productive relationship with the land.[16] Perceived as timeless children of nature, Aboriginal people made no "improvements" to the land precisely because they had no vision for the future.

Over 200 years later, historians still know surprisingly little about Aboriginal use and occupation of the Don watershed in the years before European settlement. Use of the valley in the contact period appears to have been sporadic and seasonally motivated. Anecdotal evidence from early European observers suggests that both the Seneca, an Iroquoian group who established village sites at the mouths of the Humber and Rouge Rivers in the 1660s, and the Algonquian Mississauga, who settled in the Toronto area after the Seneca withdrew at the end of the seventeenth century, hunted and fished in the valley but established no permanent village sites along the river.[17] Elizabeth Simcoe's description of Native people ice fishing for "maskalonge" and "pickerell" near the mouth of the Don in the winter of 1794 illustrates this seasonal use of valley lands: "the Indians have cut holes in the ice," she wrote, "over which they spread a blanket on poles, and they sit under the shed, moving a wooden fish hung to a line in the water by way of attracting the living fish, which they spear with great dexterity when they approach."[18]

Two Aboriginal names were recorded for the Don, Algonquian words written by early surveyors as *Nechenquakekonk* and *Wonsco-tonach*. A translation for the latter appears in the letters of surveyor Augustus Jones as "back burnt grounds," which historian Henry Scadding interpreted as "the river coming down from the back [or possibly black] burnt country, meaning probably the so-called Poplar Plains to the north, liable to be swept by casual fires." Presumably Scadding referred to the rolling countryside of the Oak Ridges Moraine at the river's headwaters. An alternative (and likely more accurate) translation by Anishinaabe linguist Basil Johnson suggests a meaning of "burning bright point or peninsula" or a point bright with fire, which may refer to the peninsula near the mouth of the Don (later the Toronto Islands).[19] Interestingly, the Native names place more emphasis on the lands at the river's origin (or at the river's mouth) than on the river itself: for Native people of the contact period, the Don appears to have been less significant than other, larger rivers in the area. That the Don was passed over as a settlement site for larger rivers in the region places in greater relief Simcoe's peculiar choice of the river's marshy lowlands as the eastern anchor point for his town of York.

References to the presence of Aboriginal people in the Don Valley, and in Toronto more generally, decline precipitously after the early decades of the nineteenth century. While chroniclers such as Elizabeth Simcoe and later Paul Kane documented their sightings of Native peoples in and around the tiny settlement of York, by mid-century Aboriginal people had largely disappeared from depictions of Toronto, their legacy firmly relegated to a pre-settlement past. As Freeman argues, this "disappearance" of Native people from the social fabric of early Toronto is indicative of the degree of invisibility that Aboriginal people had attained. No longer the romanticized, heroic Indians of Toronto primeval, Aboriginal people in the post-contact period were less likely to be perceived as an object of spectacle. As domestic workers, labourers, students, and visitors, those Aboriginal people who continued to live in and frequent the city were relegated to the background.[20]

More significantly, however, this is a story of dispossession. The 1787 Toronto Purchase, prompted by a growing number of petitions for land grants in the area in the 1780s, saw the Mississauga relinquish some 100,000 hectares of land between Ashbridge's Bay in the east and Etobicoke Creek in the west, and running forty-five kilometres north from

Lake Ontario. Widely divergent interpretations of the land to be surrendered undermined the legitimacy of the treaty from the beginning.
The eastern boundary of the land surrender proved to be especially
contentious: the Crown interpreted the boundary as running north
from the lakeshore at the eastern end of Ashbridge's Bay; the Mississauga insisted they had not surrendered any lands east of the Don
River, including the Toronto Islands, to which they had long awarded
sacred significance.[21] For the Mississauga as for the nineteenth-century
city builders who followed them, the lower river represented an important boundary both materially and symbolically. As settlement pressures increased in the early decades of the nineteenth century, further
surrenders restricted the Mississauga to a small fraction of their former
territory. In 1847, Toronto-area Mississauga relocated ninety kilometres
southwest to the Six Nations Reserve in Brantford, a move that effectively removed them from the story of the city's development.

But the conclusion that the Don watershed was used only sporadi-
cally by Aboriginal groups in the contact period obscures the longer
history of Aboriginal occupation of the Toronto area. For eighteenth-
century observers like Elizabeth Simcoe and Joseph Bouchette, the
valley's Aboriginal past would have extended into the era of the
seventeenth-century French fur trade, and likely little further. Not
until the late nineteenth century, when decades of agricultural cultivation revealed artefacts from previous Aboriginal settlement, did an
awareness of a deeper human past in the Toronto area develop. In 1886,
road-building activities near Broadview Avenue and Gerrard Street
unearthed a cache of bones suggestive of an Aboriginal burial site.
The discovery captured the interest of archaeologist David Boyle, who
supervised the excavation of what would become known as the Withrow site. The site contained human remains and artefacts both from the
Archaic period (pre-3000 BC) and from a much more recent Iroquoian
village site (roughly 1400–1500 AD).[22]

Subsequent archaeological evidence from the valley confirms a history of occupation and use dating back millennia. Research has shown
that small bands of nomadic hunters moved into the Great Lakes region
about 11,000 years ago, soon after the continental glacier retreated, pursuing caribou, mammoth, and other large game animals. Evidence of
their presence is scant: camps were small and often ephemeral, and
as lake waters fell and then rose again, many sites became submerged
under the present reach of Lake Ontario.[23] Small bands began to settle into more defined hunting territories about 4,000–5,000 years ago,

congregating in the spring and summer in large camps at the mouths of area rivers to fish, trade, and gather provisions for winter. Archaeologists estimate a population of roughly 10,000 people in southern Ontario in this period; they speculate that "each of the rivers flowing into Lake Ontario through and around the Toronto area may have supported a regional band of 500 people."[24] One of the oldest sites in the Don watershed dates from this period. Located on Deerlick Creek, a tributary of the East Don River, the site shows evidence of repeated use over thousands of years.[25] Urban development in the upper watershed in recent decades has resulted in the discovery of several other Late Woodland (1000–1700 A.D.) Iroquoian sites. In each case, archaeological investigations revealed long-term settlements surrounded by substantial maize plantations; carbon analysis of skeletal remains showed substantial dietary reliance on fish and other resources from the Lower Don.[26]

Thus, while post-contact use of the valley may have been seasonal and selective, evidence from the archaeological record shows the valley supported permanent settlements in the Late Woodland period and possibly earlier. The range of resources provided by the river – rich soils in the river flats for maize plantations; fish, waterfowl, and plants and animals from the river's marshy lower reaches – sustained small village populations for several centuries at least. Sites that have been discovered, furthermore, are not necessarily reflective of sites that once existed: over 200 years of agricultural settlement and urbanization have worked to occlude the archaeological record.[27] This potential for obliteration is especially pronounced for the Don: running through the centre of the city, the watershed has seen significantly more development over the last one hundred years than its counterparts in the east and west ends of the city (current estimates place the watershed at almost 90 per cent urbanized). While urban developments in a few cases have led to the discovery of archaeological sites, in many others evidence of past occupation went unnoticed or ignored before the plough or the excavator.

Valley Pastoral

In the early years of European resettlement, valley lands held considerable value as an integral part of Simcoe's imagined future for the colony. Anchoring a vision of nature transformed in Britain's image – in place of vast forests and wetland wastes, a compact urban settlement supported by a grid of surrounding farms, woodlots, and industries – the valley served the economic aspirations of the colony. As the site of the fledgling farms and country estates of the elite, it also fulfilled important social and political functions of the colonial project. Military officers and favoured officials within Simcoe's inner circle received generous farm lots to the north and east of his town plot. Proximity to the Don River appears to have been a significant consideration in these awards. Lots running east of Yonge Street and north of Bloor, for example, were laid out east and west "to equalize the river frontage" (see figure 1.3).[28] Simcoe himself claimed a 200-acre parcel on the west side of the river, north of the government reserve. He awarded the 250-acre parcel opposite him, on the east side of the river, to his Secretary, John Scadding, and the lot north of him to George Playter, a respected military captain. For many grantees, holdings along the Don complemented already valuable properties closer to town. They could dabble with farming along the flats of the river with little pressure to create viable operations. Some, like Scadding, farmed their holdings with relative success.[29] Others chose instead to erect lavish suburban mansions on their lands overlooking the valley. This was particularly true west of the river along Yonge and Davenport Streets, where country estates such as Rosedale prevailed until mid-century and beyond.

Valley landscapes appealed to early European settlers in part because they complied with European conceptions of beauty and productivity. As Maria Tippett and Douglas Cole have observed, early explorers and colonial officials appraised Canadian landscapes based on European aesthetic ideals, with a preference for "extensive vistas with gentle hills, luxuriant meadows interspersed with clumps of trees and the glimpse of a cottage or mansion."[30] Descriptions of valley landscapes in this period typically drew upon pastoral tropes, combining a sense of the inherent "good" of Britain's orderly, industrious landscapes with a note of nostalgia for the familiar landscapes of home. On a visit to Captain George Playter's farm on 4 July 1796, Elizabeth Simcoe walked through pasture that reminded her of "Meadows in England."[31] The river itself her husband named for a river in South Yorkshire, presumably for its likeness in size and character (historically, the English River Don meandered along a circuitous northeasterly route from its headwaters in the Pennine mountains through marshy lowlands to spill into the River Trent roughly one hundred kilometres to the south).[32] Half a century later, W.H. Smith penned a narrative tour of the valley with the goal of attracting future settlers. The land near the river mouth, he wrote, is "low and flat, forming excellent grazing ground. As you ascend the

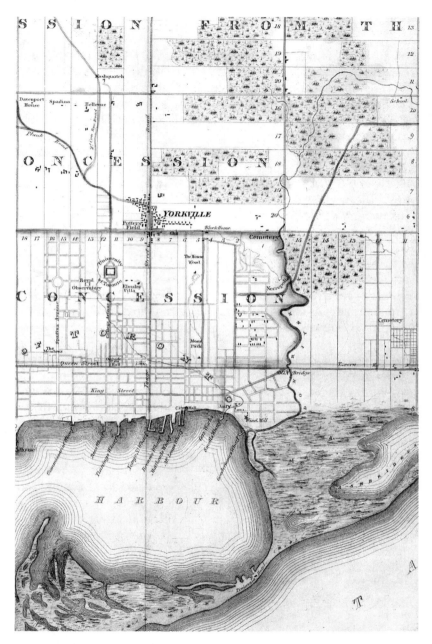

1.3 River frontage lots in the second and third concession north of the bay, 1851. The map shows lots running horizontally on either side of the Don, east of Yonge Street and north of today's Bloor Street (intersection at Yorkville, left of centre). Forested portions of lots are shaded. (Detail from J.O. Browne and J. Ellis, *Map of the Township of York in the County of York, Upper Canada*, 1851. Toronto Public Library, 912.71354 B68. Courtesy of Derek Hayes.)

river you perceive that it flows through a beautiful and fertile valley, which is bounded on either side by a range of hills."[33]

For the Simcoes, the river valley held additional significance as part of an imagined future of familial ties to Canada. In the fall of 1793 they set out to construct a small dwelling on their riverside lot, ostensibly to comply with settlement obligations. Elizabeth Simcoe wrote on 29 September 1793: "We went 6 miles by water & landed, climbed up an exceedingly steep hill or rather a series of sugar loafed Hills & approved of the highest spot from where we looked down on the tops of large trees ... The height of the situation will secure us from Musquitoes [sic]."[34] Construction of "Castle Frank" began the following spring. Named for their five-year-old son Francis, heir to the property, the cottage was located on a bluff rising above the west bank of the lower river, immediately south of today's Bloor Street Viaduct. The structure was much more modest than its name suggests (see figure 1.4). Thirty by fifty feet in size, and constructed of clapboarded pine logs, it hinted whimsically at grandeur with its columned facade of peeled pines, built, as Elizabeth noted, "on the plan of a Grecian Temple."[35] The interior of the house was rough and never fully completed, but its large, open room was the scene of numerous social occasions during the Simcoes' brief sojourn at York.

A country retreat in a settlement still only roughly hewn from the vast forests around it, Castle Frank seems to have served as a kind of pastoral refuge for the Simcoes, and particularly for Elizabeth. By reshaping the landscape to their own aesthetic conventions, the Simcoes projected an attitude of permanence and good husbandry vital to the colonial project in the 1790s. Travelling up the Don by sleigh in winter or through the woods in summer, Elizabeth hosted picnics for friends on the promontory overlooking the valley, sketched local wildlife and scenes along the river, and retreated to the modest cottage with her children when they took ill. A retreat from political life, it was also a retreat *to* the healing and inspiring environment provided by the height of land and the impressive views of the valley below. She wrote on 18 April 1796: "Francis has not been well. We therefore set off to C. Frank today to change the air intending to pass some days there." And two days later: "the Porticos here are delightful pleasant & the Room cool from its height & the thickness of the logs of which the House is built, the Mountain Tea berries in great perfection. Francis is much better & busy in planting Currant bushes & Peach Trees."[36] Castle Frank was still under construction when the Simcoes returned to England in 1796. Despite imaginings of ongoing ties to Upper Canada through the holdings of their eldest son, the Simcoes' story held a

1.4   Elizabeth Simcoe, *Castle Frank*, 1796. (Elizabeth Simcoe Loose Sketches, Archives of Ontario, F 47–11-1-0–228.)

different future. Francis was killed in action in Spain in April 1812, and the Simcoes never returned to Upper Canada. Castle Frank burned to the ground in 1829, and in the years that followed, the Simcoes sold all of their landholdings in Upper Canada.

Agricultural settlement and country estates, modest or otherwise, were just one component of the colonial vision for the Don River Valley. The valley's promise as a site for industrial activities was another. In the "excellent timber" that clothed the banks of the Don near the harbour, and the stands of straight white pine further upriver, Simcoe saw ship masts to replenish naval fleets in the event of war and accessible lumber to construct needed homes and buildings for the new capital. Rich clay deposits in the lower valley promised raw material for potteries and brickworks. Fish and riparian wildlife offered ready sources of sustenance, and the flow of the river itself, however modest, could power future milling operations.

Desperate shortages of lumber in York in the 1790s led to an unofficial competition to establish the first sawmill to serve the settlement. Simcoe first set his sights on the larger and more powerful Humber River west of the settlement, financing the construction of a government-owned sawmill there in the spring of 1794. Recurrent problems with tenant millers and milling equipment, however, soon drove him to push for a privately owned mill closer to York, on the Lower Don.[37] In 1794, the colonial government granted a piece of land at "the first fall in ascending the river" to Isaiah and Aaron Skinner, sons of a Loyalist miller in Niagara, with the condition that they build a sawmill on the property at their own expense. By the winter of 1795, the Skinner brothers had constructed what was arguably the first sawmill on the Don, along the Lower River south of the Forks.[38] The following year Simcoe granted Isaiah Skinner permission to construct a grist mill on the site, going so far as to supply "a pair of mill stones and a complete set of grist mill irons" from the government stores "as an encouragement for him" – evidence of the urgent need for experienced milling services in the settlement.[39] The Skinner sawmill provided precious lumber for shipbuilding and house construction, supplying material for "nearly every important house in early Toronto."[40] The grist mill, in turn, "was kept at work night and day." As local landowner William Lea told an audience at the Canadian Institute in 1881, "people brought their wheat as far as from Hamilton, and many other ports on the lake. The grain was taken up the Don in boats to the Sugar Loaf Hill, and thence up the flats by ox teams to the mill."[41]

The site, which became known as the Don Mills, grew to become York's first industrial complex in the first decades of the nineteenth century. In addition to lumber and flour, the Don Mills also sold vegetables and fish to families in town. Salmon migrating up the Don were caught, salted down, and shipped in barrels downriver.[42] By 1821, the site included a brewery, a distillery, and a second grist mill. A paper mill was added in 1827, the second of its kind in Upper Canada (see figure 1.5). The community that grew up around the mills extended for about a mile from what is now Pottery Road to the flats west of the river. Named Todmorden by mill owner John Eastwood in the 1830s, after his Yorkshire home, the community was home to about 300 people by the 1890s, including industrial workers, proprietors, and their families.[43]

1.5 D.C. Grose, *Taylor Brothers Paper Mill on the Don River*, ca 1860. The mill was located on the east side of the river near Pottery Road. (Toronto Public Library, Historical Pictures Collection, B 3–27c.)

At the peak of water-powered milling in 1860, the watershed supported over fifty mills producing paper, lumber, flour, and wool. With the exception of the Don Mills, all of these operations congregated along the upper reaches of the river, where gradients were higher and flow rates faster. Milling on the Don, however, was a precarious business. Mill owners faced heavy investments in costly milling equipment and volatile markets for their products. Mills often changed hands quickly or failed after a short period of operation.[44] The river, too, was capricious. Annual spring freshets and ice jams frequently washed out mill dams, destroyed equipment, and flooded buildings. Almost as devastating, occasional periods of drought in the summer months reduced flow rates, bringing operations to a halt for many mill owners in the watershed. Berczy's "German Mills," for example, located on German Mills Creek near its confluence with the East Don River, struggled to survive due to insufficient flows. On Taylor-Massey Creek, where flows were even lighter, three sawmills established in the 1810s failed due to lack of water.[45] Reductions in the volume of flow were greatly exacerbated by widespread deforestation in the watershed, which increased surface run-off and limited groundwater absorption. This cycle only became more pronounced as the century progressed. As Graeme Mercer Adam wrote in 1885, "the volume of the stream, once considerable, has greatly diminished, owing to the clearing of the country, and it is no longer available for milling uses."[46]

The process of inscribing a colonial vision of a productive and picturesque agrarian society upon the eighteenth-century landscape of the Don River Valley had dramatic effects upon valley ecologies. As early as 1850, clearing for agricultural settlement had significantly reduced forest cover in the watershed. Browne and Ellis's 1851 *Map of the Township of York* gives some sense of the amount of clearing that had taken place in the lower valley by mid-century (see figure 1.3). Some caution must be assumed here, however, as areas represented in white were likely still partially treed in this period.[47] By 1890, further clearing for agricultural purposes and heightened demand for cordwood saw the decline of remaining woodlots in the watershed.[48] These observations are corroborated by J. David Wood in his study of landscape transformation in nineteenth-century Ontario. By the 1850s, he finds, southern Ontario had lost one-third of its original forest cover to land clearance and fuel consumption; three-quarters had been removed by the 1880s; and 90 per cent by the beginning of the First World War. Customary practices of wetland drainage, Wood adds, coupled with pro-drainage legislation in the late 1860s, also disrupted the hydrology of local ecosystems.[49] Without trees to absorb surface water and anchor top soils, groundwater reserves became diminished, soils were eroded, and surface run-off increased. The steep slopes of the valley and the absence of lakes in the watershed to absorb run-off would have exacerbated these conditions, contributing to sudden and severe floods in times of heavy rainfall, and extremely low flow in the river during periods of drought.[50]

Animal populations also suffered. By the late nineteenth century, agricultural settlement and urbanization had dramatically reduced viable habitat, and domesticated sheep, pigs, goats, and horses displaced many native species throughout the watershed. Commentators of the period felt compelled to reminisce about the valley's once-bountiful wildlife. Journalist and publisher John Ross Robertson recalled that "the lands bordering the stream were alive with genuine game, grouse, quail, woodcock, snipe, plover, sandpiper and wild duck of various denominations."[51] Toronto historian Henry Scadding, who grew up on a farm on the east bank of the lower river, described the diversity of animals that frequented the river of his youth:

> After a light fall of snow in the night, the surface of the frozen stream would be marked all over with foot-prints innumerable of animals, small and great, that had been early out a-foraging: tracks of field-mice, minks and martens, of land-rats, water-rats and musk-rats; of the wild-cat sometimes, and of the fox; and sometimes of the wolf.[52]

In the century since Elizabeth Simcoe had described the "flights of wild Pidgeons [sic]" that "darkened ... the air" each spring and fall,[53] the valley had become a tamer place more welcoming to humans and their animals than to their wild counterparts.

For aquatic wildlife, the rapid expansion of milling operations along the three major branches of the river between the 1820s and the 1850s had discernible consequences. The river provided not only the energy to power milling operations, but also a convenient means of waste disposal: sawdust, grain chaff, excess dyes from woollen mills, and other milling by-products dumped in the river were carried away to become someone else's problem. Nineteenth-century mill sites are often the subject of nostalgic portraits of "pioneer life," their mill races and water wheels suggestive of simplicity, continuity, and a certain harmony with the natural elements that fuelled them.[54] And yet, as Gillis and Allardyce have shown in studies of the environmental impacts of early Canadian sawmills, their presence had significant impacts on the ecologies of local streams and rivers. Unlike their steam counterparts that used mill wastes for fuel, Gillis explains, water-powered sawmills were designed "so that edgings, butts, and sawdust dropped through the floor-boards into the water." The refuse was then carried by currents until it washed into bays and shallow areas and sank, "forming shoals of rotting material which obstructed navigation, destroyed fish spawning grounds, made the water objectionable to drink, and contributed to the formation of various gases which ... were prone to explode due to spontaneous combustion."[55] While the Don never saw the scale or longevity of lumbering activity experienced on other Ontario rivers, sawmills on the river nevertheless played a role in the destruction of local fish populations. W.H. Smith said of the river in 1851, "it was once a tolerable trout stream, as well as full of salmon, but the erection of machinery, more particularly sawmills, has nearly exterminated the fish."[56] Other factors associated with deforestation, such as low flow, rising water temperatures, and higher volumes of debris-laden run-off, also contributed to fish habitat loss along the river. Already much reduced by overfishing on Lake Ontario, salmon stopped spawning in the river entirely in the 1860s. The last native salmon on the Don was reputedly speared with a pitchfork at Taylor's paper mill near Pottery Road in the early 1870s.[57]

Centre to Periphery

Colonial approaches to the river and its valley differed in important ways from those that would follow. From reconnaissance expeditions to surveys, land surrender treaties, and resettlement efforts, imagined futures in this period consciously strove to establish a permanent European presence in the region through the institutions of agriculture, commerce, and private property. Specific in conception and practice to colonial imperatives of claiming and remodelling the geography of the New World, these imagined futures positioned the Don River and its valley as central to the development of the future capital. The practices that flowed from these ideas had visible and lasting effects upon valley ecosystems. They also displaced, and then replaced entirely, existing Aboriginal land uses. As we shall see, however, colonial practices in the river valley took quite different directions than Simcoe originally projected: while certain colonial practices found purchase in valley landscapes, others floundered due to factors unforeseen to Simcoe in his 1793 assessment.

Among the most successful of colonial land uses in the valley were industrial operations such as brickworks and water-powered mills. In the lower valley from the 1840s well into the twentieth century, brickworks took advantage of their situation in the former lake bed of the ancient Lake Iroquois to tap clay deposits over 200 metres deep in places. Water-powered mills peaked earlier and declined sooner, but their significance as sites of production anchored the development of a number of communities along the city's north-south axis. As steam came to replace water power in mills in the 1860s and 70s, and deforestation limited timber supply for area sawmills, the Don lost its attraction as a site for sawmills in particular. By 1885, most sawmills had closed; grist mills also suffered, but a number converted to steam and remained in operation, some into the early twentieth century.[58]

Valley lands proved less useful as sites for agricultural resettlement. With the exception of the river flats south of Pottery Road, relatively poor soils throughout the lower valley reduced the potential for successful farming initiatives. A series of attempts through the 1810s and 20s to dispose of 400 acres of reserved lands within the government reserve or "Park" on the west side of the lower river (see figure 1.2) provides an early indicator of the waning desirability of valley holdings through the nineteenth century. In an effort to generate revenue from the reserved lands, the colonial government commissioned a survey of the Park in 1811. In his response, Deputy-Surveyor Samuel Wilmot delivered disappointing news. "The land," he wrote, "consisted of poor thin soil with the timber principally destroyed, but ... with good management it might answer for pasture." The only valuable timber, he continued, "was close to the lakeshore." He estimated annual lease values of six to twelve pounds for most of the lots in the Park Reserve, considerably short of government expectations.[59] A second survey conducted in 1817 by Deputy Surveyor Reuben Sherwood generated some interest among a group of wealthy land speculators in York (particularly for holdings along King Street, the town's principal commercial corridor and eastern connector to the highway to Kingston), but few actual sales.

Following these two abortive attempts to generate revenue from the eastern park reserve, the Crown in 1819 granted the entire reserve lands to a group of trustees for the purpose of raising funds for the construction of a hospital for the Town of York.[60] The land grant, estimated by government authorities at a value of 6,000 pounds, was issued to match funds donated by a charitable society towards the construction of the hospital.[61] However, sales were neither as expedient nor as lucrative as the hospital trustees had hoped.[62] In his appeal for support from the provincial government in 1824, hospital trustee Justice William Dummer Powell reported that the trustees could proceed no further in their fundraising efforts due to the fact that "the sale of the ... Lands granted in Trust for the Hospital ... failed in producing the disposable funds estimated."[63]

As surveyor Wilmot's comments suggest, lagging sales could be attributed in part to the poor agricultural potential of the area. The steep valley walls between Bloor and Gerrard further limited agricultural potential and complicated access to valley holdings. Unpredictable riparian conditions brought more headaches for landowners: seasonal floods washed out bridges and roads and occasionally threatened livestock and outbuildings, and unexpected droughts reduced water flow, threatening mill and agricultural operations alike. For property owners east of the river, the limited number of bridge crossings over the Don, and the poor quality of those that did exist, made access to their holdings especially challenging.

By far the most damning for valley land holdings were persistent perceptions of unhealthiness associated with the marshy landscape of the lower river and Ashbridge's Bay Marsh. From the earliest days of European settlement, certain problems were especially pronounced in the east end. A notice in the *Upper Canada Gazette* on 18 May 1799, for example, cautioned York residents to guard their crops against the "swarms of insects" driven from the eastern marshes by prevailing spring winds.[64] More serious still than damage to garden produce was the fever or ague that tormented settler populations each summer. Characterized by alternating symptoms of severe fever and shaking chills, the "ague" or "lake fever" was an almost inevitable, if rarely fatal, aspect of life in Upper Canada in the late eighteenth and early nineteenth centuries.[65] Now understood as a strain of malaria, a disease spread by the bite of the *Anopheles* mosquito, at the time the ague was thought to result from inhaling "bad air" (hence mal/aria). In a letter to a former employer in Quebec City in September 1801, Toronto printer John Bennett wrote:

> I am just recovering from a severe fit of fever and ague which confined me to bed for ten days past – no body can escape it who pretends to live here ... There is a marsh about [half] a mile from where I live from which a thick fog arises every morning – people attribute [the fever] in great measure to that and to the low and uncultivated state of the Country.[66]

Gases produced by decomposing organic matter took on the ominous label of "miasmas" – disease-producing vapours – and the places where such organic matter accumulated, such as swamps and wetlands, became places to fear, avoid, and destroy through drainage and fill.

Before the discovery of the malaria parasite in 1880 and subsequent discoveries of mosquitoes as vectors of transmission, place itself bore the mantle of disease risk. Certain environments were considered more "unhealthy" than others. In 1803, for example, Sir Isaac Brock reported in a letter to military secretary James Green that the soldiers quartered in the Block House at the mouth of the Don "are falling ill of the Ague and Fever in great numbers" while the garrison at the west end of town "continues in perfect health." The evidence confirmed his suspicions about the environment around the lower river, "[shewing] plainly that the character given of the situation of the Block House is ... well founded."[67] A quarter-century later, petitioners to the Upper Canadian Legislature in 1830 stressed the "inconvenience and unhealthiness" of the site of the recently burned Parliament House, located at the foot of Parliament Street just west of the Don marshes, in their call to reconstruct the parliament buildings near the lieutenant-governor's residence in New Town (west of the original town plot). "No person having a regard to health would select [the site near the Marsh] for a residence," they argued; "the untenanted State of houses adjoining the said Marsh, confirm them in this opinion."[68] Simcoe's vision of a secure and prosperous settlement at the east end of Toronto Bay had been dashed.

Conevery Bolton Valencius has provided useful context for this notion of "unhealthy" landscapes in her 2002 monograph *The Health of the Country*. For nineteenth-century Americans, Valencius reminds us, "the environment [did not stop] at the seeming boundary of the skin." Instead, "the surrounding world seeped into [one's] every pore, creating states of health that were as much environmental as they were personal."[69] Just as elevated sites with fresh, circulating air were considered salubrious, so low, marshy areas where air and water alike were thought to stagnate were considered unhealthy and malevolent.[70] Miasmas "entered the body as breath or fluid, and they operated within it just as they did within terrain. They carried the environment's imbalance, disturbance, or putrefaction into the depths of the body, expressing within the individual the sickly tendencies of the locale."[71] For Brock's soldiers and the petitioners to the Upper Canadian parliament, then, the marshlands around the mouth of the Don were inherently unhealthy. Ironically, despite mistaken theories about the origin of disease, fears of miasma were not entirely misplaced. Brock's observations about the disproportionate frequency of ague among soldiers at the eastern blockhouse corroborate other anecdotal sources in suggesting that malaria cases were more numerous in areas adjacent to the marsh.[72] Indeed, the slow-moving waters of the Don marshes would have provided an excellent breeding ground for mosquitoes, and efforts made to avoid these "unhealthy places" and to shut out the dangerous "night air" often had the effect of shutting out mosquitoes as well. Even before significant industrial development in the area, the marshy lowlands of the lower river were experienced, and imagined, as a diseased landscape.

Not surprisingly, perceptions of unhealthiness had significant implications for the area's development. In an 1833 letter to Viscount

Goderich, Secretary of State for the Colonies, Lieutenant-Governor John Colborne explained that the westward expansion of the city was the only reasonable option: "the Eastern part of the Town is affected by the effluvia of the marshes of the Don, and the rapid increase in the population requires that the Town should be extended towards the Westward, the most salubrious and convenient site."[73] Toronto did, indeed, "lean west" in the decades that followed, pulling away from the site of the original town plot near the mouth of the Don. Parliament moved to new and more fashionable quarters in the west end of town (at Front and John Streets) in 1832, escalating with its relocation the desirability of west-end real estate (and the corresponding undesirability of the east end).[74] When the city incorporated in 1834, the lower river came to represent an official margin, its curving course forming the eastern border of the city between Bloor and Queen streets. The largely undeveloped area between Parliament Street and the Lower Don was further marginalized by its placement within the city liberties, an ambiguous administrative status that meant residents neither enjoyed full city rights and services nor paid full city taxes. Like other suburban areas around the city, development here was slower and more sporadic than in the more desirable and (marginally) better-serviced areas of the centre, and tended to concentrate along central access routes.[75] From 1834 until the abolishment of the liberties in 1859, the Lower Don occupied an urban margin, both within the everyday experience of the city's residents and in the official sphere of city maps and jurisdictional boundaries.

And yet, as much as these considerations played a role in reducing the desirability of lands in and around the lower valley, particularly for middle- and upper-class buyers, they always existed in tension with pressure in various periods to expand the city eastward. With undesirability came incentives: cheaper land prices; lower taxes for property owners; and, as the century progressed, proximity to industrial employers.[76] As access improved and population pressures increased throughout the century, development increased in the area despite associations of risk. By the 1840s, the Park had become "chiefly a quarter of workmen's cottages."[77] Proximity to a growing number of industrial employers in the 1860s and 70s attracted more working-class residents to neighbourhoods on both sides of the lower river, a trend not lost on land developers who advertised the "walk to work" attractions of new subdivisions in the area.

Clustered around "railyards, noisome factories and packinghouses," the neighbourhoods around the Lower Don were among several impoverished working-class districts in the city, J.M.S. Careless has noted, that emerged between the high-value properties of the centre and the wealthy enclaves in the outlying districts."[78] Here, working-class families "had mainly to be content with little clapboarded or rough-cast cottages ... [where] at least, they had gardens and some space around them, while yet being within walking range of work."[79] An urban periphery had been created, a designation that would become even more pronounced as industrial activities further transformed the valley in the late nineteenth century.

Conclusion

With its forested slopes, rich clay deposits, and running water, the Don Valley fuelled the growth of the nascent town of York. From the first years of European settlement in the 1790s until the early 1830s, the lower valley and eastern waterfront featured significantly in imagined futures for the colony. Here Simcoe located his parliament buildings; here, too, the government park reserve for future government buildings. At once a provider of raw materials and a corridor for people, animals, and goods, the valley served well Simcoe's vision for a settlement at the eastern end of Toronto Bay.

Unforeseen difficulties surrounding the location of Simcoe's settlement, however, coupled with the arrival of rail transportation across the eastern waterfront in the 1850s, would transform material uses and perceptions of the valley in the latter half of the nineteenth century. With the decline of milling operations in the 1860s and 70s, the Don River Valley was increasingly seen more for its problems than for its possibilities: steep ravines, poor soils, and an unpredictable riparian environment circumscribed the agricultural potential of the area; persistent perceptions of danger and unhealthiness associated with the marshlands of the lower river provided further disincentive for development. The particular geography of the river valley, combined with these larger political and economic developments, ultimately redirected settlement activities away from their origins at the eastern end of the harbour. For the river valley, the ramifications of this shift in the city's development were significant. Colonial visions of the valley as a fitting site for agricultural resettlement gradually eroded, to be supplanted by a new and industrial imagined future, one that cast the valley as a hub for industrial development and a sink for industrial and municipal wastes.

2 Making an Industrial Margin

Every city that has manufacturing industries has a district set apart therefor, and the Don is the district that nature and expedience have set apart for Toronto.

Toronto World, 8 May 1884

By the 1880s, the Lower Don River was widely perceived as an "objectionable stream" and a persistent threat to public health. Years of waste and sewage disposal by local industries and municipal authorities, combined with changes in the river's hydrology caused by deforestation, soil erosion, and water diversion for agricultural and industrial purposes, contributed to highly polluted conditions in the slow-moving, serpentine reaches of the lower river and the massive reach of marshland at its mouth. As one area resident commented in a letter to the *Daily Globe* in 1874, "the water and marsh [at the mouth] of the Don continues to be filled with a foul combination of [wastes] … so that whenever the wind sets to a particular quarter, and agitates the water, the result is [an] abominable smell … injurious to the comfort [and] the health of all within its reach."[1] Associations of the valley as a polluted and unhealthy space built upon environmental perceptions that had been in place since the early 1800s.

In the early 1890s, a group of Ashbridge's Bay property owners set about to compel the city to abate the nuisance. A number of sewage outfalls along the north shore of Ashbridge's Bay[2] constituted part of their grievance, but the dominant source of stench and contamination, they claimed, came from the Gooderham and Worts cattle byres, located on the shores of the marsh east of the bend in the river mouth.[3] Soon after launching his distillery operations in 1837, William

Gooderham recognized the capital benefits to be gained by fattening cattle and hogs with the waste products of the distilling process. Grain "wash" or "swill" converted into marketable meat products created a neat and profitable feedback loop in the company's operations; waste products, in the form of liquidized cattle manure, found a convenient sink in the adjacent marshlands. Gooderham and Worts's cattle operations eventually comprised seven byres or cattle sheds with a capacity for over 4,000 cows.[4] A piggery on the same grounds added to the olfactory cocktail.

Complaints, primarily focused on the stench of the operations, began to accumulate. In 1874, a Reverend Baldwin, resident of Ashbridge's Bay, submitted a series of letters to the editors of the *Daily Globe* complaining of the unpleasant and unhealthy smells emanating from the marsh as the result of the effluents from the distillery's cattle byres. Gooderham and Worts responded with a letter of their own, suggesting that Baldwin go "to some quiet watering place and [spend] his summer, as he has often done before" rather than "drawing the attention of his neighbours to any smell he [perceives]." The cattle byres were only one of many industries near the mouth of the Don, the distillers pointed out, including "coal oil refineries, packing houses, slaughterhouses, lard-rendering establishments, breweries, &c, that do at times smell disagreeably." "Shall we do away with all these industries," they concluded, "and make Toronto the nice little watering place that would suit Mr. Baldwin, or shall we allow Toronto to make her way up to a first-class city, and let Mr. Baldwin seek for some place more congenial to his sense of smell!"[5]

Gooderham and Worts's sneering response to Baldwin prompted further letters in Baldwin's defence by others without the means of escaping the city in summer.[6] A poem in Toronto's weekly satirical magazine *Grip* was particularly effective in skewering the "Don Dictators" and their arrogance:

Ye of the squeamish stomachs; ye dwellers by the Don;
Ye who about the "Eastern Smells" so woefully take on;
Ye of the weak olfactory nerves and irritable humours;
Ye autocrats of impudence, ye insolent presumers
Who, holding dainty noses, rush daily to the papers –
I want to say a word to you about these foolish capers.
Why all this fuming, fury, fuss – why all this letter-writing?
'Tis wholly useless labour – just so much vapour fighting;
For if you're not content to breathe the odours with good grace,

> You'd better move your families to some nice watering-place.
> A *fig* for the "Authorities," the people of the Press!
> They've tried their strength with us before – and *we* run this stench, I guess.
> Don't care a continental who the "foul effluvia" hurts –
> It's part of our big business – Us – Gooderham and Worts!!
> You pay your honest taxes and ought to draw your breath
> Without inhaling poison, malaria and death?
> Well; if you *want* to rid yourselves of this here "Eastern Pest,"
> Go to some quiet watering-place, or, leastwise, friends, "Go West!!"[7]

Apparent in this correspondence is the gulf between those residents who could afford to remove themselves in summer when noxious odours were at their most foul, and those, as one respondent wrote, "whose occupation or circumstances [did] not permit them to accept Messrs. G & W.'s generous advice," but who nonetheless "[had] a right to be protected from the injurious effects of poisoned air and water."[8] As Andrew Hurley and others have shown, the politics of who suffered most from the effects of environmental pollutants had much to do with social stratification along lines of race, class, and gender.[9] In the case of late-nineteenth-century Ashbridge's Bay, both class and ethnicity were at work as determinants of environmental risk: those with the least amount of flexibility in escaping the effects of industrial pollution were certainly the area's workers and their families, many of whom had immigrated from Ireland at mid-century.[10] While the bulk of complaints about pollution in Ashbridge's Bay and the Lower Don in the 1870s and 80s centred on issues of smell and "bad air,"[11] water contamination from the byres and other area industries posed a much more serious risk to area residents.

This chapter explores some of the circumstances that led to the selection of the Lower Don lands as a space "set apart" for industrial development. Between 1850 and 1890, the expansion of manufacturing operations on the Lower Don established a pattern of industrialization that persisted and intensified in later years. Concentrations of particularly noxious industries, including tanneries, packing plants, and oil refineries, contributed to perceptions of the lower river as an urban wasteland. The expansion of sewerage systems served to further marginalize valley environments, reinforcing the separation between spaces for "people" and spaces for their wastes. As Michèle Dagenais and Caroline Durand observe in their study of wastewater systems in nineteenth-century Montreal, the implementation of sewerage systems resulted in the separation of "spaces reserved for human waste and its evacuation" from the places where "commerce, socialization, and family life took place."[12] Toronto's Don River in the late nineteenth century was one of these "spaces apart": a place designated to receive and process the city's wastes, and a place that carried with it both the dangers and the stigma of this designation. This chapter examines the ways that people responded to these changes and the threats they placed upon public health within the context of the conflict over the Gooderham and Worts cattle byres in the latter decades of the nineteenth century. Here, issues of class, corporate control, and the city's emerging (and reluctant) role as regulator and protector of the public interest appear as facets in the debate over environmental quality at the mouth of the river.

A Corridor of Wastes

As perceptions of unhealthiness and poor agricultural potential dampened the desirability of valley land holdings in the 1830s and 40s, and the status of the valley as an urban periphery solidified, new land uses began to take hold. Whereas water-powered mills continued to congregate along the upper branches of the river in this period, the lower river took on new significance as an attractive site for factories producing a broader array of goods after 1850. The arrival of the Grand Trunk's east-west rail line across the Toronto waterfront in 1856 drew tanneries, breweries, foundries, and, later, packing plants, soap factories, and oil refineries to locations along the lower reaches of the river and the river mouth. With them came working-class housing, from isolated cottages in the early years to ethnic and mixed-origin neighbourhoods such as Cabbagetown, Corktown, and Riverside in the late nineteenth century.

Early firms attracted others, creating constellations of mutually supportive operations. Soapworks in the lower valley, for example, took advantage of local supplies of tallow from nearby animal processing plants, while tanneries produced leather belts used for power transmission in early factories and mills. In the 1860s and 70s, widespread adoption of steam power stimulated industrial expansion across the city. The existence of a growing industrial hub on the Lower Don, with its established benefits of affordable land and convenient rail and shipping access, provided the foundation for further industrial growth. The 1880s and 90s would see greater expansion still, with the infusion of state funds to straighten the river and create new industrial lands. By the turn of the century, the lower reaches of the river and the river mouth had been transformed into a built environment especially conducive to industrial production.

Industrial aspirations for the lower river imagined a geography decidedly different from the colonial visions of John Grave Simcoe. While Simcoe sought to lay claim to valley lands and to harness their natural resources in the development of an agricultural settlement in England's image, late-nineteenth-century industrialists sought to transform the lower valley into a viable built environment for industrial capitalism. As manufacturing expanded in the lower valley, the river itself and the natural resources it provided – the clay, timber, and fish that had supported the development of the earlier city – became less important than the character of this space on the urban fringe, and the attractions it offered in terms of transportation infrastructure, affordable real estate, and remove from the discerning residential and commercial districts of the urban core. While an earlier generation of industries may have chosen a valley location for proximity to a source of water power, a stand of white pine, or a supply of tan bark, industries building or relocating in the lower valley after 1850 looked primarily to proximity to rail and shipping depots. An increasing reliance on imported raw materials such as coal and iron ore, and an orientation towards national and international markets, made access to transportation sites vital for success. Sweeping technological change in the latter half of the nineteenth century – notably the advent of steam, hydraulic, and electrically powered machinery – produced changes throughout the entire production system, creating new demands for large, space-consuming modern facilities.[13]

Industries congregating along the lower river and the river mouth in the latter half of the nineteenth century shared in common the relatively noxious character of their operations: extreme noise, "dirtiness," rank odours, or unsightliness were among their defining features. Land uses that endangered surrounding buildings also found a place in what urban geographers have called the city's "backyard" – the waterfront and low-lying spaces along the edges of the urban centre.[14] Activities and materials that posed a risk of fire typically fell within this category, including coal and lumber storage, stables, and industries such as foundries that operated steam engines or employed high-temperature processes. These land uses built upon established patterns. Noxious industries were the first, and for many years the only, industrial uses on the lower river. Tanneries, for example, had existed on the lower river since 1820; distilleries and rendering plants, since the 1830s and 1840s.

Valley lands also had a history of hazardous materials storage: in the early 1800s, a powder magazine on the peninsula near the mouth of the river kept flammable material away from the homes of early Toronto residents. The 1858 Boulton Atlas for the city shows a second powder storage site on the west side of the river near Winchester Street.

In the location of these land uses at the urban fringe, both push and pull factors were at work. Nuisance by-laws and public pressure played a role in pushing these types of industries to the edges of the city, but as Robert Lewis reminds us for Montreal in this period, "in most cases ... firms sought out locational assets being created on the city's unbuilt fringe."[15] The establishment of two oil refineries – Duncan and Clarke, and McColl Brothers – along the west bank of the lower river in the 1860s and 70s is illustrative. Like other North American refineries in this period, the Don plants produced mainly kerosene for illumination purposes and a variety of waxes and lubrication products. The location of these industries in what was gradually becoming an industrial suburb at the city's edge was not incidental. As Raphael Fischler points out, as early as the 1860s Toronto City Council took action to prohibit the establishment of oil refineries and storage facilities in the city centre due to the flammability of their products and processes.[16] But locational assets also played a role. Reliance on imports of coal and later petroleum made access to transportation facilities imperative; as facilities modernized and markets expanded, the need for greater space made newly created industrial lands around the river mouth especially attractive. McColl Brothers relocated to the river mouth in 1890, continuing to expand before being purchased by Texaco in the 1930s.[17] By 1911, oil refineries dominated the area around the mouth of the Don; they would persist in the area through the first half of the twentieth century (figure 2.1).

Locational assets did not simply exist on the fringe; they were actively created by urban elites and supported by the state in the form of the municipal government. In the case of the Lower Don, two features of the area operated to attract manufacturing firms in the latter half of the nineteenth century: the availability of cheap land and the creation of transportation infrastructure. As we saw in chapter 1, the stigmatization of valley lands due to associations of unhealthiness, challenging access, and poor agricultural potential had the effect of suppressing real estate values and transforming the demographics of the area from elite to largely working-class landowners by the 1840s – developments viewed favourably by industrialists. The extension of the Grand Trunk

2.1 Bird's-eye view of the Lower Don River, 1893. Note the oil refineries to the right (east) of the bend in the river, and the marsh stretching south and east of the river mouth. The large Gooderham and Worts distillery building sits at the southeastern corner of the harbour, west of the river mouth. The Gooderham and Worts cattle sheds lie on the opposite side of the river, immediately east of the bend. (Detail from Barclay, Clark and Co., *City of Toronto, 1893*, Toronto Public Library, Historical Pictures Collection, 916-2-1.)

Railway (GTR) across the eastern waterfront in 1856 and the completion of the Don Improvement Project in the early 1890s, with its north-south rail corridor and newly created industrial lands, compounded incentives for industry.

Rail development in the 1850s created its own spin-off industries and attracted others, dramatically changing the landscape of the area around the river mouth. By 1857, the GTR had constructed a number of workshops, depots, and a station immediately west of the river mouth at the eastern end of Front Street. Here the role of the state in guiding and legitimizing these land uses is evident: Toronto City Council permitted waterfront access to the railway company with the condition that they restrict their engine house and depot to a location near the Don River.[18] As in other cities, rail's high material demands attracted a range of supportive industries, including those supplying metal, wood, and leather products.[19] In Toronto this was epitomized by the massive Toronto Rolling Mills, which opened just south of the GTR yards in 1857. At the peak of its operation in 1867, the company employed 300 men producing iron rails and re-rolling worn rails from the Toronto to Montreal section of the GTR.[20] Other industries took advantage of the benefits created by rail access to build or relocate along the riverfront. William Davies's decision to relocate his expanding pork packing business to the eastern end of Front (now Mill) Street in 1879 is a case in point. The new site granted him more space and better rail access; significantly, it also provided him with ready access to a supply of ice from the Don River. A huge ice house located on the site allowed Davies to stockpile and preserve his ice supplies through the summer months and thus to operate year round (see figure 2.2). Easy rail access combined with proximity to ice supplies enabled him to ship his products to destinations across North America and beyond. Davies's pork-packing plant became the first in Canada to slaughter, cure, and process pork products continuously and on a large scale; it later amalgamated with another packing firm to become Canada Packers.[21]

The outcome of these changes was a grossly polluted waterway. It is important to remember, too, that this was a small river – a river you could throw a stone over. The effects of pollutants would have been more pronounced, and more rapid, than in other more sizeable urban-industrial waterways like the St Lawrence or the Allegheny. For most industrial operations along the Don, the river offered a convenient disposal site for industrial wastes. Animal carcasses, lime from tanning operations, corrosive lye from soapworks, and industrial by-products such as gasoline all found their way into the river. Organic wastes such

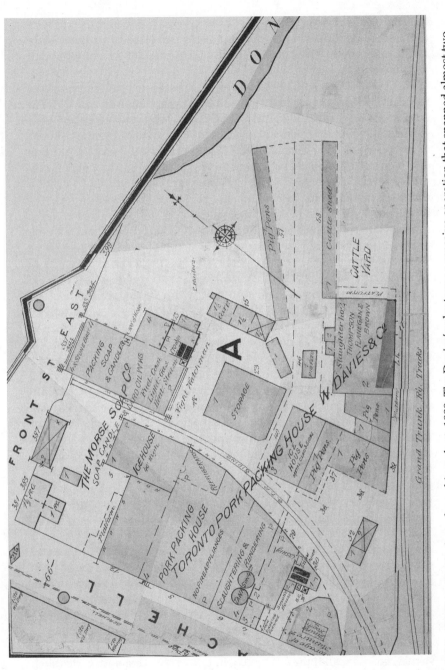

2.2   William Davies's pork-packing plant, 1889. The Davies's plant was a massive operation that spanned almost two acres northwest of the river mouth. (Detail from Charles E. Goad, *Insurance Plan of the City of Toronto, Ontario, 1889.* Courtesy of the University of Toronto Map and Data Library.)

as animal offal and manure put heavy stress on the river's supply of dissolved oxygen, a vital ingredient for the maintenance of aquatic life and the decomposition of wastes. In limited quantities, organic wastes will be broken down by microorganisms present in river water. As tanneries, breweries, and other industries multiplied along the lower river in the latter half of the nineteenth century, however, the river's ability to assimilate these wastes would have been seriously compromised.[22] Consumption of land around the river mouth also removed porous wetlands, further reducing the river's capacity to process pollutants.

Sewage pollution added to the cocktail. Sewage disposal in the river was largely incidental until the 1880s and 90s, when the city extended the sewer system to the east and ran several outfalls into the Don. Conditions along the lower river and Ashbridge's Bay marsh worsened rapidly. An article in the *Toronto Mail* of 20 March 1894 described the lower river as a "pestilential channel" whose waters had taken on "a yellowish green colour, and a slimy, soup-like consistency." In the hot days of summer, area residents complained, the river "[gave] off noxious and undesirable vapours." "Sewage from a large district," the *Mail* observed, "is constantly being poured into [the river]," and "the slowness of its current is not enough to clear off [these] impurities." Rosedale Creek sewer appears to have been the most offensive of the outfall points constructed south of Bloor Street in the 1880s and 90s. Formerly running as an open sewer into the Don near Winchester Street, the creek was sewered in 1888 or 1889 in response to the concerns of local residents and the city's medical health officer.[23] Draining "a vast area comprising the north and north eastern portions of the City," the sewer caught the attention of engineer W.T. Jennings in 1890, who reported on "a present and growing evil caused by the discharge of sewage in the waters of the River Don at Winchester Street."[24] Conditions worsened as additional outfall points were constructed on the east side of the river in the early 1890s, and even more of Toronto's rapidly growing population had their homes connected to the sewage system.[25]

Sewage and industrial pollution undoubtedly had serious consequences for riverine ecology. More clearly demonstrable from the nineteenth-century records was the effect of pollution (and sewage pollution in particular) upon human health. While the city would see its last outbreak of cholera in 1866, the incidence of other water-borne diseases such as typhoid fever remained high until the end of the century.[26] As nineteenth-century observers increasingly suspected, the principal problem lay in the location of the city's water intake pipe at the foot of Peter Street in the Toronto harbour, only one-eighth of a mile from the

Yonge and Bay Street sewer outfalls. While city water was initially used mainly for firefighting and industrial purposes, a growing number of homes tapped in to the water supply in the 1870s and 80s.[27]

Nineteenth-century responses to the problem were few, and those improvements that were conducted were grossly inadequate.[28] In 1875, for example, the city succeeded in moving the water intake pipe out of the harbour to the lake side of Toronto Island; an ineffective filtering and delivery system, however, meant that citizens continued to "rely on fetid harbour water at their peril."[29] A break in the pipe in August 1890 led to one of the city's most devastating typhoid fever outbreaks, killing almost 500.[30] Other initiatives, such as the prohibition of ice cutting on the Don, Ashbridge's Bay, and Toronto harbour in 1889,[31] and efforts by Toronto's medical officer of health to remove sources of "filth" from the city's streets likely had some effect in improving public health. Measurable improvement is certainly evident in the city's death rate, which fell from 21.3 per 1,000 in 1883, to 15.2 per 1,000 in 1896.[32] The fundamental issue of sewage contamination in Toronto Bay, however, remained unaddressed. Repeated calls for a trunk sewer to carry wastes into the deeper waters of the lake were either ignored by Council or refused by over-burdened ratepayers.[33]

Like other cities across North America at this time, a series of factors worked against the implementation of pollution controls on local waterways. As urban environmental historian Joel Tarr has observed, competing ideas about the origins of disease, widespread belief in the effectiveness of dilution in treating sewage wastes, and "a municipal disinclination to spend public funds for improvements that did not promise any material return" contributed to the heel dragging among municipal governments in responding to sewage pollution problems. The decision to invest in water treatment, rather than sewage treatment and disposal technologies, also delayed the implementation of pollution controls.[34] By the early 1890s, conditions in the harbour and adjacent Ashbridge's Bay had become so foul, and effective responses so unlikely, that for some beleaguered residents and harbour users, litigation seemed the only option.

The Price of Prosperity?

In 1884, ten years after the initial complaints, the issue of Gooderham and Worts's cattle byres pollution resurfaced in the press. A debate developed around the question of whether pollution was an inevitable consequence of prosperity. The press, for its part, saw pollution as a by-product of a vibrant metropolitan economy. Media coverage of the conflict largely absolved the distillery owners of wrong-doing, pointing to the importance of their establishment in fuelling the city's prosperity and identifying the range of other industrial offenders in the area that added to the nuisance.[35] The Lower Don in these depictions appears as a providential setting for the city's wastes, and pollution an inevitable side effect of the process of industrialization. As the editors of the *Toronto World* reasoned on 8 May 1884,

> Every city that has manufacturing industries has a district set apart therefor, and the Don is the district that nature and expedience have set apart for Toronto. It is not frequented by the fastidious, it possesses excellent railway and shipping accommodations, the land is cheap, there is good accommodation for working people, and it is accessible to the business centres by the street cars.[36]

Not everyone agreed with this assessment. Among the few dissenters was William Canniff, Toronto's first medical officer of health. For Canniff, the pollution in Ashbridge's Bay conflicted with, rather than exemplified, notions of modernity: "That cow-byres are still allowed to exist within the city bounds," he wrote in his final report to the city before resigning in frustration in September 1890, "is an indication that the public does not realize the fact that Toronto is no longer a village or small city, but a metropolis of goodly proportions, requiring corresponding conditions."[37] The modern city, for Canniff, defined its success not simply by its prosperity, but by its ability to protect the public interest.

As it had in the 1870s, the debate fissured along class lines. The *Toronto World* concluded that most area residents supported the industrial development of the Lower Don, despite the costs to their comfort. "It is a comparatively few property holders," the editors asserted, "who are holding to sell for villa lots who feel aggrieved."[38] Class conflict over the pollution issue became especially pronounced in May 1884, when a group of industrial workers submitted a petition to city council defending the distillery and other industries near the mouth of the Don as employers and supporters of their livelihoods. Written in response to an earlier petition by Ashbridge's Bay residents "respecting the offensive and unpleasant odour ... near the mouth of the river Don" and a subsequent commission appointed by the city to report on the issue, the petition argued that the offending industries employed a large number of workers, many of whom owned homes in the area. Removing the industries would thus "be a serious blow to the prosperity of this portion of the city," an area "peculiarly adapted … for the location of manufactories." The problem would be best solved, petitioners concluded, by having the city install a "complete system of drainage" that would "encourage rather than discourage the carrying on and commencing [of] the industries … in question."[39]

Signed by over 800 individuals, including the executive and employees of a number of industries around the river mouth,[40] the petition presented a potent statement not only of worker loyalty to the offending industries, but of workers' interests as homeowners with investments in the future of the district. Like so many subsequent conflicts between jobs and environmental integrity, jobs were placed in direct opposition to environmental reforms: pursuing one would negate the other. The fact that the language of the petition reflects so closely earlier letters from the Gooderham and Worts executive, together with the presence of Gooderham and Worts's signatures among other executive signatories, suggests at the very least the involvement of company owners in drafting a text that reflected their interests as much as those of their employees. For workers and their families, the issue was likely not as black and white as the petition suggests. Like other area residents, they were probably bothered by the smell of the cattle byres and other industries; the threat to their livelihoods, however, was likely more worrisome than the potentially dangerous health effects of offensive smells. Workers' roles in perpetuating representations of the marsh as a providential site for industry point to the failure of environmental justice arguments (linking class and race with environmental risk) to fully capture the complexity of the historical processes that create such landscapes, and the perceptions attached to them.[41]

Despite the intensity of debate through the 1870s and 80s about the pollution of the marsh, and the role of Gooderham and Worts's cattle byres in particular, attempts to address the problem were half-hearted and ultimately fruitless. A litigation attempt by the Dominion government in 1884 proved unsuccessful. Details on the outcome and nature of the case are frustratingly thin, the evidence limited to a comment in Jeffrey Stinson's history of the Port Industrial District that "the out-of-court settlement included an unusual requirement for the company to plant 1,000 trees."[42] Four years later, in the fall of 1888, the city responded to pressure from area residents by dredging a narrow channel (Coatsworth's Cut) from the eastern end of Ashbridge's Bay to the lake to allow for greater circulation in the bay.[43] While initial reports from health authorities were promising,[44] by July 1891 the shallow channel had filled almost completely with sand and conditions had again deteriorated.[45]

In 1892 the city attempted again to abate the pollution problem in Ashbridge's Bay. A survey of conditions in the summer of 1891 by Dr Canniff's replacement, medical health officer Norman Allen, documented the effects of the pollution upon local residents. Notably, the language of the miasmatic theory of disease persists in his association of "fog" and "scum" with disease:

> In warm weather bubbles of gas arise from the bottom of the Bay, especially in the vicinity of the sewer outlets; a green scum forms rapidly upon the water, and in the early morning a dense fog hangs over the weeds and rushes. When the scum forms, the residents in the immediate neighbourhood state that they suffer extremely from sickness, indeed all whom I consulted complained of illness in their families – diphtheria, sore throat, malaria, nausea, loss of appetite, lassitude and inability to work.

Gooderham and Worts's cattle byres again appeared, in Allen's assessment, as "one of the worst sources of pollution."[46] Conditions had only deteriorated by the following summer, prompting the Ashbridge's Bay Property Owners Association to threaten the city with litigation if actions were not taken to abate the nuisance.[47] In the meantime, officials from the Provincial Board of Health (PBH) predicted that cholera would reach Canada by the summer of 1893, increasing the pressure to address conditions around the mouth of the Don during the 1892 season.[48] The PBH intervened in June 1892 with a mandate to clean up the bay. The mandate, to be implemented by Toronto's local Board of Health, included four recommendations: (1) to dredge an east-west channel through the marsh between Ashbridge's Bay and Toronto Bay; (2) to dredge a second channel through the sandbar at the far east end of Ashbridge's Bay, opening it to Lake Ontario; (3) to extend the sewers discharging into Ashbridge's Bay into deeper water; and (4) to direct Gooderham and Worts to immediately implement alternate waste disposal measures or face legal action by the Local Board of Health.[49]

The city was forced to act. Less than a month later, Council advised the city solicitor to take legal action against Gooderham and Worts to prevent their further pollution of the marsh and bay. The company received notice that they would be prohibited, after 15 October 1892, from discharging wastes into the marsh. In November 1892 the city engineer reported that the company was in the process of implementing a system to filter liquid wastes from the byres.[50] At the same time, the city applied for permission from the Dominion government to breach the Government Breakwater separating Ashbridge's Bay from the harbour in order to create an east-west channel between the two bodies of water. Their application was refused, partly in response to a deputation from the Toronto Harbour Commissioners, who feared that the migration of flotsam from the marsh would interfere with harbour navigation. Facing an injunction from the province preventing them from "opening any more sewers into the Bay," together with several pending suits for failing to abate the nuisance in Ashbridge's Bay, the city was pressed to address the problem.[51]

In October 1892 Council asked city engineer E.H. Keating to develop a proposal for putting Ashbridge's Bay "in a sanitary condition." Keating's emergency relief plan, adopted in November, contained two main components: the dredging of a wide channel from Toronto harbour east along the northern boundary of Ashbridge's Bay and then south through the sandbar into the lake (Coatsworth's Cut); and the diversion of the Don directly south to meet with this channel (colour plate 1).[52] Significantly, Keating viewed the plan as a temporary measure to allow for better circulation of the waters in the bay in advance of a permanent remedy, the construction of a trunk sewer: "No reclamation scheme," he wrote, "can be regarded as perfect which does not either provide for or anticipate the exclusion of faecal matter from the Bay."[53] Permission to breach the breakwater was finally granted by the federal government in March 1893, and construction of what would become known as "Keating's Cut" began that spring.[54]

In reality, the implementation of Keating's plan was considerably more modest than his original proposal: the channel was dredged to a width of only ninety feet, significantly short of the projected 300 feet. Coatsworth's Cut was completed to specifications at the eastern end of Ashbridge's Bay, but, as we shall see, the diversion of the Don south into the new channel was not completed until many years later.[55] Pollution of the marshlands persisted: in 1893 an Ashbridge's Bay resident sued the city for negligence, blaming conditions in the marsh for the severe illnesses of his children.[56] Twenty years later, in 1913, boat builder Richard Schofield brought legal action against the city and the Toronto Harbour Commissioners, claiming difficulty in maintaining water access to his boat works due to sewerage construction in the area. Sludge from these sewers accumulated around his wharves, damaging boat hulls and threatening the health of his employees.[57] In both cases, the plaintiffs were unsuccessful in their claims.

Not until 1908, when population pressure had compounded an already abominable situation, and the germ theory of disease had gained a strong foothold among expert authorities and the general public alike, did the Toronto electorate finally approve expenditures for the construction of a trunk sewer, sewage treatment, and water filtration plants.[58] By 1910, a secure water intake pipe extended well out into the lake, and a new filtration plant on Toronto Island cleansed incoming water before pumping it across the harbour to expanded reservoir facilities. A primary sewage treatment plant opened at Ashbridge's Bay the following year. The combined effect of these two developments significantly reduced water-borne disease rates: typhoid was virtually eliminated from the city after 1911, and Toronto's annual death rate fell from 15.18 per 1,000 in 1896 to 11.2 per 1,000 in 1914.[59]

Conclusion

By 1880, the "Don problem" and related concerns about the marshlands at the river's mouth were well established in the public consciousness. Because the Don was conceived as a "space apart" and a providential site for the city's wastes, the resulting foul odours and polluted waters were seen by many observers as the price of prosperity and of keeping other parts of the city more habitable. As Joel Tarr has shown for American cities in the same period, businesses repeatedly chose the "cheapest sink" for wastes unless prohibited by law, and public officials typically responded only in times of crisis. Overburdened municipal budgets and fluctuating political will contributed to the tendency to adopt quick-fix solutions – solutions which, more often than not, failed to solve the problem, but only transferred it to other locations.[60] Visions of a sanitary and predictable waterway as a hub for industry and a corridor for transportation would eventually compel the city to initiate the Don Improvement Project in 1886.

3 Taming a "Monster of Ingratitude"

From the moment that the peninsula raised its protecting head above the waters, and screened the Don from the surges of the Lake, the Don, like a monster of ingratitude, has displayed such destructive industry as to displace by its alluvial disgorgings by far the greater part of the body of water originally enclosed by the peninsula. The whole of the marsh to the East, once deep and clear water, is the work of the Don, and in the Bay of York, where now its destructive mouths are turned, vegetation shews itself in almost every direction, prognosticating the approaching conversion of this beautiful sheet of water into another marshy delta of the Don.

Hugh Richardson, Captain of the *Canada*, ca 1834

But the Don, the poor unconscious object of all this invective, is in reality no more to blame than is the savage because he is a savage, not having had a chance to be anything else. In proceeding to lay the foundation of a delta of solid land at its mouth, the Don followed the precedent of other streams, in conformity with the physical conditions of its situation. When at length the proper hour arrived, and the right men appeared, possessed of the intelligence, the vigour and the wealth equal to the task of bettering nature by art on a considerable scale, then at once the true value and capabilities of the Don were brought out into view.

Dr Henry Scadding, *Toronto of Old*, 1873

Hugh Richardson's and Henry Scadding's comments on the Don – Scadding's made in response to Richardson's words almost forty years earlier – provide apt bookends for a discussion about human frustration with, and human alterations of, the Don River and its seasonal processes of flooding and silt deposition. For Richardson, the silt and detritus that the river deposited each spring in Toronto Harbour created hazards for shipping traffic. Unwary ship captains faced damage to ship hulls from floating debris, or the grounding of their craft upon a steadily accumulating ridge of silt stretching southwest from the river mouth.[1] In his later role as harbour master from 1850 until his death in 1870, Richardson saw his dreams for a deep and navigable harbour continually frustrated by the silting actions of the river. For Scadding, the Don was not so much a malignant presence as an undervalued resource, its "true value and capabilities" lying dormant and unseen until the "right men appeared" to take up "the task of bettering nature by art on a considerable scale." Scadding's assessment anticipates the modern, technocratic approach to the river adopted by proponents of the Don Improvement Project in the 1880s and 90s. For Scadding and his peers, nature was fundamentally knowable, predictable, and malleable.

The "Don problem," as it was known, had three central components: pollution and related concerns about water-borne disease; flooding; and the accumulation of silt around the river mouth. A series of improvement projects, beginning in the 1870s, attempted to address these problems. In each case, the projects proved more complicated and time-consuming to implement than planners originally thought. Even more damning was the fact that they largely failed to fulfil expectations. Conflicting institutional priorities between the city, concerned primarily with upstream flooding and pollution, and the Harbour Trust, concerned with siltation at the river mouth, complicated efforts to resolve the problem. Further challenges arose as a result of the planners' failure to adequately comprehend the environment they were working with. In the end, engineers' attempts to transform a complex riparian system into a "flush" for wastes and debris and a viable corridor for shipping and rail traffic were too willing to assume a blank slate – a river patiently awaiting the revelation of its "true value and capabilities." For all the apparent success of projects elsewhere to transform urban environments into working components of the industrial landscape, the Don and its seasonal processes proved extremely difficult to contain. Fixing one problem, as successive generations of engineers and planners discovered, too often created another.

The Harbour, the River, and the Problem of Silt

In city council minutes and Harbour Trust documents, engineers' reports and editorials in city newspapers, Richardson's 1834 frustration with the Don's "alluvial disgorgings" was restated again and again, albeit less colourfully. Sediments deposited near the mouth of the river clogged access routes to industrial wharves, limited the approach of deep-hulled craft, and threatened navigation in the eastern portion of the harbour. Problems arose not only from the quantity of material deposited, but also the quality: as riverfront industry expanded in the latter half of the nineteenth century, depositions of "sludge" became increasingly foul.

Like all rivers, the Don carries suspended silts scoured from upstream riverbanks and tributary creeks, organic debris such as tree branches, and a host of human-generated refuse. Items that are not caught up in tree roots or washed ashore in an oxbow turn find their way to the river mouth. As water flow decreases near the river mouth (the result of opposing currents or a widening of the river channel), silt and other fine particulates fall out of suspension and sink, forming in many cases broad deltas of rich alluvial soils – Ashbridge's Bay marsh is an example of this process. Seasonal flooding along the river accelerates this process of sedimentation. As Hugh Richardson was all too aware, the predictable annual cycle of fall rainstorms and spring freshets brought especially high concentrations of silt and debris into Toronto harbour.

Further exacerbating these processes was the incremental deforestation so central to the process of Euro-Canadian settlement in Upper Canada. Resulting increases in soil erosion and surface run-off produced sudden and severe floods in times of heavy rainfall, and extremely low flow during periods of drought.[2] Reviewing the growing register of complaints by harbour industrialists, ship captains, and officials from mid-century on, we can draw a rough correlation between rising percentages of upstream deforestation and increased levels of silt in the harbour. Contemporary observers also noted this connection. "Even the cultivation of the country," Hugh Richardson wrote in 1834, "increases the destructive powers of the Don, for the plough of the husbandman annually loosening the soil, the rain storm furnishes the river with a much larger tribute of alluvial matter, than when it only washed in its descent the matted foot of the wilderness."[3]

Changes in the shape and quality of the harbour through the nineteenth century prompted a series of reports and predictions by harbour officials, city engineers, and experts imported from the United States and England, but very little action. In 1833, the province appointed three harbour commissioners to report on problems in York harbour and make recommendations for its improvement. In their 1834 report, the commissioners identified sediment deposits at the mouth of the Don as one of several major threats to the viability of the harbour. The solution, they proposed, lay in damming the river's outlets into the harbour and diverting its flow east into Ashbridge's Bay marsh.[4] The commissioners' recommendations went unheeded, victim to a general reluctance by the province to invest in costly and potentially fruitless harbour improvements. As MPP W. Hamilton Merritt commented twenty years later, recalling the 1834 report, "the harbour has continued in its present state time out of mind ... some natural cause must have preserved its present depth of water." Let us not, he warned, "assume the responsibility of destroying one of the best harbours on Lake Ontario by undertaking an expensive and useless experiment."[5] Merritt's bid for caution here and his recognition of the little-understood natural forces in the creation and preservation of the harbour are all the more remarkable in light of his history as a central promoter and overseer of the 1820s Welland Canal project, which created a shipping corridor between Lake Ontario and Lake Erie that bypassed Niagara Falls. Presumably, he held no objection to the idea of improvement.

Studies and interventions in the following decades illustrate this fundamental uncertainty surrounding harbour processes, attributing the siltation problem to the river or to the sand-bearing currents entering the harbour from the lake. Attempts to solve one problem, as several generations of harbour authorities learned, typically exacerbated the other. In December 1852, a storm caused a narrow breach at the east end of the peninsula, creating a temporary separation between the harbour archipelago (today's Toronto Islands) and the mainland. Anxiety about the potential repercussions for the harbour, combined with ongoing concern about annual sediment deposits from the Don, led to a new flurry of reports and recommendations in the early 1850s. In 1854, the Toronto harbour commissioners held a competition "for the three best reports on the means to be adopted for the preservation and improvement of the Harbour of Toronto." Contestants were asked to comment specifically on the anticipated effects and proposed remedies for the "eastern gap," and the relationship between the Don, the harbour, and Ashbridge's Bay. Cash prizes went to three reports: the first to University of Toronto chemistry professor Henry Youle Hind, the second to civil engineer Sandford Fleming, and the third to provincial surveyor Kivas Tully. Differing in their recommendations for the harbour,[6] the contestants came closest to agreement in their suggestions for the Don. Echoing the findings of the 1834 committee, all three report authors saw the benefits of damming the Don's outlets to the harbour and diverting its sediment-bearing waters into Ashbridge's Bay marsh. For Tully and Fleming, the river offered added potential as a useful conduit for carrying the city's sewage into the natural "sink" of the marsh. Only Fleming identified sand-bearing lake currents as the main source for harbour sedimentation; by comparison, he found, the sediment loads of the Don were "inconsequential."[7]

No action was taken on these recommendations, and in April 1858, the Harbour Commissioners' fears materialized: a severe storm breached the repair work in the narrows of the peninsula. High lake waters destroyed the Peninsula Hotel and created a channel four to five feet in depth. Within a month, the breach was wide and deep enough to accommodate steamer traffic into the harbour.[8] The influx of lake currents through the newly formed gap brought greater quantities of sand into the harbour, exacerbating existing sedimentation problems. In his May 1858 report to the Commissioners, Harbour Master Hugh Richardson commented that the long north-south sandbar or "cross-beach" separating Ashbridge's Bay from the harbour had almost completely disappeared: "I observed the water had made passages over the cross-beach ... Toronto Bay ... is laid open to Ashbridge's Bay, and Ashbridge's Bay is widely opened to the lake, consequently the water flows freely from the west to the east or east to west."[9] The effects of this increased circulation at first seemed positive: Richardson reported to the Commissioners in 1862 that "the water in the bay is purer in summer and freer from ice in the winter, and the health of the city better assured."[10] Open communion between the harbour and the marsh, however, would soon produce more problems than benefits.

Throughout the 1860s, the Toronto harbour commissioners responded to urgent requests from area industries to widen and deepen a continually contracting channel at the Don's northern outlet to the harbour. Frustrated with the mounting expense and ultimate fruitlessness of these dredging activities, harbour engineer Kivas Tully finally suspended dredging operations in 1866. Three years later, in 1869, Tully produced a plan and budget for the construction of a breakwater extending along the south edge of the channel parallel to the lakeshore. Such a structure, Tully hoped, would deflect sand and detritus drifting into the harbour through the eastern gap. The first remedy to the siltation problem to be implemented, the Don Breakwater, was completed in 1871 (figure 3.1). Like many subsequent developments along the lower river and harbour, however, it seems the breakwater was constructed in anticipation of developments that didn't materialize. Plans by the Toronto and Nipissing Railway to establish terminals on the south side of the channel[11] were abandoned, and another industry on the channel, the Toronto Rolling Mills, ceased operations in 1874. By 1886, much of

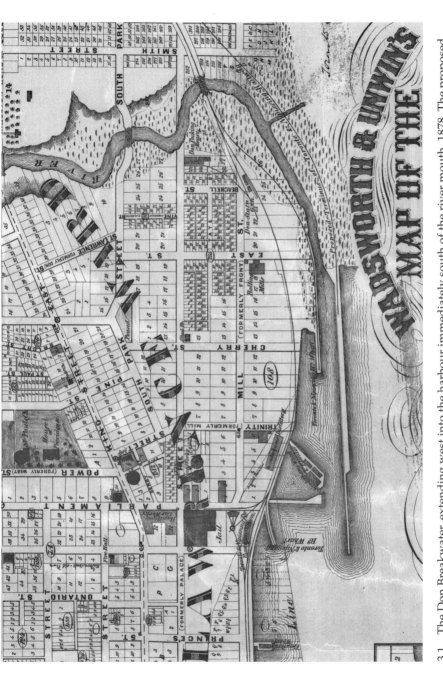

3.1   The Don Breakwater, extending west into the harbour immediately south of the river mouth, 1878. The proposed Toronto and Nipissing Railway terminal is indicated at the eastern end of the breakwater. Toronto Rolling Mills is visible at the intersection of East and Mill Streets, north of the GTR rail line. (Detail from V.B. Wadsworth and C. Unwin, *Map of the City of Toronto*, 1878. Library and Archives Canada, National Map Collection, NMC-25641.)

the breakwater was rotten; the spring freshets of that year destroyed it completely.[12]

In the decade following the construction of the Don Breakwater, the shape of the harbour continued to change, often confounding the predictions of its observers. By the early 1880s, the ongoing necessity for costly dredging caused by persistent silt deposits from the Don and navigational hazards posed by floating detritus from the marsh resulted in yet another expert opinion on the eastern harbour and its problematic tributary. In 1882 the federal Department of Public Works commissioned Captain James Buchanan Eads, a prominent marine engineer from St Louis, to recommend a course of action for harbour improvements. After surveying present conditions and reviewing past recommendations, Eads recommended the construction of a dyke or breakwater between Ashbridge's Bay marsh and the harbour, and the closure of the eastern gap. Like Fleming's assessment thirty years earlier, he argued that the effects of the Don on the harbour were inconsequential: whatever injury was produced by the small quantity of sediment that the Don brought into the harbour, he noted, was compensated for by the increased current it provided when in flood. The large expenditure required to divert the Don into Ashbridge's Bay could only be justified as a public health measure, and not, he argued, as a means of preserving the navigability of the harbour.[13]

In response to Eads's recommendations, the Dominion government embarked upon what would be the first major step to reconfigure the harbour. By 1885, a long dyke had been constructed roughly along the line of the original cross-beach, stretching from the disintegrating breakwater at the northern outlet of the Don south to the eastern edge of the eastern gap (figure 3.2). The dyke, or Government Breakwater as it was known, effectively blocked all water passage between Ashbridge's Bay marsh and the harbour. It also sealed off the Don's southern outlet (identified in early maps of the harbour as the river's primary outlet), giving the river only one passage point into the harbour at the northeast corner of Toronto Bay.[14] Eads's recommendations were only partially fulfilled, however: the eastern gap was never closed, presenting as it did a valuable shortcut for westbound shipping traffic.

Like those before him, Eads failed to take into account the unpredictability of natural systems and the complexity of their interconnections with established human systems. By fixing one problem (the drift of detritus from the marsh into Toronto Bay), he had created another. The reduction of water currents into the marsh led to increasingly unbearable conditions for area residents and industrialists. Contained on

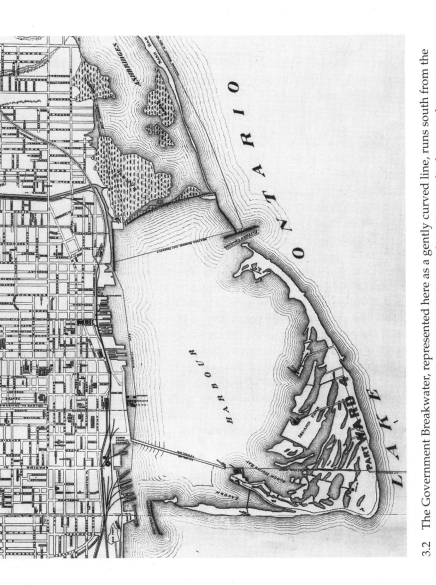

3.2   The Government Breakwater, represented here as a gently curved line, runs south from the lakeshore and divides Ashbridge's Bay marsh on the east from Toronto harbour on the west. (Detail from Copp Clark Co. Ltd., *Plan of the City of Toronto* [Toronto: City Engineers Office, 1894]. Courtesy of the University of Toronto Map and Data Library.)

three sides, water in the marsh stagnated, and any flushing action the marsh had once provided to process pollutants was dramatically reduced. Former harbour commissioner James G. Worts perhaps said it best in an 1878 report to Toronto's mayor and city council: "I consider reports on the Harbour to be of very little value ... No person, be he ever so learned, can foresee with any certainty the effects the different currents and winds will have."[15] Unintended consequences, as Worts predicted, would continue to dog harbour improvement projects well into the twentieth century.

Inundation

Intimately connected to the problem of siltation was the problem of flooding on the Don. Viewed from the perspective of harbour officials, the central concern with flood waters was not the water itself but the silt and debris it carried with it. From the perspective of riverside farmers and industries, however, flood waters endangered lives and threatened properties, livestock, and livelihoods.

Earlier inhabitants of Toronto's river valleys and table lands may have been more likely to see annual flood events for their advantages as well as for their inconveniences. As a 1950s study on the history of the watershed noted, "the yearly enrichment of the meadows or 'flats' made it possible to grow corn on them year after year, so that the Indian villages near the river could remain on the same site for long periods." The high water, furthermore, "enabled a skilled traveller to navigate many parts of the river which at ordinary times were too shallow to be worth attempting."[16] European settlers, in contrast, tended to view these seasonal events with a mix of resignation and dread. Newspaper coverage of annual spring freshets marked the level of potential danger posed by flood waters and described in detail ensuing damages and inconveniences. While severe and sudden floods were likely less frequent and less intense in the years before widespread deforestation in the watershed,[17] limited surviving evidence suggests that they did occur periodically. In late July 1808, for example, mill owner Parshall Terry drowned while crossing the river on horseback near the Don bridge (at today's Queen Street). An account of his death in the *York Gazette* suggests that the approaches to the bridge had been washed out "by an excessive flood," forcing Terry to wade or swim his horse across the flooded river.[18]

Flooding events became more severe as the century progressed. With more milling infrastructure along the river over time, they also became more destructive. Detailed tracking of nineteenth-century flood events on the Don reveals a total of thirteen major floods between 1801 and 1881. Given fluctuating coverage of items of local interest in the Toronto newspapers, these numbers are likely very conservative.[19] Flooding in 1850 and 1878 was especially severe, causing deaths and destroying riverside industries along the Don. As the *Globe* reported on 6 April 1850, heavy rains on 3 and 4 April, combined with a rapid melt of accumulated ice and snow, led to enormous flooding of Toronto-area rivers; losses were apparently greatest on the three branches of the Don. Nine mill dams were destroyed on the east branch of the Don and a stable full of horses and cows was wrenched from its moorings and lost downstream. A man was drowned crossing Mount Pleasant Creek, a tributary of the Don, and many houses were flooded on the west branch of the river. Flooding was most devastating, however, along the Lower Don south of the Forks. The Taylor Brothers' paper and sawmills suffered heavy damages: the mill dam and "three large bridges" on their property were destroyed, while "the whole of their farm [at] the flats [was] laid under water" and "fences, hay stacks, and cordwood" were swept away. Two bridges on the lower river – the plank road bridge at Winchester Street and the Don bridge at Queen, were lost to the force of water and accumulated debris.[20] Described by the *Globe* as "the most disastrous freshet that was ever known in the vicinity," the 1850 flood was the largest on record until that point. Devastating as it was, the damage was not nearly as great as that caused by the flood of 1878.

"Never before in the history of Toronto," began the coverage for the flood of 10–13 September 1878, "has the Don presented such an appearance as it did yesterday, and at no previous time have its waters occasioned so much damage."[21] At the height of the flood, waters on the Don rose to a record of eight feet above normal levels. The *Globe* described the scene as "wild and picturesque in the extreme": "hundreds of trees floated down the stream, the leafy tops above water. Many of them anchored in the mud at various points throughout the wide expanse of waters, thus forming what looked like a miniature archipelago."[22] Four of the six bridges spanning the Lower Don were destroyed, the exceptions being the South Park Street bridge south of Pottery Road, saved when the waters instead washed out the approaches on either side, and the Grand Trunk Railway bridge, a heavy iron and stone structure that withstood the pressure of the flood. Wreckage from bridges and buildings upstream crashed into the bridges below them, creating a domino effect of destruction. For onlookers, the loss of the Queen Street bridge was especially climactic. All afternoon, a mountain of debris had accumulated on the upstream side of the bridge, including barrels, piles of wood, wheelbarrows and carts, and buildings. It finally gave way when the McColl Brother's oil refinery warehouse, which contained a number of barrels of oil, was swept down. "It came with great speed, and being of itself heavy, it set the thousands of tons of material already accumulated in motion, and this pressing on the bridge, proved its destruction." The bridge itself then "swept down the river with irresistible force, carrying everything before it, and followed by the whole of the stuff which during the day had been gathering above it."[23]

The flood claimed a heavy toll on industries along the Don and communities in the Lower Valley. At least two people lost their lives: those confirmed included a nine-year-old girl swept from the river bank near Don Mount, and a man who had attempted to cross the Queen Street bridge shortly before it collapsed.[24] Thirty mill dams and twenty bridges were lost on the east branch of the Don alone, and losses experienced by riverside industry brought damage estimates to $200,000 to $400,000. In the riverside neighbourhoods south of Gerrard Street, and particularly south of King, sidewalks were uprooted, houses and cellars flooded, and people's belongings were washed away or destroyed by the high waters.

The events of September 1878 prompted changes in the city's relationship with the river. For the *Globe*, the disaster reinforced the city's folly in failing to construct adequate bridges at the river's major crossings. Only a few months before, the editors pointed out, the city engineer had "condemned every one of the Don bridges."[25] In the aftermath of the flood, bridges were rebuilt with higher spans and stronger materials; riverside properties were in many cases removed to a safer distance; and mill owners, fewer in number by the 1880s, began to adopt the practice of opening floodgates in advance of a freshet.[26] Due at least in part to these changes in practice, annual spring freshets through the final decades of the nineteenth century produced little damage in comparison with earlier years. Nine years later, however, when riverside landowners and industrialists voted in the referendum for the Don Improvement Project, the devastation caused by the Great Rainstorm of 1878 would still have been close to mind.

The severity of the 1878 flood and its consequences underlines a recognition of the power and ultimate unpredictability of nature. The image of the upstream bridge creating a domino effect of destruction is a useful metaphor: improvements implemented in one location did not typically take into account the potential for upstream influences and forces at work in other parts of the watershed. As James Worts commented in the same year as the flood, there is value in recognizing and accounting for the limits of human knowledge. How this played out in the readiness of late-nineteenth-century publics to accept major improvement projects is difficult to ascertain. The flood seems to have reinforced for those most affected the need for technological interventions to tame an unruly river. Whether others saw in the rising floodwaters a confirmation that human interventions are necessarily partial is impossible to know from the evidence that has survived.

The Don Improvement Project

The "Don problem" of flooding, siltation, and pollution propelled the involvement of two distinct institutional authorities with an interest in its amelioration: the Harbour Trust, concerned primarily with problems of siltation and its consequences for harbour navigation, and the city, pressured by a range of stakeholders to respond to problems of pollution and flooding. Overstretched and poorly resourced, the city still commanded greater authority throughout the nineteenth century than the Harbour Trust, which had limited capital and jurisdiction.[27] Not until the establishment of the Toronto Harbour Commission in 1911, with its considerable land resources and greatly bolstered jurisdictional control, would the tables begin to turn. Until that time, projects directed at the Don problem would prioritize the city's interests over those of harbour officials: namely, the Lower Don and its potential for shipping and industrial development.

Concentrating on a portion of the lower river between Winchester Street and the Grand Trunk Railway bridge at Eastern Avenue, the Don Improvement Project proposed to straighten the river channel, deepen it to 12 feet below lake level, and widen it to 120 feet. The works were designed to meet four central objectives: (1) to improve the sanitary condition of the area; (2) to make the Don a navigable stream for large vessels; (3) to accommodate rail traffic into the city; and (4) to create new lands for industrial purposes.[28] Flood control was considered an associated benefit.

For residents of Toronto's east end, the idea of the improvement conjured images of prosperity and revitalization for an area that had long been relegated to the margins of the city. Throughout the early 1880s, they regularly petitioned council to take action in implementing a river improvement scheme. Their dreams for the area were ambitious. Memories of the devastating flood of September 1878 and daily experience of the lower river's sluggish and fetid condition likely fuelled their visions for a rationalized Don River. At a public meeting to discuss the project in October 1881, landowner J.P. Doel "pleaded on behalf of the health of the neighbourhood and city for the straightening and deepening of the Don," imagining a future where the Don would become "the great shipping centre for Toronto."[29] Alderman Thomas Davies, who owned a manufacturing firm along the river, perhaps best expressed the vision of area residents in his submission to the city's committee on works in early January 1882:

> This great scheme ... will afford sites and facilities for all kinds of manufacturing enterprises, coal yards, lumber yards, and many factories we may not now think of, the establishment of which will most assuredly go far towards making Toronto, what I believe it is destined to become, a great manufacturing as well as a business centre ... The miasmatic atmosphere with which this locality is too often troubled will be dispelled and the healthfulness greatly increased. Freshets and ice-jams will be things of the past, and the current in the River unobstructed.[30]

The project, he concluded, will "make [the area] as it ought to be – as healthy as any other part of the City."[31] Imagined futures for the Don received even more breathless expression in real estate broadsides for the period, which referred potential east-end buyers to the proximity of the improvement and its potential to "materially advance the value of surrounding districts." As one 1887 advertisement read, "that hitherto despised stream" will soon become "the commercial shipping centre of Toronto, not only for lake and river, but for railway commerce as well."[32] The improvements, in sum, would turn a stigmatized and peripheral area into a productive district of the city, producing revenue for the municipal government and local landowners alike.

While area landowners and industrialists sought to remove the uncertainty and insalubriousness of their surroundings, city council members saw the improvements as an opportunity to augment paltry assessment revenues and to address flooding and pollution concerns that increasingly carried the threat of litigation. Early project proponents would likely have been aware of the success of other urban centres in transforming listless urban waterways into bustling hubs for industry.[33] In early February 1880, Toronto City Council resolved to form a special committee to report "upon the state and condition of the Don River ... from a sanitary point of view" and to develop a scheme to abate the nuisance. In conjunction with this resolution, council members suggested the employment of convicts from the Don Jail "in straightening the River Don between Gerrard Street Bridge and Winchester Street Bridge."[34] Little action seems to have been taken until the following year, when Mayor McMurrich, in his 1881 inaugural address, identified the river as an important force in the city's future development. Positioning "the eastern end of the City along the banks of the Don and the marsh" as a site "specially fitted by nature ... for manufactures of all descriptions," he argued that a project to straighten the river and "[make] it navigable for a considerable distance" would greatly enhance property values in the area.[35]

While the city pondered the potential of the improvements, a group of local businessmen worked to set out in concrete terms a vision for a navigable and disciplined waterway as a centrepiece of economic revitalization in Toronto's east end. Organized under the name of the Don Improvement Company, the syndicate released a circular in early January 1881 addressed to landowners on both sides of the river. "A few gentlemen," the advertisement stated, "are willing to form themselves into a company for the purpose of widening, straightening, deepening and otherwise improving the Don River so as to allow vessels drawing fourteen feet of water entering and navigating the same." Progress on the project would not proceed, it advised, until landowners on each side of the river agreed to sell "all the land ... [required] for the purpose."[36] By mid-February, the syndicate had placed a petition before the Dominion government requesting incorporation of the company, with the purpose of "[straightening] the course of the river between the line of Winchester-street ... and the bay." To effect these improvements, the company requested the right to expropriate lands up to 500 feet on either side of the river.[37] Particularly galling to area landowners was the implication that they would be compensated for their lands "at a valuation, after the manner of railway companies for lands taken by them." While owners would "have the privilege" of repurchasing their lands after the improvements were complete, it would be at a grossly inflated value.[38] The bill had passed through the House of Commons and awaited approval from the Senate by the time the Toronto City Council organized a response. Indignant with the company's presumptuousness in neglecting to inform municipal authorities of their plans, council resolved on 7 March that representatives of the city in the House of Commons and the Senate should "use their influence to postpone the passage of the ... Bill."[39] The bill was eventually withdrawn from the House, and the efforts of the syndicate were abandoned.[40]

As developments in the following months would show, however, it wasn't the company's proposed object of improving the river that area landowners and council members objected to as much as their approach to the project and the question of who stood to benefit. In September 1881, the death of United States President Garfield took Mayor McMurrich to Cleveland, where he was apparently "struck at the way in which manufactures had clustered round a little stream [the Cuyahoga River] which had been likewise improved," leaving him with "no doubt that in East Toronto they would find the same result with reference to the Don."[41] Here was a comparable context: a relatively small urban waterway that was subject, like the Don, to chronic problems of flooding, siltation, and pollution, but transformed with dredges and piledrivers into a vital industrial corridor in its lower reaches. McMurrich returned to Toronto resolved to push forward an improvement scheme for the Don. In early October he joined long-time project proponent Alderman Davies in calling a public meeting of ratepayers to discuss the question. Well attended by area property owners, the meeting reinforced ratepayer support for the project under the auspices of the municipal Local Improvements Act (whereby ratepayers shared improvement costs with municipal councils). It concluded with a unanimous resolution by area ratepayers to shoulder their portion of the costs of the improvement and to request cooperation from the councils of York and Toronto to bring the project to fruition.[42] The ratepayers' consent in hand, Alderman Davies set about convincing Toronto City Council of the project's viability. The improvement would soon pay for itself, he argued, by way of the "immense benefit that will accrue to the city by the increase of taxation as soon as the scheme ... is accomplished."[43] Despite Davies's enthusiasm for the project and the support he enjoyed from the mayor, plans for the project stagnated in circuitous discussions about the advisability of carrying out the project, the legislation and funds required to complete it, and proposed methods of carrying it out.

The interest of a new and powerful stakeholder finally propelled the project out of the council chambers and onto the ground in 1886. The Canadian Pacific Railway Company, which had attempted since 1881 to improve connections to the city from their east-west lines, succeeded in the spring of 1886 to win the support of then-mayor William Howland to create an eastern entrance to the city along the west bank of the Don

Improvement.[44] The timing of the CPR's interest in the project is significant: the improvement would be completed within the context of larger
municipal efforts to accommodate railway development in the city. A
straightened river would facilitate the laying of tracks into the city; filled
land in the former meandering river channel would create additional
space for railside industry. And for several aldermen with manufacturing firms along the river – Davies among them – the relocation of the
river channel would extend their property and increase its value through
proximity to the railway. Railway interests also shaped the nature of
the improvement project, shifting the emphasis from the development
of a navigable shipping canal to a rail and road corridor, from the river
itself to the space alongside it. The improvement would become, in John
Stilgoe's words, a "metropolitan corridor" with all its associations of
modernity and prosperity.[45] Adding the interests of a powerful railway
company did much to secure project fortunes, and in March 1886 the Don
Improvement Act was passed by the provincial legislature, empowering
the city to borrow funds and expropriate lands to complete the works.[46]

Having secured the necessary legislation to carry out the project,
city council had only to obtain the approval of the qualified electorate.
On 18 August 1886, council adopted a bill "to authorize the straightening and improvement of the River Don."[47] The bill established the
estimated cost of the improvement, including the cost of lands to be
expropriated, at $300,000, one-third of which would be paid by the city
and the remaining two-thirds assessed against the properties benefit-
ing from the improvements. It granted the city the right to expropriate lands within the boundaries of the improvement, extending to a
maximum of 400 feet on either side of the centre line of the river from
Lake Ontario to Winchester Street. (Original plans had extended the
area for improvement north to Bloor Street. In order to contain costs,
this section was excluded from the bill.) On Saturday, 18 September,
2,724 voters returned a majority of 1,594 in favour of the by-law. Not
surprisingly, wards abutting the river (St David's Ward on the west side
of the river, St Matthew's on the east, and St Lawrence's straddling the
river to the south) registered decisive support, while wards in the west
end of the city showed ambivalent or negative returns.[48] The bill was
passed into law on 27 September 1886.[49]

Contractors A.F. Manning and R. MacDonald began work on the
project in the fall of 1886; by the spring of 1887, dredging work had
begun on the new alignment of the river channel. The area for improvement was divided into three sections: section one, from the lakeshore

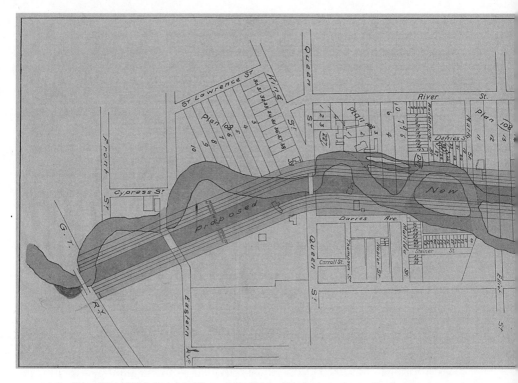

3.3   *River Don Straightening Plan*, 1886. (City of Toronto Archives, fonds 200, series 725, file 12.)

north to the Grand Trunk Railway (GTR) bridge (immediately south of Eastern Avenue); section two, from the GTR bridge north to Gerrard Street; and section three, from Gerrard Street north to Winchester Street. In a decision that would frustrate officials at the Harbour Trust, the city postponed work on section one, focusing their efforts instead on the portion of the river between Eastern Avenue and Winchester Street (sections two and three) (see figure 3.3). The work in this first phase would straighten the river channel from Winchester Street to the GTR bridge, deepen the channel to 12 feet below lake level, and widen it with piles or cribs to 120 feet. A total of 52 feet would be reserved for railway purposes, and 50 feet for roadway. Existing bridges would be replaced with stronger structures of wood and iron, and the lowlands adjoining the river would be raised to three feet above the high-water mark of the lake.

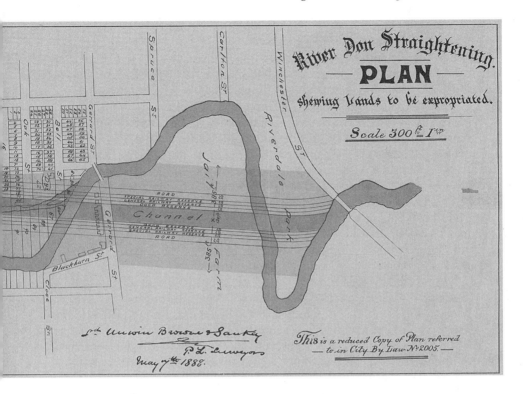

Work on sections two and three carried on steadily throughout 1887. By the end of the year, the bulk of the piling for the new river channel had been completed, and the channel from the GTR bridge to King Street nearly finished. Visible progress on the ground prompted Mayor Edward F. Clarke to speculate in his inaugural address for 1888 "that the whole of this improvement [sections two and three] will be finished about the fall of this year."[50] While the city engineer's reports and council minutes provide a general outline of work completed, monies expended, and problems encountered, newspaper coverage for the period fills in the colour and gives a sense of the magnitude of the work on the ground. A July 1887 article in the *Globe* portrayed the sensory experience of the works, from the dredge at the south end of the improvement and its "huge iron spoon sinking, filling, rising, swinging and dropping," to the piledrivers upriver, "black, and ladder-like," which drove trimmed cedar piles into parallel rows to demarcate the new channel. Around the machines, men worked digging out the new channel, pushing wheelbarrows of excavated material and floating on rafts hauling logs for piling. High banks of sand "dotted with men and horses" stood along the river banks "as far as the eye can reach up the valley," while full wagons and carts moved down the sand piles to dump into the former river channel. Incongruously, in the midst of this industry, "numerous small boys ... div[ed] out of scows or jump[ed] off the piles ... laughing, shouting, swimming and spluttering." With the completion of the work, the reporter anticipated, the "crooked stream" of the Don "will really be nothing more or less than a canal."[51]

Despite Mayor Clarke's optimism for the project in January 1888, the magnitude and ambitiousness of the project soon became apparent in a series of unforeseen difficulties. Problems with contractors, disputes with area residents and industrialists, protracted negotiations with project stakeholders, and unanticipated challenges with the environment itself all contributed to delay project progress and increase the amount of required funds. Both the cost of lands expropriated and the work performed to date, council minutes reveal, "far exceeded the original estimates, owing to the increased value of the former and unforeseen difficulties in carrying on the latter." Out of the original $300,000 borrowed in the fall of 1886, only $3,000 remained to apply towards the improvement in October 1888. The following month council passed a by-law authorizing the city to borrow an additional $150,000 to carry on the works.[52] By January 1889, cost overruns for the Don Improvement reached 50 per cent over original estimates.[53] On top of its excessive costs, the improvement also ran considerably over its original time estimates. Sections two and three of the improvement were not completed until 1891, three years later than originally planned. The largest roadblock that the city encountered came from the project's most powerful stakeholder group, and one who stood to gain the most from the improvements. A protracted dispute with the CPR over their claim to exclusive use of tracks on the west side of the Don Improvement hampered project progress throughout the 1880s. The dispute was finally settled in 1890 by the Railway Committee of the Privy Council, which granted the CPR a perpetual lease of two tracks on the west side of the Don Improvement in exchange for an annual fee to the city.[54]

Another area where expenditures of time and funds dramatically exceeded predictions was the expropriation of lands along the route of the improvement. Requested in 1885 to evaluate the value of lands between Winchester Street and the marsh that would be subject to expropriation, the city's assessment commissioner N. Maughan reached a figure of $75,000, an amount he felt was "ample to remunerate all parties interested for the loss of land and for any buildings which may be interfered with."[55] Claims ranged from expropriated landowners and riverside manufacturers who lost buildings and property to the improvements, to small businesses such as ice cutters and boat builders, and recreational interests such as the Don Rowing Club, whose loss of access to the river forced them to fold or relocate.[56] Disagreements and delays in negotiations over particular properties translated into delays, as contractors could not proceed over lands still subject to settlement. Increased land values in the area were partly to blame for the attenuated settlement process; bureaucratic foot dragging and tardiness in issuing payments for land purchases and damages was another. In January 1889, the Assessment Department estimated that total expenditures on land purchases and damages for sections two and three of the improvement would reach $167,000, well over double the original estimate.[57]

Attempts to satisfy multiple and often competing objectives also contributed to cost and time overruns. Having lost the original contractor for section three (Gerrard to Winchester Street), the city decided to proceed with the work by day labour, satisfying frequent demands by the public to use the improvements as a means of employing out-of-work labourers.[58] Throughout the winter of 1886–7, the "unemployed poor" were set to work cutting into the steep banks on the east side of the river below the Don Jail. Political expediency outweighed pragmatism, however, as the scheme proved to be expensive and inefficient. In a report to council on 8 February 1887, city engineer Charles Sproatt responded defensively to allegations of extravagant labour expenses, calculating the expenditure for labour at 27.5 cents per cubic yard of material excavated. Costs associated with commencing the work so late in the season – and particularly the challenge of conducting the work "through three feet of frost" – combined with the changing of the men weekly, he wrote, resulted in a labour expense "somewhat in excess of what it should be."[59] Ultimately, the city decided to cease the use of day labour in section three and award the contract to Manning and Macdonald, a decision that involved more expenditure: Manning and Macdonald's estimate ran $16,000 over the original contractor's bid.[60]

As Sproatt's statement above suggests, the environment itself also contributed to overruns in project expenditures and timing. Winter conditions slowed progress in cutting through steep valley banks. More problematic, and less foreseen, were the dense clay and shale deposits encountered along the course of the new channel north of Queen Street. By the summer of 1888, Sproatt was forced to admit that "the quantity of shale found on the line of the new channel is much larger than estimated," necessitating additional costs for its removal and the subsequent cribbing of the channel with horizontal planks of wood (rather than vertical piles) to provide extra support.[61] As a result of these discoveries, council elected to dredge the channel north of Gerrard to a depth of only eight or nine feet, rather than the twelve feet originally proposed.[62] These modifications had significant repercussions for project objectives: lost in that difference of three to four feet of channel depth was the vision of a navigable channel north of Gerrard Street. Flood protection and "pollution flushing" objectives may also have been compromised in creating a wide and ultimately shallow channel, rather than one with the ability to accommodate higher flows. In a retrospective on the Don Improvements in 1902, the *Mail and Empire* derided the project for its dubious results and excessive expenditures, "the greater proportion [of which]" were "thrown away in an abortive attempt to dredge the river to a depth of fourteen [sic] feet. This proved impracticable, as the clay in the river proved impervious to the dredge."[63]

Shortages of funds and political will, then, had produced a project that was necessarily fragmentary: only a portion of the river had been modified, rather than the full distance from Bloor Street to the lake contained within the initial 1886 proposals (see map 2). For the Harbour Trust, the improvement was a farce: in ignoring the river's mouth, it failed to address its central concern with siltation in Toronto harbour. Echoing a chorus of engineers and harbour officials who had since 1835 recommended the diversion of the Don into Ashbridge's Bay as a means of turning "what is now a positive evil ... into a benefit – and a profit to the City,"[64] the Harbour Trust saw the Don Diversion as a pivotal part of their plan to create industrial lands in Ashbridge's Bay marsh and to rid the harbour (and their annual budget expenditures) of the menace of accumulated river silts.

For a brief moment in 1883, before the main improvement work began further upriver, it appeared that the diversion of the Don into Ashbridge's Bay would at last be accomplished. An agreement between city council and the Harbour Trust in early May 1883 enabled the Trust to cut a channel from the GTR bridge south into the marsh. The work, which was carried out that summer at the Harbour Trust's expense, was viewed by the city as "turning the first sod" in its larger project to

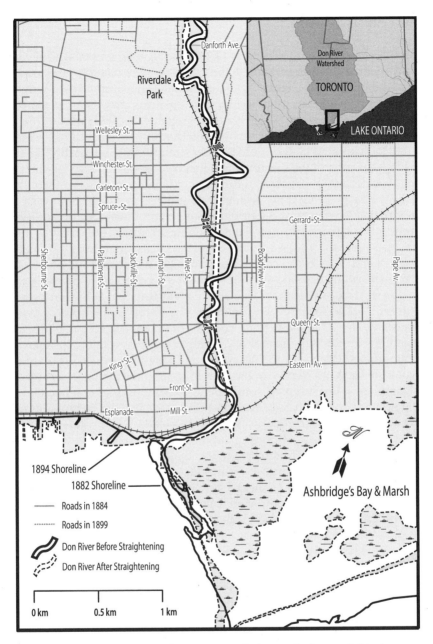

Map 2   Lower Don River and major streets before and after straightening, 1882 and 1894. (Map composed by Rajiv Rawat using shoreline data from the University of Toronto Map and Data Library and road map data from Byron Moldofsky, GIS and Cartography Office, Department of Geography, University of Toronto.)

straighten and improve the river Don.[65] The river, however, was never fully diverted. Requests made to the GTR to place a dam of "stop logs" across the old river channel (which fell along their right of way) met with resistance, and, mollified by city council's promising plans to straighten and improve the river on a larger scale, the Harbour Trust abandoned the project.[66] While the 1886 Don Improvement Project initially incorporated plans to run the river straight south into Ashbridge's Bay, section one of the improvement had been set aside indefinitely by the time dredging work began further north on the channel in 1886.

By the early 1890s, daily accumulations of sewage and cattle wastes in the shallow waters of Ashbridge's Bay led provincial health authorities to raise the spectre of a potential cholera outbreak, forcing the city to act at last. In 1892, council approved city engineer E.H. Keating's plan to construct a channel running east-west along the northern perimetre of the marsh, with cuts through the government breakwater on the west side of the marsh, and through the sandbar at the northeast extremity of Ashbridge's Bay, in order to intercept north-south sewer lines and carry wastes further out into the lake (see colour plate 1). Keating viewed the channel as a temporary intervention to relieve pollution in advance of the necessary and inevitable construction of a trunk sewer.[67] His plan saw the Don diverted into the new east-west channel on a line running south of the existing improvements. Having secured funds on loan from the province, and the permission of the Dominion government to breach their 1882 breakwater, the city set out to implement Keating's plan in 1893. Once again, however, the work that was carried out fell significantly short of proposed improvements. "Keating's channel" was dredged to a width of only ninety feet, much narrower than the 300 feet proposed in his original plans. Coatsworth's Cut was completed to specifications at the eastern end of Ashbridge's Bay, but the Don was not diverted into Keating's channel as proposed.[68]

Tensions between the city and the Harbour Trust reached a new high, and by the spring of 1897 harbour officials had threatened legal action in an attempt to compel the city to divert the river.[69] Urged by the Board of Trade, who sought to make the harbour receptive to new ocean-going traffic enabled by the deepening of the St Lawrence River, engineers from the city and the Harbour Trust came together in 1898 to produce a joint scheme to divert the Don.[70] Initially supported by the promise of a federal loan, funds for the project were revoked in 1902 on the grounds that the Don was not a "navigable stream" that warranted federal intervention. The 1902 decision also revoked all future federal funding for waterfront improvements until the city addressed the fundamental problem of sewage deposits into the harbour.[71] Another obstruction had been pushed into the course of the Don Diversion.

Not until 1906 would the Don Diversion finally get off the ground, the city having received the support of the electorate to borrow $200,000 to straighten the river south of the GTR bridge to the lake, and to improve the surrounding lands in Ashbridge's Bay.[72] Work finally began in September 1908, and by mid-July 1909 the river had been diverted from its curving westerly course into Toronto Bay to run instead south to an outlet in Keating's Channel.[73]

Final adjustments to the mouth of the river occurred within the context of the newly incorporated Toronto Harbour Commission's 1912 Waterfront Plan.[74] Under the leadership of THC chief engineer E.L. Cousins, a series of studies through 1912 presented different alternatives for the creation of new industrial land within Ashbridge's Bay marsh. Two options were proposed for the mouth of the Don: the first, to extend the existing north-south river channel further south through the marshlands to empty into a proposed ship channel; the second, to divert the channel west along a route slightly south of its original path into Toronto Bay (see figure 3.4). The rationale for the second alternative, which seemed to confound the commissioners' long-held objective to remove the menace of river silts from the harbour, lay in providing additional space for dockage and in allowing for the construction of a roadway across the old channel to provide access to the west bank of the Don. In September 1912 the THC made a decision to adopt the second of the two alternatives, despite its considerably greater expense.[75] The river would curve southwest from the GTR bridge, then south to meet with a widened and reinforced Keating Channel before entering the harbour. Objections by the British American Oil Company, whose property lay along the line of the proposed diversion, led to the final amendment in the long history of plans to alter the river mouth. Rather than curving through the BA Oil property, the river would continue straight south to connect at a right angle with Keating Channel – the same jarring alignment that persists today (see map 3).[76] The new Keating Channel – wider and slightly south of its previous alignment – was dredged in 1914; by the spring of 1915, the channel had been reinforced and the river diverted for the final time.[77]

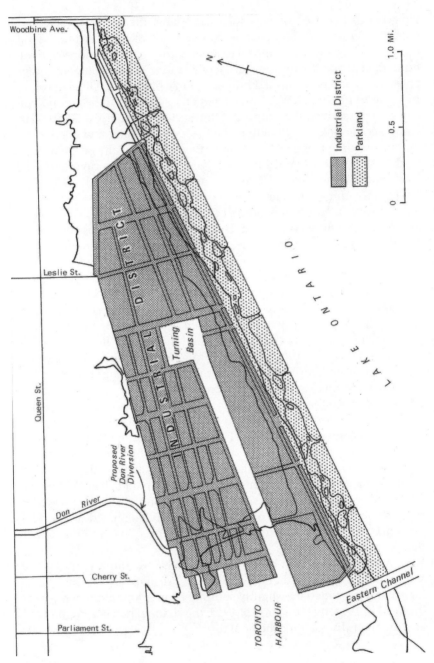

3.4 Toronto Harbour Commission, proposed Don River Diversion and Port Industrial District, 1912. (Map by C. King, Cartographic Lab, Department of Geography, York University. Courtesy of Gene Desfor.)

Woodbine Ave.

N

1.0 Mi.

0.5

Industrial District

Parkland

0

Leslie St.

Queen St.

INDUSTRIAL DISTRICT

Turning Basin

Proposed Don River Diversion

Don River

Cherry St.

Parliament St.

LAKE ONTARIO

TORONTO HARBOUR

Eastern Channel

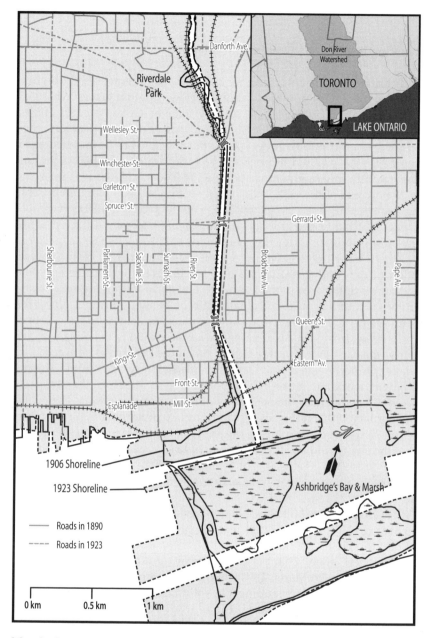

Map 3   Lower Don River and major streets before and after final realignment of river mouth, 1906 and 1923. (Map composed by Rajiv Rawat using shoreline data from the University of Toronto Map and Data Library and road map data from Byron Moldofsky, GIS and Cartography Office, Department of Geography, University of Toronto.)

Looking Back on the Don Improvements

In February 1897, a columnist for the *Globe* commented that "the Don
Improvement was one of those mysterious infatuations to which all
men are subject when acting in corporate or Governmental affairs.
There are few who cannot look back and puzzle over the past advocacy
of some absurd public undertaking. But it is hard to be laughed at by
the men who profited more than even the landowners by our monumental folly in straightening the river."[78] The columnist was referring
to the owners of the CPR, who had recently reached a very favourable
agreement with the city for annual rents to access the Don Improvement.[79] Certainly, the city and its ratepayers had paid a high price to
encourage industrial development in the east end.

Whether their efforts would pay off was still far from clear. The creation of new industrial land along the improvement attracted some
industries to the area in the late 1890s and early 1900s, especially those
in the oil and gas sector. The failure to erect swing bridges along the
improvement[80] and the compromises made in channel depth forever
dashed the dreams of a navigable Lower Don lined with docks and coal
yards and bustling with ship traffic. As for the benefits to be accrued by
higher property values, and Davies's faith that the work would "become
a paying work and a profitable undertaking to the City," the prospects
were still not clear at the beginning of the twentieth century. Reporting
in February 1902 on the city's plans to repay project debts through lev-
ies on "improved" properties, the *Mail and Empire* expressed scepticism
that the city would be able to demonstrate any measured improvement
on the lands involved: "it will be rather difficult to establish that the
ratepayers along the Don have reaped any material advantage from the
straightening of the river."[81]

The project had failed in other ways as well. Pollution continued
unabated. As early as 1894 it was apparent that faith in the project's
ability to "flush" contaminants and detritus through a deepened and
straightened lower channel had been misguided. An article in the
Toronto Mail on 20 March 1894 presented a satiric account of the city's
"great Improvement," lauding the solid construction of the new Isolation Hospital while pointing to the irony of the "pestilential" river
channel running below it. While the river "has been 'improved' so far as
its width is concerned," the *Mail* noted, the fact that it receives sewage
from a large district makes "its present state ... altogether deadly. The
Don is ... nothing more or less than a big open sewer. The slowness of

its current is not enough to clear off the impurities that are daily poured into it."[82] Not surprisingly, public health continued to suffer. Two to three hundred cases of typhoid fever per year remained the norm in the late 1880s and early 1890s. In 1891 a severe outbreak infected almost 900 people across the city, killing 170 of those infected.[83] While exposure to contaminated water in Toronto Bay was the main cause of typhoid deaths in these years, the contribution of heavily polluted waters from the Don certainly exacerbated the problem.

Chronic problems with flooding, ice jams, and siltation also persisted, making mockery of Alderman Davies's 1882 prediction that "freshets and ice-jams will be things of the past, and the current in the River unobstructed." An ice jam that formed near the river mouth in late February 1902 caused considerable flooding along the lower river, submerging cellars, washing out roads, and temporarily blocking the railway lines.[84] The spring freshet of April 1912 was more serious, destroying six mill dams along the river and prompting the *Mail and Empire* to describe the condition of the Don as "a rampage which baffles the memory of the 'oldest inhabitant' in the Valley."[85] Memories of the devastating damage caused by the 1878 flood must have run short. The inconvenience caused by repeated floods throughout the 1910s and 1920s finally led the GTR in 1928 to elevate their rail line, which crossed the Don south of Front Street, onto an earthen viaduct six metres in height.[86] Having failed in their efforts over the better part of a century to divert the Don into Ashbridge's Bay, the Toronto Harbour Commissioners faced the ongoing drain of dredging expenditures at the mouth of the Don through the twentieth century. Today, civic agencies spend an average of $500,000 annually to dredge sediment from the Keating Channel.[87]

Important to recognize in all of this is that the Don is a small urban river, bearing little resemblance to great rivers such as the Thames or the St Lawrence that have been harnessed by other cities for urban infrastructure projects. Why, then, had Toronto been so desperate to make it into something it wasn't? At the time the Don Improvement was being implemented, other North American cities were taking advantage of steam power and railways to create new industrial hubs outside of city centres, and moving away from their former dependence on rivers as drivers of industry. Toronto, conversely, chose to invest considerable public funds into the development of a minor river relatively close to the city centre.

For contemporaries of the project and for today's Toronto residents looking back on the legacy of the Don Improvement, it is difficult, indeed, to pinpoint any concrete benefits that accrued for the residents of the city and for those who continued to live near its banks. Certainly, stronger bridges at the major crossing points along the Lower Don allowed for more reliable travel between communities east and west of the river. The completion in 1892 of the CPR's Don Valley Subdivision from Leaside (southwest of the Forks) through the lower valley to the waterfront, and the opening of a passenger rail station at Queen Street in 1896, allowed greater mobility for east-end residents. The level of industrialization that did occur along the river south of Gerrard Street brought jobs for the area's growing working-class population. But the major problems it set out to address – flooding, poor sanitary conditions, and the lack of navigability of the lower river – persisted for years after the dredges had retired and the money had been spent.

Losses to the human experience of the Lower Don would also have been apparent to area residents. As George Rust D'Eye comments in *Cabbagetown Remembered*, the improvement "included the removal of five small islands between Queen and Winchester Streets, and the straightening of three big meanders and two small ones," while "fill taken from the hillsides surrounding the Don Valley permanently altered the appearance of the landscape."[88] In what would become an established trend in the history of the Don, corridor functions were prioritized over competing claims to valley spaces.

On top of these losses came additional expenses in the form of damages. As late as 1914, for example, the city and the Toronto Harbour Commission faced court action when two boat-building companies were denied access to the lake during the construction of Keating Channel.[89] Consequences for the river's ecology are more difficult to assess, imbricated as they were with other factors such as the disposal of raw sewage into the river further upstream and the subdivision and clearing of remaining forested lands further north in the watershed. Accelerated urbanization in the watershed in the first half of the twentieth century saw the filling of more wetlands and the pouring of more concrete over previously porous soils, exacerbating flood conditions in the watershed still further. In the end, the Don continued, as it had always done, to fuel the vitriol of Toronto residents. After all the money and effort spent to transform it into a productive economic engine for the city, it remained, in Hugh Richardson's words, "a monster of ingratitude."

Etched into the landscape and its ongoing ecological processes, the Don Improvement presents a legacy of late-nineteenth-century approaches towards urban environments. Perhaps most obviously, it demonstrates the challenges faced by contemporary engineers in rationalizing a dynamic river system already linked in complex ways to the city's metabolism. As early as 1834, Captain R.H. Bonnycastle recommended something resembling a trunk sewer as an essential component of any strategy to address the Don problem. His recommendations were repeated through the century by seasoned observers of harbour processes, including architect and engineer Kivas Tully, railway engineer Walter Shanly, and British sanitary engineer James Mansergh.[90] That the city failed consistently to act on these recommendations explains in part the failure of other harbour improvement projects. As the Dominion government recognized in 1902, until sewage was diverted from the harbour, support for other waterfront improvement projects was pointless. Not until 1908 would the public finally grant support for the construction of a trunk sewer and sewage treatment plant; the project was completed in 1913.[91] In the decades that followed, water-borne diseases were virtually eradicated in the city.

Looking back on the Don Improvement with the benefit of hindsight, we can identify some of the reasons why it failed. On one level, limited financial resources and unforeseen circumstances resulted in a scale-back of original project plans, handicapping opportunities for success. Large quantities of clay and shale in the substrate of the channel path slowed construction work and resulted in considerable cost overruns. Faced with dwindling resources and construction objectives that continued to slip from reach, municipal authorities elected to eliminate certain aspects of the project that, ironically, were critical to its success: reductions in the channel depth north of Gerrard and the elimination of swing bridges condemned to failure early visions for a navigable shipping corridor; the omission, early on, of the section stretching south to the lake ensured that sewage and other pollutants would continue to accumulate in the river's lower reaches. The dramatic growth of the city's population in the same period only increased sewage quantities, making conditions along the lower river even worse than before. By sloughing off as too costly, ambitious, or extravagant significant components of the original plan as the reality of funds and time became apparent, the city created a project of half-measures, reducing considerably its ability to meet expectations.

The competing priorities of proponent institutions – the city with its interests in flood control and raising property revenues through industrial development and land creation; the Harbour Trust with its concerns of siltation and interference with harbour navigation – also worked against project success. Conflicts between these institutions slowed project progress, particularly around the mouth of the river: the Don Diversion so long advocated by the Harbour Trust did not materialize until almost thirty years later, and even then in considerably modified form. Finally, the plan's rigid construction allowed little flexibility to accommodate dynamic and often unpredictable ecological processes. Its failure to adequately assess the particularities of the environment account, at least in part, for its ultimate shortcomings.

4 Refuge and Subsistence in an Urban Borderland

Not far from the spot where, at present, the Don-street bridge crosses the river, on the west side and to the north, lived for a long time a hermit-squatter, named Joseph Tyler … His abode on the Don was an excavation in the side of the steep hill, a little way above the level of the river bank … To the south of his cave he cultivated a large garden, and raised among other things, the white sweet edible Indian corn, a novelty here at the time; and very excellent tobacco.[1]

Henry Scadding, *Toronto of Old*, 228–9

Henry Scadding's 1873 description of Joseph Tyler's cave is the first detailed record in what would become a long history of homelessness in Toronto's Lower Don River Valley. According to Scadding's account, Tyler was an industrious and inventive recluse, a veteran of the American Revolutionary War who manufactured and sold "pitch and tar" to merchants in town and ferried the Helliwell brewery's beer in his "magnificent canoe" when the roads were too muddy to use. He was a puzzling figure – Scadding notes the "mystery attendant on his choice of life of complete solitude [and] his careful reserve." His choice of location was equally mysterious: the Lower Don River in Tyler's time (the 1820s and 30s) was separated from the town of York by the woods of the government reserve, making Tyler a man distinctly on the margins. Whether Tyler chose to live on the Lower Don or was pushed there by circumstance is difficult to determine. Certainly his livelihood of pitch and pine knot production would have been facilitated by a location close to the forest, and the river provided easy transportation into town. The uncertainty surrounding Joseph Tyler is emblematic of the history of people on the margins – indeed, the fact that he is named and some details of his life are recorded is more than we have for most of the people who found themselves living in the valley, for various reasons, over the last 200 years.

We have seen the Don move, in public perception and experience, from a place central to the development of the town of York to a place increasingly peripheral to the centre and increasingly polluted as industry concentrated along the banks of the lower river through the latter half of the nineteenth century. With the lower river tracing the eastern boundary of the city until the annexations of the 1880s, the river valley was in the mind's eye of those residents fortunate enough to enjoy some distance from it a "place on the edges," with all that that implied. Material conditions of the late nineteenth century, particularly sewage and industrial pollution, coupled with public perceptions of the valley as a source of disease and danger, cemented these assessments of marginality.

We saw, too, a distinct shift in land ownership patterns in the valley. As early as 1830, tradesmen and middle-class merchants replaced York's prominent inhabitants as principal landowners in the lower valley. By mid-century, the area's reputation for unhealthiness, together with other factors such as the growing distance from the centre as the city expanded west, accessibility challenges posed by steep ravine slopes, few and unreliable bridges, and reputedly poor soils for agricultural purposes, made it undesirable for all but the most speculative or poorly resourced of buyers – those motivated by lower taxes, cheaper land rates, and rising population pressures in the centre. As manufacturing enterprises congregated in increasing numbers along the lower river and the waterfront, more and more working-class inhabitants were attracted to the area. By 1880, rising tenancy rates, typically small dwelling sizes, and a tendency towards lots with multiple dwellings characterized an area populated largely by working-class families.[2]

This chapter further explores the area's reputation as an urban wasteland, and the implications it had for people who called the valley home temporarily or for longer periods of time, in the late nineteenth and early twentieth centuries. The ways in which the Don was conceived as a semi-rural space at once isolated and proximate, restorative and befouled, had implications for the kinds of uses to which it was set, and the opportunities it allowed for those living on the edges of society. In the 1860s, a cluster of institutions were established in the lower valley that drew upon this rhetoric. For the Industrial House of Refuge (later the Riverdale Isolation Hospital) and the Toronto Jail in particular, complementary goals of reforming and isolating their inmates found purchase in the semi-rural landscape of the lower valley. The rationale these institutions employed for selecting the lower valley as a location, and the controversies that accompanied that selection process, are explored here as a way of elucidating the stigma of valley lands and the limited options that corporate landowners faced for their holdings. Conceptions of the valley as an "outlaw space" – a harbour for criminals and illicit activities – are examined in the second part of the chapter through a case study of the trial of members of the Brooks Bush Gang for the murder of newspaper editor and MPP John Sheridan Hogan in 1859. Finally, I draw upon two episodes of "visible" homelessness in the valley in the early twentieth century in an attempt to reconstruct, as far as possible, the lived experience of people "living rough" in the valley and the reactions that their presence drew from middle- and upper-class Toronto residents.

My focus here is not on the working-class communities that grew up alongside the industrialized areas of the lower valley, but rather on people who experienced even less security – those who turned to the valley itself for refuge. Throughout the chapter, I return to a central dialectic between perception and experience: the tension between the ways the valley and its inhabitants were perceived by the more privileged residents of the centre, and what was happening, as best we can discern from the limited sources that exist, "on the ground." Here, place itself becomes a source for insights into the experiences of people who occupied the edges of society. The kinds of things people sought in that space, and the opportunities it presented – expected and otherwise – give some sense of the motivations of marginalized groups in choosing the valley over other options for relief housing.

A connection exists between perceptions of the river valley as a polluted wasteland at the edge of the city and its function as a repository for marginalized people. Toronto is not the only city to witness a connection between ravines or "lowlands" and marginal housing: Kellogg's 1909 *Pittsburgh Survey* reported on "squatters" and "disreputable families" living in the polluted area of "Skunk Hollow"; Minneapolis's "Bohemian Flats" shared a similar reputation among nineteenth-century reformers.[3] Despite substantial work on marginalized groups and, in the environmental history literature, on degraded spaces, few studies have examined the links between those places and people relegated to the margins of urban environments. Certainly, land value and perceptions of risk were at work. Ken Cruikshank and Nancy

Bouchier's study of squatters and working-class families in nineteenth-century Hamilton demonstrates the geographic connections between industry, polluted and poorly drained lands, and working-class neighbourhoods.[4] And yet, while most historical studies of environmental inequality describe the unequal distribution of environmental hazards in racialized or working-class neighbourhoods,[5] few investigate the congregation of marginalized populations in already degraded spaces or in urban borderlands. Even fewer explore the link between homeless people and degraded environments.[6] The way in which such spaces were constructed as marginal and the attractions they held for homeless travellers have yet to receive detailed treatment.

The connections between degraded spaces and marginalized populations may best be grasped with reference to the structures of power at work in designating people and places within the framework of centres and peripheries, insiders and outsiders. Just as poor or racialized groups resisted the intrusive improvement initiatives of late-nineteenth-century reformers, cementing their status as inferior outsiders, environments that resisted improvement, that proved somehow difficult to occupy, to make industrious, or to gain value from, were classified as marginal or "waste" spaces by state authorities. Mountainsides and ravines, deserts and wetlands fell into this category. Valerie Kuletz makes this connection in her work on nuclear testing areas in the American southwest, arguing that scientific discourses cast deserts as barren wastelands in a hierarchy of value not unlike the one that cast the people of the region – American Indians – at the bottom of the ladder of economic productivity. By illuminating the place-based experiences of a marginalized people, Kuletz aims, as I do, to "make visible the centers of power that have made [such] landscape[s] a reality."[7]

Marginality, in other words, is not an inherent characteristic of landscapes or of human populations, but one that is actively produced. Kay Anderson documents this spatial production of marginality in her work on Vancouver's Chinatown, where city municipal policies and practices worked to create a racially demarcated district within the city and, through material realities such as overcrowding and the absence of municipal refuse collection, reinforced popular associations of the Chinese with squalor, disease, and social deviance.[8] The Don Valley, of course, differs markedly from the dense urban grid of Vancouver's Chinatown, but the processes that identified it as marginal were similar. In its tendency to represent everything the city was not – wooded, wild, undeveloped, difficult to traverse – it was imagined in ways that reflected elite anxieties about their own lack of control over and within such spaces. This tendency to imbue space with moral characteristics had discernible consequences. As in Chinatown, the ideas and practices of municipal authorities and landowners contributed to the material reality of the Don – its undeveloped ravine slopes and polluted lowlands – just as they contributed to the social and economic circumstances of the people who sought refuge there.[9] By attending to this connection between environments and populations understood as "marginal," we can see the ways in which perceptions of space operated in tangible ways to subordinate areas and their inhabitants.

Institutions at the City's Edge

In 1855, the Toronto General Hospital relocated from the central city to a four-acre site west of the Don River. The original hospital property had dramatically increased in value in the thirty years since the building was erected, and, seeking to expand their facilities, the trustees of the hospital resolved to erect a larger building on a plot of land in the former park reserve east of Parliament Street – land they had held in trust since 1819 and from which they had failed to generate adequate revenue. The downtown lots were leased in 1853, and the trustees used the resulting revenue to commission architect William Hay to design a grand new hospital building on the Don lands east of Parliament.[10]

The relocation of the hospital was not without controversy. An 1853 editorial in a local scholarly medical journal outlined three arguments against the east-end location. The first and strongest of these was the disadvantages it placed on the public due to its distance from the city centre. "Only picture to yourself," the editors wrote, "the necessity of conveying in the middle of winter, perhaps upon a shutter, any poor man who may chance to meet with a serious accident at the western end, a distance of four or five miles, before he could be received into hospital." Second, they expressed concerns about the site's proximity to the ague-producing marshlands of the Don, located 1.5 kilometres to the south. Acknowledging that the proposed site of the hospital was comparatively high in elevation and the building "thoroughly ventilated" – features that would mitigate "the baneful influences of malaria" – they were less sure that the intended site would be "completely removed from all the influences of marsh miasmata, engendered by the alluvium drifted down the River Don, and located at the eastern end of the harbour." "When we consider," they argued, "that during the past summer ague has prevailed very extensively throughout the east part of the city, so that scarcely a house has been free from its visitation, how shall we expect the new General Hospital to escape its influence?" Finally, the editors pointed out the considerable inconvenience that the proposed location would place upon medical students obliged to walk the almost four miles between the Medical School at Trinity College and the hospital "in search of practical knowledge."[11]

The concerns outlined in the *Journal* met with a spirited editorial response in the pages of *The Leader* in the summer of 1853. Published by James Beaty, one of the hospital trustees, and edited by William Lyon Mackenzie's son-in-law, Charles Lindsey, *The Leader* was a forum for conservative views in Toronto. The editorial dismissed the medical journal's complaints as "most whimsical and extraordinary." It pointed out that the present location of the hospital "in the extreme west end of the city" was equally distant from the east end, and never produced "the terrible results which the *Journal* conjures up as certain to flow from its future location at the east." In response to the risk of ague, Lindsey argued that "the western and central portions [of the city] have supplied as many cases, in proportion to the quality of the inhabitants, as the eastern." Falling outside these calculations, he went on to explain, were those "poor quality" inhabitants, who, as members of the labouring class, were "miserably housed ... in tenements pervious to the night air, and in a constant state of dampness." Combined with a "want of ... scrupulous attention to cleanliness" and a "general addiction to intemperance," such conditions rendered this class "more susceptible of receiving and being affected by the poison of ague." Neatly dismissed here, then, are the predominantly working-class inhabitants of the lower Don lands – the area surrounding the proposed hospital. With respect to the inconvenience placed upon medical students, Lindsey rejected the journal's concerns, referencing the inadequacy of the current facilities at Trinity College and the school's plans to construct new facilities near the site of the new hospital. He noted, in conclusion, that the selection of the hospital site, with "all the advantages which are to be derived from an airy and unconfined position ... has met the general approbation of the public."[12] Construction went ahead at the location west of the Don in 1854, and the hospital opened its first wing to the public in 1856.[13]

In the years that followed the hospital's relocation, two other public institutions were constructed in the semi-rural lands of the lower valley north of Gerrard Street. In 1857, the women directors of the Toronto

Magdalen Asylum negotiated a charitable lease from the city of five acres on the east side of the river for the location of a shelter and reformatory for "the poor and indigent ... idiots ... the dissolute and the vagrant members of the community."[14] The Industrial House of Refuge opened on the site three years later. In 1865, after a series of setbacks, the Toronto Jail and Industrial Farm opened immediately south of the House of Refuge (figure 4.1). While the Lower Don was not the only location for reformatory institutions – others, such as the Provincial Lunatic Asylum, were located in the city's west end – it undoubtedly emerged as an important site of moral and physical rehabilitation in the geography of nineteenth-century Toronto.

The rationale for the location of two of these institutions – the Toronto General Hospital and the Toronto Jail – and the controversies they generated, provide some interesting clues into elite perceptions of the area around the Don. When hospital trustees and city politicians, respectively, deliberated on the benefits and drawbacks of siting their institutions in the Lower Don Valley, they drew upon perceptions of the undesirability of lands on the city periphery and the people who lived within these margin zones. The working-class inhabitants of the lower valley were considered people of "lesser quality" who brought misfortune upon themselves through their lax habits. The land on which they lived, too, was "lesser" – poorer in agricultural potential, plagued by threat of disease, and haphazardly developed.[15] Not quite urban, and not quite rural, the area presented both opportunity and challenge for urban expansionists: cheap land prices and limited development controls beckoned, while notoriety and distance from the centre constrained potential. Frustrated in their attempts to convert their holdings into profitable uses such as residential building lots, corporate landowners conceived of other eventualities, including institutions and parkland. They capitalized on nineteenth-century urban conceptions of the countryside as a more virtuous and wholesome environment to fulfil simultaneous goals of isolating and reforming the "poor ... criminal and disorderly" of society.[16]

The decision to relocate Toronto's prison to the east side of the river north of Gerrard balanced economic constraints with the city's desire for self-sufficiency in the housing of its prisoners. At the time of the relocation, Toronto faced escalating annual fees to incarcerate a portion of its prisoners in the county jail outside of city limits. Seeking to reduce costs, the city elected to construct a larger facility for its prisoners. The rationale for these plans emphasized the value of prisoners' labour in

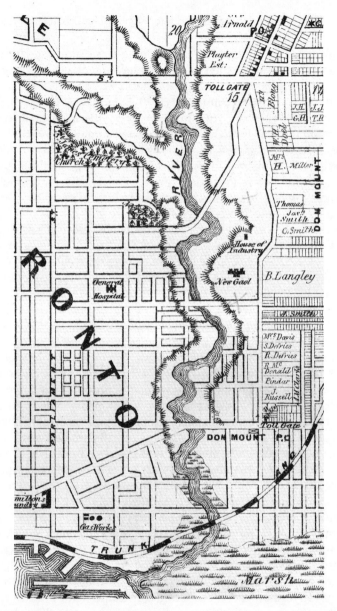

4.1 Institutions of the Lower Don Lands, 1878. The Toronto General Hospital appears several blocks west of the river near the centre of the map. The Industrial House of Refuge (labelled "House of Industry") and the Toronto Jail and Industrial Farm (labelled "New Gaol") appear on the opposite side of the river north of Gerrard Street. (Detail from the *Illustrated Historical Atlas of the County of York* (Toronto: Miles and Co., 1878.) Courtesy of the Canadian County Atlas Digital Project, McGill University and the University of Toronto Map and Data Library.

offsetting the costs of their maintenance and the availability of a site with significant agricultural potential to support the operation of a jail farm.[17] In April 1856, Toronto City Council's Police Prisons committee initiated a search for a suitable site "for a house of correction and Industrial Farm," and in late October of the same year, the committee tabled an offer from the heirs of the Scadding property of 135 acres on the east side of the Don south of Bloor Street. Committee chair John Wilson recommended its purchase, noting in his report to council that it was "in every respect suitable for the purpose desired."[18]

Developments in subsequent years would place in doubt the Police Prisons committee's assessment of the value of the Scadding property for agricultural purposes and stall the construction of the jail. Shortage of funds and mounting controversy around works expenditures caused setbacks in 1857.[19] In 1858, an investigative committee of city council accused the Police Prisons committee of awarding lucrative contracts in conflict of interest and attacked their selection of the Scadding property as a suitable site for revenue-producing agricultural labour. "The selection of ground more suitable for [cultivation] would have been preferable," they argued, speculating that of the entire one-hundred-acre area proposed for the industrial farm, "not more than thirty acres can be brought under cultivation without expenditure of a very large amount of labour."[20]

Council considered abandoning the jail project altogether in the spring of 1859, noting the "very heavy expenditure" necessary for jail construction, the "perpetual drain" from the area's unproductive character," and its "distance from the Courts" as factors that could place the institution "upon the revenues of the City for its maintenance."[21] Kivas Tully, then chairman of the Board of Jail Inspectors, reported on the issue to council later that year. His conclusions demonstrate more a sense of resignation to the decisions made and money spent to date, together with an acknowledgment of the broader economic recession gripping the city, than an endorsement of the Don Valley site. The property, he reported, "could not be put to any other profitable use by the City, or be sold for one half of what was paid for it."[22] Tully's words reflect a familiar theme in the history of the lower valley: the steep, sloping land on either side of the river was difficult to develop. Its use for institutional purposes and later parkland[23] was largely determined – as the hospital trustees learned earlier in the century – by its lack of profitability for residential or industrial sales. Construction of the jail finally began in October 1859 and proceeded with much of the same bad luck

4.2   The Industrial House of Refuge (left) and the Don Jail on the east side of the Don River. "On the Don River, Toronto, Canada," postcard, ca 1906–13. (City of Toronto Archives, fonds 70, series 330, file 54, item 37.)

with which it started. A fire in 1862 destroyed the building just as it neared completion; it was reconstructed based on the original plans, finally opening in January 1864.

For both the Toronto General Hospital and the Toronto Jail, the primary reason for relocation to the lower valley lands was economical: land was cheaper there than in other parts of the city.[24] In the selection of a suitable site, economic considerations and the paucity of options for valley land holdings outweighed considerations of the unhealthy character of the area and its distance from the centre. The directors of the House of Refuge likely arrived at a similar conclusion, pleased as they must have been to receive a site from the city on such favourable terms.

And yet, beyond this bare economic rationale lay other considerations. Concerned as they were with isolating and reforming their inmates, these institutions deliberately sought a location more rural than urban in character.[25] Each chose to relocate beyond city boundaries: the site of the new Toronto General Hospital lay within the liberties east of Parliament Street; the Toronto Jail and the Industrial House of Refuge fell under the jurisdiction of the County of York until the annexation of Riverdale in 1884. For the Toronto General Hospital, distance from the city centre was used as an argument against the site near the Don. But for both the Toronto Jail and the House of Refuge, the benefits of a certain "remove" from the city likely factored into their selection of a site east of the river. Deliberations over the agricultural potential of the Scadding property offer evidence of this goal for the Toronto Jail.

The search for an ideal site – rural, yet close to the city – illustrates some of the paradoxical ideals about rural space in the mid-nineteenth century as well as the changing land uses and valuation of land along the lower river. When the city purchased the Scadding property in 1856, the area east of the river was still largely rural in character. Market gardens interspersed with older farm estates, and a smattering of industry, clung to the banks of the river south of Gerrard. The Scadding estate itself had a few decades earlier supported considerable agricultural production, including fields of wheat, oats, and maize, fruit tree orchards, beds of flowers and vegetables, and pasturelands.[26] While the property may not have been quite so productive when the city purchased it in the 1850s,[27] it evidently presented enough of a rural, agricultural character to allow city council's prison committee to imagine its use as an industrial farm. The area north of Gerrard also enjoyed considerable remove from the stench and filth of the marshlands near the mouth of the river. While the river itself would likely have assaulted the senses, the lands surrounding it in this part of the valley still carried the pastoral character of the valley lands further north.

Nineteenth-century writing about the countryside infused the landscape with powerful symbolic meaning. The idea of the country carried connotations of virtue and wholesomeness. In comparison with perceptions of the city as a place of industry, disease, and moral depravity, life in the country was understood to be slower, more natural, and more in keeping with human rhythms.[28] For nineteenth-century social reformers, hard work in a rural environment became a form of therapy and social regeneration. Mid-century prison reforms, influenced by the ideas of English social reformers such as John Howard, reflected the belief that criminals were a product of their environment. Just as past prisons strengthened criminal tendencies through corporal punishment, idleness, and lack of segregation of experienced and inexperienced criminals, future prisons would seek to reform prisoners through a "morally superior" routine of hard labour, structured routine, and

separate confinement for repentance and reflection.[29] Jail farms served
the dual purposes of reducing the costs of the institution through revenue from agricultural produce and providing training and moral reform
to prisoners through healthful labour in a peaceful environment.

Such romantic portraits of the countryside have little bearing on the
"real history" of rural spaces, which have encompassed a wide variety
of practices and forms of social organization over time.[30] The tendency
of outsiders to portray rural environments in paradoxical terms – at
once liberating, health-giving, and beneficial; marginal, backward, and
unregulated – reflects the expectations and prejudices of the viewer
more than it does the nature of the place. This concept of the divide
between outsiders' essentializing viewpoints and actual lived experience in place is useful in thinking about the Lower Don Valley in this
period in that, as a semi-rural space, it had the ability to feed desires for
a landscape of rural harmony while absorbing the effects of urbanization from the adjacent city. Crossing the Don bridge at Queen Street,
the urban dweller confronted a landscape in transition, a bricolage of
small industrial establishments clustered along the riverbanks, scattered dwellings on newly subdivided land, and larger agricultural
holdings. Evidence of the "country" past and the inevitably "urban"
future would have been immediately apparent.

The institutions that were established east of the Don in the 1850s
and 60s embodied these paradoxical ideas about rural spaces. Perched
high above the riverbanks and surrounded by sloping hillsides and the
cultivated fields of the Industrial Farm, the House of Refuge, and the
Toronto Jail occupied what they considered to be a restorative landscape. From this vantage, the city, with its corrupting influences of
overcrowding, poor sanitation, and moral laxity was distant enough to
be incapable of harm but close enough to act as a reminder for inmates
in the process of their moral education. And yet, in their remove, these
institutions also isolated undesirables – criminals, vagrants, the impoverished elderly, prostitutes, and the mentally ill – from contact with the
supposedly uncorrupted residents of the centre. Here again, the river
valley was at once idyllic landscape and repository for things – in this
case, human individuals – considered unpleasant or unsightly. Moral
geographies of the lower valley worked in powerful ways to shape
space and experience.

This pattern of isolating sources of danger, corruption, or disease
"over the Don" and outside the city limits continued into the twentieth
century. The House of Refuge was converted into an isolation hospital

during the smallpox epidemics of the 1870s. In the early 1900s, the site came to house the Riverdale Isolation Hospital, Toronto's treatment and teaching centre for infectious diseases. A second isolation hospital opened on the west side of the valley in the same period.[31] North of Danforth Avenue at Todmorden Mills, the Second World War saw the establishment of a prisoner-of-war labour camp in the valley. A satellite to the larger internment camp at Mimico, the camp housed mainly German merchant sailors who laboured at the nearby Toronto (formerly Don Valley) Brick Works.[32] It seems the establishment of the camp in the valley followed a similar rationale as the Don Jail and Industrial Farm: proximity to a site for labour and relative remove from the centre.

Valley Underworld

Linked to perceptions of the Don Valley as a "space for undesirables" was its reputation as a frontier of sorts, a place that harboured and facilitated a certain degree of lawlessness. Stories of attacks and robberies on pedestrians and carriages crossing the Don bridge at Queen Street were commonplace in nineteenth-century Toronto, and the area acquired a reputation as a place of danger and unpredictability for travellers moving to and from the highway to Kingston. These perceptions of risk were wrapped up within the history of an urban periphery consistently marginalized by elites. As we have seen, the lower valley had become, by the 1860s, a repository for urban discards – for sewage and industrial wastes, for prisoners, for the institutionalized poor, and for people who in other ways failed to measure up to nineteenth-century liberal values of rationality, moral rigour, and self-advancement. Related to this, the valley also featured in the elite imagination as a place of uncertainty and danger. Its difficult landscape of steeply sloped, tumultuous ravines and marshy lowlands meant that parts of the valley remained, at mid-century, relatively undeveloped and inaccessible. Ravine lands following tributaries into the Don were often still largely wooded, and patches of woodland still existed in the farm lots immediately east of the river. Sloped and partially forested, the valley acted as a kind of "underworld" to the city above, bringing with it images of darkness, unpredictability, and other-worldliness: things could happen here that were less likely to happen on the streets above.

Such fears were at least partially justified. For much of the nineteenth century, Toronto's police jurisdiction paralleled the city limits in extending only to the west bank of the Don between Queen and Bloor

Streets. Not until 1884, with the incorporation of Riverdale, did city police have jurisdiction over the east bank of the river north of Queen Street. North of Danforth Avenue, valley lands remained unincorporated until the early twentieth century. The east side of the valley north of Queen Street, then, was an area beyond the scope of Toronto police powers, and likely little monitored by the scant policing resources of York county. Nineteenth-century police surveillance, furthermore, differed substantially from the active presence we are familiar with today. In 1858 sixty-five police constables monitored a population of about 44,000 inhabitants, a ratio of about one policeman to every 677 inhabitants (today's ratio is closer to 1:474).[33] Not only were police constables fewer per capita but the nature of surveillance differed significantly, focusing primarily on the suppression of rebellions and the regulation of working-class behaviour rather than on "crime fighting" per se. Enforcing Sabbath laws, regulating merchants, trades, and taverns, and making arrests for public drunkenness, vagrancy, and prostitution were the kinds of tasks that constables performed regularly; routine surveillance of areas of sparse population and difficult access, such as the Don Valley, was unlikely to have occurred.[34]

Sporting Taverns on the Urban Fringe

This relative lack of police presence in the lower valley presented possibilities for behaviour less likely to be tolerated in the more effectively regulated districts of the centre. Taverns on both sides of the river earned reputations as "sporting houses" that hosted a range of rough entertainments aimed at a working-class clientele. Among them was the Don Vale House, which operated from the late 1840s until about 1875 immediately west of the river, at the foot of Winchester Street (see figure 4.3). The tavern served travellers and farmers on their way to market in Toronto; it also catered to a local clientele of working men seeking rougher entertainment. As George Rust-D'Eye notes in his 1984 history of Cabbagetown, the tavern was a "frequent resort of the sporting fraternity"; boxing contests, crude fighting, cockfights, and gambling were among the activities staged in its various outbuildings.[35] Anecdotal references to sporting activities in these taverns in the late nineteenth century give some sense of their illicit flavour (gaming of all kinds was banned in taverns by provincial statute)[36] and the role of the valley in giving them harbour. In an interview with Toronto journalist John Ross Robertson, former Toronto resident Bob Givins recalled the

4.3 Don Vale House, ca 1870. (John Ross Robertson, *Landmarks of Canada*, vol. 3 [Toronto: Toronto Public Library, 1967], opposite p. 302.)

Castle Frank Brewery on the west side of the valley in the early 1860s, where he and his friends met on Saturday afternoons to box in a "24 foot ring staked out to the old brewery." "Now," he continued, "when I pick up a paper and read the report of a prize fight, dog fight, chicken dispute or any other horrible enterprise, my mind reverts to the old brewery in the valley."[37] On the east side of the river between today's Danforth and Sparkhall Avenue, William Vine's Butcher's Arms tavern was a destination for blood sports in the 1870s. The tavern reputedly backed onto a "deeply wooded valley, easy to escape into if the authorities showed up."[38]

While the sporting tavern may have been considered, as Peter DeLottinville has suggested, a "moral hazard" for respectable travellers in the latter half of the nineteenth century,[39] the area of the valley around the Queen Street (Don) bridge presented more serious threats to passersby. In the late 1850s and early 1860s, a group known as the "Brook's Bush Gang" were frequently accused of bullying residents in the area. An amorphous group of loosely associated men and women that varied in number depending on the year and the season, the so-called "Bush Gang" occupied a forty-acre woodlot east of the Don Jail known as "Brook's Bush." Using a "deserted barn in a clearing in the heart of the forest" as a base, the group apparently ran stills and gambling operations out of the bush, and regularly harassed and robbed area residents.[40] In the spring of 1861, several gang members were implicated in the murder of John Sheridan Hogan, Reform member of the legislature for Grey County and former editor-in-chief of the *British Colonist*. The murder inquest and subsequent trial attracted huge crowds and received detailed coverage in Toronto's *Daily Globe*, making household names of the gang members and further bolstering images of danger attached to the Lower Don Valley. Over seventy years later, in August 1931, the Hogan murder was the subject of a retrospective article in *MacLean's Magazine*. The case placed a spotlight on the underworld of the Lower Don Valley at mid-century: through the testimony of witnesses, including many members of the Brook's Bush Gang itself, we learn something more about the people who "lived rough" in the valley at this time, and the interactions they had – or were said to have had – with members of the wider society around them.

The Murder of John Sheridan Hogan

At around eight o'clock on the evening of 1 December 1859, John Sheridan Hogan left the home of Sarah Lawrie on Terauley (now Bay) Street, purportedly to visit Samuel Thompson, the new editor of the *British Colonist*. She never saw him again. Lawrie and Hogan had known each other for seven years, and he visited her frequently, often staying for a night or more. Months passed, and though his friends pressed for information as to his whereabouts, nothing surfaced. Rumours circulated in the local press, suggesting suicide or sightings in the United States; a reward of $600 posted by the provincial government in October 1860 proved fruitless.

On 30 March 1861, sixteen months after Hogan disappeared, James Bright went duck shooting with three of his nephews near the mouth of the Don. They found a body floating in shallow water between the mouths of the "big" and "little" Don (the river's north and south entrances into the harbour), its head caught in the crotch of a branch that was frozen into the mud. Thomas Bright, presumably the eldest of the three nephews, tied a rope around the body and towed it with his skiff to the Gooderham Wharf across the bay. In the coroner's inquest that followed, Bright testified that he regularly frequented the marshlands around the mouth of the Don, and as early as a week before had not seen the body. He believed it to be "carried to the spot by the recent freshets" of the Don.[41] The body was badly decomposed, but items of Hogan's clothing allowed for a positive identification by his friends. Sarah Lawrie had sewn a new collar on Hogan's "under flannel shirt" the day before he disappeared, and she identified the variance of colour between the collar and the body of the shirt, together with a safety pin she had used to take in his underwear. Hogan's vest, his shooting jacket (an overcoat), and one of his shoes were missing from his body. The post-mortem that followed could discern no obvious indicators of violence, and the case was sent on to the Police Court for investigation.

Despite a lack of physical evidence of foul play, it didn't take long for the papers to reach their own conclusions. An article in the *Globe* the following day placed great weight on the absence of papers or bills found on the body in speculating upon Hogan's demise: "It is extremely probable," the editors concluded, "that poor Hogan fell a victim to some portion of a gang of miscreants who at the time of his death infested the eastern part of the city, but who have since been sent to the penitentiary."[42] The known presence of gang members in the area, and their reputation for hassling or accosting people moving along Queen Street after dark, certainly gave cause for suspicion. George Allen apparently stated in court that Hogan had told him of being stopped on two occasions by members of the Brook's Bush Gang while on his way home. Sarah Lawrie later testified that Hogan was on friendly terms with the gang members: "He once or twice said to me that parties belonging to the Brook's Bush Gang had stopped him, and that he had had some difficulty in getting through, but immediately added, that they knew him well, and he was sure they would not hurt him."[43] Still, evidence that Hogan may have been carrying a significant amount of cash on him the night he died seemed to sway observers from the press, at least, towards the gang attack hypothesis.

On 8 April 1861, sixteen men and women reputedly involved as members of the Brooks Bush Gang were brought to the Police Court from the jail. Only two of the prisoners, Jane Ward and James Brown, were brought before the court; the rest were called as witnesses. A week previous, James Colgan, a detective officer contracted by the Toronto police, had encountered Ellen McGillich, a woman known to be affiliated with the gang, at a boarding house while investigating another case. She told him her version of the events of 1 December 1859. According to McGillich, she had left the bush that night with Jane Ward, James Brown, John Sherrick, Robert Wagstaff, and Hugh McEntameny. They crossed the Don bridge towards town and stopped for a drink at Kingsbury's Tavern before walking back towards the bridge along King Street. They encountered Hogan west of the Don bridge. Hogan spoke with them, and Jane Ward took his arm and walked with him towards the bridge. McGillich apparently walked on ahead, and waited at the east side of the bridge while Hogan and Ward talked. She then saw Ward strike Hogan with something. He cried out and staggered towards the bridge, and the four men, who had been waiting at the west end of the bridge, rushed in and took hold of him. She heard Hogan say to his assailants not to take his coat from him, as Ward had already taken all the money he had. Ward apparently said, "God damn him, fling him over!" McGillich screamed as she saw Sherrick and Brown pick up Hogan and throw him over the railing into the river. Ward then ran towards her and hit her in the mouth, drawing blood. During this encounter, McGillich spotted a handkerchief with a stone in it tied to Ward's belt. She took hold of it, and Ward told her: "The man I struck with that will never tell another tale." McGillich was apparently too afraid to return with the others to the bush that night, and sought out shelter in a shed behind Squire's Tavern. She returned to the bush the next day with Brown and Sherrick, who, on spotting blood on the bridge railing, stopped to whittle it away with their penknives. She later saw the two of them in the bush with the victim's overcoat and vest.[44]

On hearing her story, Colgan secured four or five constables from the police chief and headed to Brook's Bush around midnight. They succeeded in locating six of the gang members in an old barn; two others were arrested the next day. John Sherrick was located in the Kingston Penitentiary; McEntameny had since died in hospital. McGillich was promised immunity as a Crown witness, and on 29 April, Ward and Sherrick were tried at the spring assizes. Two witnesses corroborated parts of McGillich's story: Maurice Malone, a "dissipated youth ... of respectable parentage,"[45] who confessed to having witnessed the first part of the struggle with Hogan before fleeing the scene; and Dr T.C. Gamble, a respected physician who testified that he witnessed a struggle on the bridge while returning from visiting a patient at a farmhouse east of the Don. Two other pieces of evidence aided in substantiating her story. Hogan's missing vest was found in the possession of an associate of the gang; and an analysis of the section of the railing over which Hogan had apparently been thrown revealed traces of blood, though tests could not determine whether the blood was human or animal. Contradictory evidence emerged, however, which established some doubt in the minds of the jury: an acquaintance of Hogan's, Robert McGillivray, claimed that Hogan had been with him in the north part of the city at nine p.m. on the night of his death (and not, as the other witnesses agreed, on the Don bridge at that time).

As a result of this conflicting evidence, together with some contradictory statements in McGillich's testimony, the jury acquitted Jane Ward. John Sherrick was acquitted upon the production of a convincing alibi, and James Brown was held over to be tried in the autumn assizes to allow the detectives more time to produce relevant testimony against him. Brown was tried on 8 October 1861. Although the evidence against him was much the same as that produced in the Ward and Sherrick trial, the jury took a different view, and found him guilty. An appellate jury reached the same conclusion on 10 January 1862.[46] Brown was sentenced to death and was hanged three months later on 10 March 1862.

The trial had a lasting impact on the popular imagination. At the time, many people believed that Brown should also have received the benefit of reasonable doubt that had been granted Sherrick and Ward. In late February 1862, two weeks before Brown was scheduled to hang, a petition "numerously signed" was submitted to the governor general requesting that Brown's sentence be commuted to life in prison. The governor general, however, would not be swayed.[47] In the decades that followed, commentators reflected what seemed to be a widespread belief that the trial failed to bring the guilty parties, and particularly Jane Ward, to justice. John Ross Robertson wrote in 1885, over twenty years later, that the "really guilty parties escaped punishment, while a comparatively innocent man underwent the extreme penalty of the law."[48]

Beyond the sensationalism attached to the trial and the notoriety it granted the accused, the trial and its coverage by the local media present a fascinating record of the lives of those living rough in the valley in the late 1850s and early 1860s. The circumstances that brought them to "the bush" near the eastern bank of the river, and the kinds of strategies they employed to survive there, appear as contextual detail in places throughout the media record of the trial. Of the men and women accused and those brought to the court as witnesses, most described themselves as "resorting to Brook's bush" for three years or more. For many, the bush seemed to represent an important fallback option for lives that moved between the jail, the hospital, various rooming houses, and, occasionally, the home or outbuildings of a friend or acquaintance. The frequency of periods spent in prison, typically for larceny or disorderly conduct, is especially noticeable. McGillich tells the court in the trial of Sherrick and Ward 29 April 1861: "I have often seen robberies committed, and have committed them myself. I am a married woman, but I have been away from my husband four years. In that time I have been twenty-five times in gaol." As the so-called gang members are called upon to testify, each in turn refers to periods spent in the jail. Ana Maria Gregory, for example, recalled being in the jail for two months in the winter of 1859; the police clerk confirmed she received two weeks in the jail in November 1859 for disorderly conduct; she had been on the street only two weeks when she was again apprehended and sentenced to two months for larceny.[49] Time in prison was often interspersed with time in hospital. Two members of the bush gang, McEntemany and Hannon, had apparently died in hospital before the trial began; another, Biddy Donnelly, was called from the hospital to act as a witness.[50]

Alcohol played a prominent role in the daily lives of most of the men and women who frequented the bush. References to taking whisky in various drinking houses are scattered throughout the trial record; in the bush itself, however, where gang members reputedly operated stills, the drinking was heaviest. Mary Crooks, who spent time with James Brown in the bush, describes "getting drunk" there; she apparently never saw McGillich in the bush "unless she was staving drunk and not able to leave it."[51] McGillich later confessed to getting drunk in the bush on the night of the murder: "It takes ten or fifteen glasses to make me drunk. I often go and drink seven or eight straight off, and then stop."

Violence was also present. McGillich mentions being beaten once by her lover, Maurice Malone, in the bush. Her claim of being "boxed in the mouth" by Jane Ward on the night of the murder was corroborated by Constable Gibben, who found her on the bridge later that evening "with blood on her face, clothes, and hands," looking "as if she had been in a row."[52] In her response to one of the witnesses, Jane Ward makes reference to "a black man who was murdered three or four years ago in Brook's bush," whose body was later robbed by one of the women in the bush.[53]

Frequently debauched and occasionally violent, life in the bush at least involved some degree of shelter. The men and women who frequented the area congregated in an abandoned barn north of the Don Jail. It seems they also found intermittent shelter in rooming houses and in the outbuildings of employers or acquaintances. Mary Crooks noted that she stayed "at Mrs. Smith's on King Street … off and on." William Rhodes, a gardener who had frequented the bush for five years before moving into a house on River Street with his wife Louisa, testified that Jane Ward had lived at his house with her child from New Year's 1860 until June or July of that year; Ana Maria Gregory and Sam Hannon, and Ellen McGillich and Maurice Malone also stopped in for several nights from time to time.[54] The outbuildings at Squires', a farmhouse about fifty yards from the bush, also provided occasional shelter. McGillich testified that she "slept in Squires' shed" on the night of the murder. James Brown "slept in the cow-shed among the hay" while he was working for Squires in November 1859.[55] Numbers in the bush were much lower in winter. Ana Maria Gregory recalls that when she left the jail on 1 December 1859, she "did not go to the bush, as it was winter time." James Squires recalled that Brown "was the only one in the bush" when he worked for him in late November and December of 1859.

The men who frequented the bush seemed to support themselves, at least in part, through a combination of odd jobs in Toronto and its surrounding countryside. Robert Wagstaff testified that he was working "at the Don" with a blacksmith named Berry in December 1859; he frequented the bush at the same time.[56] James Brown worked for Squires "cutting stumps" for a number of days in November and December 1859 before heading to Mono Mills north of Toronto for work on a farm.[57]

The women seem to have had fewer options.[58] Most of the women who testified had spent time in the jail for robbery; others were referred to by witnesses or by the accused as "infamous women." Mary Ann

Pickley, an associate of the gang and witness for the defence, described Ellen McGillich as a "very bad girl."[59] And Brown, who insisted upon his innocence until the end, vehemently protested that his guilt was established on the testimony "of a prostitute and her man" (McGillich and Malone).[60] McGillich herself later traced her acquaintanceship with Hogan to the fact that she "worked about among the gentlemen who were in the habit of dining at the gaol."[61] What exactly she meant by this is unclear, but it is evident from these accounts that the women who found themselves "resorting to the bush" were those with few opportunities to support themselves.

A précis of Brown's life story sheds light on the circumstances that carried one man to life in the bush, and, in this case, to a much worse fate. In the weeks before his execution in March 1862, Brown was visited in prison by a number of clergymen who attempted to prepare him for his impending death. One of these clergymen, Reverend Fish, set about to record a sketch of Brown's life. Brown's story was published in the *Globe* on the day of his death. It reveals a trajectory of insecure, short-term work and the consequences of injury and youthful errors in judgment that narrowed his opportunities for self-sufficiency. Born in Cambridgeshire, England, in 1830, Brown learned to read and write before leaving school to work as a farm labourer and sawyer. He left England for the United States in 1855 and apparently fell into "bad company" in Buffalo, losing much of the money he had earned. Within a year he crossed the border into Canada, where he worked in a number of places before accepting a job building rail lines for the Grand Trunk. Injured on the job at the age of twenty-six, he was apparently sent to the General Hospital in Toronto to convalesce. Upon his discharge in 1857, he apparently became associated with members of the Brook's Bush Gang. Until he was arrested for the murder of John Sheridan Hogan in April 1861, Brown had never been charged with any criminal offence. Sent to the jail a few times for disorderly conduct – he was once arrested, reputedly, for "telling Mr. Sparkhall to go to the devil when the landowner objected to their trespass in his barn off Logan's Lane"[62] – he had a record that was cleaner than that of most of his compatriots. Despite expectations to the contrary by the clergymen who attended him in his last hours, James Brown never confessed to the murder of Hogan.[63]

These rough sketches of the lives of men and women who frequented Brook's Bush hint at what it was like to live on the margins of society in the 1850s and 60s. From them, we can paint only the broadest brush-strokes of the circumstances that brought people to piece together a living in the valley. And yet, hazy as these images may be, they are useful as an alternate narrative to elite perceptions of the lower valley as a place of danger and depravity. For members of the "bush gang," the bush and the valley that enveloped it was a haven to turn to when other options had evaporated, a place to regroup after months spent behind bars. Despite its occasional violence, it was also a kind of social hub for those with few other meeting places to frequent.[64] Trial evidence suggests that men bartered clothing and tobacco in the bush, and that couples spent time there together away from the discomfort of the streets and the moral censure of many rooming houses.[65] "Fallen" or "dissolute" though these individuals may have been to most observers, the trial record shows – however imperfectly and judgmentally – that they were also people with life stories, relationships, passions, and regrets.

Valley Home

In the first half of the twentieth century, political and economic circumstances around the world resulted in heightened levels of homelessness in cities across Canada. As it had in the past, but now in a much more visible way, the Don became a receiving area for those who either could not or chose not to seek out other means of shelter. While the valley remained an area of preference, it was not hermit Joseph Tyler's refuge west of the Don bridge nor "the bush" north of the Don Jail that twentieth-century transients chose. Instead, they chose areas still capable of providing refuge: the partially wooded flats of the river north of Bloor Street/Danforth Avenue, and secluded copses along the upper branches of the river north of the forks. By the early twentieth century, industrialization and major improvement projects had transformed the river south of Gerrard, and what remained of the "rural" in the valley had shifted further north.

Largely unexplored as a phenomenon in its own right in Canadian historiography, transience was central to Canadian experience in the nineteenth and twentieth centuries. Moving between city and country in pursuit of seasonal labour, moving west in search of access to land and better possibilities, and moving between provinces with disparate employment opportunities are iconic Canadian experiences. And yet, for nineteenth- and early-twentieth-century observers, transience was viewed as both an anomaly and a dangerous development.[66] Social reformers puzzled over the conundrum of the "pauperization of the poor" and the need to separate "the worthy poor" – those willing to work – from those who aimed to take advantage of charitable services. "Vagrants" almost invariably fell into this latter category: perceived as a sign of declining morality, they were singled out as targets for hard labour or restricted assistance.[67] As cities like Toronto struggled with a huge influx of unemployed men in the early 1930s, "the transient" was again singled out as less deserving of city support than the resident unemployed – a practice that eventually spurred intervention from provincial and federal levels of government in generating make-work projects for unemployed men in remote areas of the country.[68]

Like most marginalized populations, people who sought refuge in the Don Valley in the early twentieth century are largely absent from the historical record. Census enumerators walked through the neighbourhoods bordering the valley, but did not enter the wooded areas of the valley to record people living there. City reports on housing and homelessness document city-wide housing crises, particularly in the 1930s and during the postwar boom in the 1940s, but rarely reach the level of specificity needed to trace people living rough in the valley. And policemen did not regularly venture into the valley, except in pursuit of particular suspects.[69] It is precisely this absence of scrutiny that may have attracted people to the valley in the first place. As Bouchier and Cruikshank note in their study of working-class residents and squatters in Hamilton's Burlington Bay, "one of [the community's] attractions was that it was nicely secluded from the gaze of the Harbour Commission and city police authorities that workers on street corners and in busy city taverns often felt."[70]

Despite this relative silence in the official record, public interest in the unfortunate and the alien ensured some coverage in Toronto newspapers. Two groups of "undesirables" appeared in association with the Don Valley in this period: Roma immigrants who camped in the valley in the 1910s and 1920s; and the unemployed men who formed a "hobo jungle" on the flats of the river in 1930 and 1931. Drawing upon a limited record of historical photographs and newspaper articles, I will sketch the movement of people through place, and explore the ways that place – including topography and local resources – provided for and attracted populations with few alternatives.

Roma Travellers, 1910s and 1920s

In their illustrated history of immigration to Toronto, Robert Harney and Harold Troper made reference to groups of Roma immigrants who carved a space for themselves at the edges of society:

> Moving about in family groups or small "tribes," their wagons or old cars appeared in and around Toronto at certain times of year. The river valleys along the Humber and Don were their favourite campsites and those who did not come into the centre of the city to do business spent their time fishing and making sweet grass and reed baskets.[71]

As these observations suggest, Toronto's river valleys provided not only refuge from authorities (examples from other North American cities show that Roma families often faced imprisonment or ejection when confronted by local police)[72] but also a source of sustenance and livelihood. The parallels with nineteenth-century descriptions of Aboriginal peoples are striking. Here the Roma appear as "urban primitives," exotic "others" who, like Aboriginal people before them, frequented the modern space of the city for brief transactions before retreating again to what were broadly conceived as backward and incomprehensible lives lived close to nature.

Toronto photographer John Boyd Senior documented the presence of Roma families on the banks of the Humber River in 1918. His images show women gathering water from the river and cooking meals on fires fuelled by driftwood from the riverbanks (see figures 4.4 and 4.5). Although these images were captured in Toronto's other major river valley, it is clear from the documentary record that Roma families also camped along the Don. The images are rich with detail and provide an excellent companion to the scant textual records available on Roma travellers in the Toronto area in the early twentieth century. Together with their captions, they convey potent messages about mainstream perceptions of groups like the Roma in early twentieth century Canada. "Would you imagine, unless told, that this scene is within walking distance of Toronto City Hall?" exclaims the caption accompanying the first image. "The Gypsy walks as easily and gracefully with the water pail on head as without it." Likely reminiscent, for the photographer and his audience, of images of African women, the photograph becomes a performance of primitivity and difference, its (seemingly reluctant)

4.4   Roma woman carrying water at camp on the Humber River, 12 October 1918. (City of Toronto Archives, fonds 1548, series 393, item 15386.)

subject enacting for her viewers a reflection of their own assumptions. Juxtaposed with this first image of exotic grace is a performance of a different kind: the Roma woman as foil for contemporary ideals about female domesticity. In this second image, scattered objects around the tent entrance present a scene of "domestic disarray," an assessment compounded by the cigarette hanging casually (and mannishly) from the woman's lips. The caption cements the distance from the kitchens of the *World*'s Sunday morning readers: "meal-time, commencing with raw eggs. The fire is set ready for kindling in the centre, just gathered drift wood, and upon this potatoes, corn and more eggs will be fried to complete the meal. The youngsters appear to thrive on this diet." Characterized as domestically deficient, yet at the same time graceful and carefree, these Roma women fit within a larger fascination with the lives of "authentic others."[73] Similar tropes are at work in accounts of Roma encampments along the Don in the same period.

4.5   Roma woman peeling potatoes at camp on the Humber River, 12 October 1918. (City of Toronto Archives, fonds 1548, series 393, item 15391-1.)

An article in the *Toronto Daily Star* on 5 November 1910 described a Roma campsite near the west branch of the Don (near the intersection of today's Eglinton and Bayview avenues). Discernible here again is the discourse of the urban primitive, the reporter drawing upon a well-established trope of the "vanishing race" in marking the Roma's remove from mainstream Canadian experience:

> Tucked away in the bushes around the last bend of a long road to the north of the city, miles from a railroad, and a good walk from any other human habitation, are four little white tents, the dwelling place of the remnants of a gypsy tribe. They have prepared for the winter only by building leaf shelters over the doorways of the tents and there they will stay through storm and sunshine until the wanderlust seizes their gypsy fancies.

At the time, this area of the valley remained rural and largely wooded, with large farms occupying the neighbouring table lands. A different Don than the polluted environment further south, the area nevertheless occupied a margin in its rurality and its position just outside the city limits. Living at the camp "as one large family," the reporter noted, "are four men, three women, three children, two bears, and a baboon." As best he could observe, the group made a modest income by taking up collections after "the bear and monkey [gave] exhibitions on the streets" and from fortunes that "the women of the party tell ... to the unwary." It seems the reporter was left to draw his own conclusions about the possible relationship between the women and men in the camp, and the purpose of their stay in the area. "They are not the sociable summer camping party," he reported with disappointment, "that their tents might imply"; nor are they "over fond of stray callers."

Despite the relative isolation of the camp, local residents – apparently concerned that "these gypsies might have too many of the story book gypsy characteristics" – attempted "to show [the Roma] that there were other parts more favorable to their race." The article doesn't elaborate on the means with which the group was made to feel unwelcome. According to the reporter, the families responded by "promptly [purchasing]" the property. After they had "shown themselves to be law abiding citizens, and people of wealth," harassment by neighbours and authorities purportedly ceased. The reporter, however, speculated that the group would nevertheless "be off for other parts when the springtime comes around"; with them, he concluded, will go "the covered wagon and the collapsible stoves, the old hay horse, and the scratching hens that they have taken unto themselves." Here is interesting evidence of the "Other" as a dubious prospect for social belonging. While the purchase of land granted this particular group of Roma some limited respect as "probationary members" of the dominant liberal, capitalist society, their ethnicity cemented their status as outsiders.[74] No further mention of the group appears in the local papers until 4 February 1911, when the *Globe* reported that a "band of gypsies who have been encamped around Eglinton for some time" was taken in by Dominion Immigration Officers "preparatory to being deported to the United States." Apparently the group consisted of "a number of men, women, and children, four wagons, several horses, and four brown bears." While it is difficult to be certain if this was the same group described by the *Star* in November, the location "near Eglinton" suggests so. Area residents had apparently complained of the group's "persistent begging," adding to Children's Aid Society reports that children had been observed "running out in the snow barefooted."[75]

Ten years later a group of eight "Serbian gypsy" families occupied a site farther upriver, on the west branch of the Don near the intersection of Yonge Street and York Mills Road.[76] Unlike the 1910 camp, this camp was easily visible from the road. An article in the *Globe* on 1 June 1920 noted that the camp was situated "not more than one hundred yards from Yonge Street ... so that passing motorists may easily be beguiled to visit their encampment and have their fortunes told." The camp's roadside location in the valley provided the dual advantages, the article suggests, of access to the river for cooking, bathing, and drinking water, and access to a source of revenue through roadside sales and services. Men in the camp apparently worked in the city as chauffeurs and coppersmiths, and supplemented their income with roadside sales of used cars and car parts. As the reporter waited, trying to get an interview with one of the women of the camp, he observed children, apparently "too numerous to count," swimming in the Don. They swim with their clothes on, he noted, "[jumping] into the water and then [waiting] for the sun to dry them." It wasn't long before the camp raised the ire of local residents. Complaints throughout the summer of 1920 about "the condition of things at the gypsy camp at York Mills bridge" were directed to the county police and health authorities.[77] The situation was last mentioned in the *Star* on 21 August, when the columnist speculated that "the gypsies are preparing to move to their winter quarters."

While the evidence here is sketchy and laced with the prejudices of its presenters, it nevertheless supports the hypothesis forwarded by

Harney and Troper that Toronto's river valleys provided – temporarily, at least – refuge and means for subsistence for immigrant families travelling with seemingly scant resources. As Boyd's images remind us, the river valleys provided access to water for drinking, cooking, and bathing, to driftwood for cooking fires, to fish, and to grasses for basket making. They also provided a degree of refuge from "stray callers" and powerful authorities. As Marlene Sway has shown, Roma family groups in the United States and Canada used nomadism, multiple occupations, and the exploitation of readily available natural resources as strategies of economic adaptation. Descending in large part from Roma populations who came to North America during the large immigration of eastern Europeans in the 1880s and 90s, many Roma groups pursued a nomadic lifestyle due not "to wanderlust as much as to pressure exerted upon them by ... host societies." Following occupations that were typically "seasonal, temporary, marginal, and even precarious," they moved from place to place and engaged in a number of occupations simultaneously.[78] Car repairs and used car sales, occasional farm labour, scrap metal recovery, fortune telling, and other forms of entertainment were among typical overlapping and gendered occupations.[79]

The use of the natural environment as a means of subsistence and livelihood also has a long tradition in Roma historiography (as it does, of course, with nomadic groups more generally). Sway records the use of fallen branches and scrap wood to produce bowls, spoons, and children's toys, and the collection of holly and heather for seasonal sale in nineteenth-century Europe.[80] Mayall notes the use of grasses and wood from camp locations to manufacture brooms, doormats and baskets, clothes pegs, skewers, and walking sticks in the same period in rural England.[81] Many of these craft occupations were extended to North American environments. The location of Roma camps along the Don in the first decades of the twentieth century may have been due in part, these sources suggest, to access to natural resources. Strategic placement along travel corridors for fortune-telling and used-car sales occupations was also important, as the 1920 camp at Yonge and York Mills Road suggests, as was distance from the *gaje*, or non-Roma, population, which was considered both a bad influence on Roma cultural norms and a potential threat.[82]

The "Hobo Jungle" of 1930 and 1931

Transience in the valley took on much greater visibility during the 1930s, when unemployed men established a large hobo jungle in the flats of the lower valley north of Bloor Street. Sometime in the fall of 1930 a group of men found refuge in a brick factory in the valley, and rumours began to circulate about the Don Valley "kiln-dwellers." Some investigative journalism by the left-leaning *Toronto Daily Star* located the camp in early December – the reporter apparently having "tramped one night almost the full length of the Don valley searching for [the men]" before being tipped off weeks later by a young homeless man who had spent time at the site. "Last night," he reported, "during bitter winds and near-zero weather, forty-two homeless, jobless, and penniless wandering men slept on 'hot-flops' in the Don Valley yards of the Toronto Brick Co. [formerly the Don Valley Brick Works]." The reporter explained that bricks baked in a series of huge chambers, or kilns, often took up to a week to cool. "While they are cooling, [the men] climb right inside the kilns, stretch themselves out on the hard, warm bricks and seek the solace of sleep." The reporter was careful to point out that these "decent and respectable" men were not trespassers:

These men are not bums. They are not tramps. Nor are they hoboes … They are residents of the Don Valley yards of the Toronto Brick Co. as the invited guests of Frank E. Waterman, general manager of that company, who has not only issued instructions to his staff that the men are to be allowed the privileges of his brick yard, but he has on several occasions stoutly resented the intrusion of policemen and plainclothesmen."[83]

This emphasis on the men's essential respectability stands in marked contrast to perceptions of the Roma. While concerns about communist sympathies and anxieties about the presence of "professional tramps" in the jungle betrayed underlying suspicions about the character of men who had "let themselves fall" into such circumstances, overall these men received a warmer reception than those identified by their ethnicity and economic practices as hopelessly and permanently depraved. While institutional responses to Depression-era homelessness and unemployment fell back on earlier approaches – sorting the "resident" from the "alien" homeless and focusing support on married rather than single men – the public response to the men in the valley tended to be more generous. As the *Globe* reported in the last days of the camp, "[the men's] self-imposed rigor and independence, their vigorous cry for work and not charity, have appealed to the public imagination. They made good as citizens out of luck."[84] A Reverend Peter Bryce made numerous visits to the "jungle" to report on the men's well-being, and church and women's organizations across the city organized donations of food and clothing. In a remarkable document that reinforced, in their own words, representations of the valley residents as "ordinary citizens down on their luck," the "cave and shack dwellers" of the valley scripted a letter of thanks on a scrap of plywood and posted it at the edge of the valley. The letter, dated 4 August 1931, read as follows:

> To whom it may concern: this is to say that we dwellers of the Don Flats (otherwise known as the "cave and shack dwellers") do hereby wish to thank all those who have tried to help us out in any way and particularly those kind enough to send any supplies in way of food left over from picnics etc. which might have otherwise gone to waste and we'll be glad to accept in future any kindness that this notice might happen to bring to us.
> Hoping that things will soon be better we remain thankfully yours.
> [eight signatures are included].[85]

The location of the hobo jungle in the Lower Don Valley likely contributed to its acceptability. Imagining the Don as a marginal space had become something of a tradition by the 1930s. For many observers, the valley was a natural place for the hoboes to congregate. As the hobo jungle approached its second year in the summer of 1931, however, and the number of unemployed men in the valley continued to climb, public acceptance began to wane. Concerns about communist agitation centred around the Don Valley camp led to warnings in the conservative newspapers that "all drifters should be cleared out of the cities before winter" to stem the possibility of revolution.[86] The accusations were met with vehement indignation by the *Star* and, reputedly, by inhabitants of the valley camp.

Jungle inhabitants defended their choice of the valley as one that allowed them to maintain their dignity and independence. When a reporter asked why they chose the valley brickworks rather than the House of Industry or one of the city's night missions, one of the men responded, "We've still got a little pride left," adding that they found begging on the streets demeaning. This sentiment was repeated frequently in the *Star*'s coverage of the Don Valley camp, and in accounts of hobo jungles in other parts of the country.[87] It was clearly expressed in a letter to the editor of the *Star* from an anonymous jungle resident in July 1931. Identifying himself as a First World War veteran who found himself homeless in the same city in which he had enlisted years before, he wrote that he was "of a husky build and suited to manual labor." "Before I will accept charity or line up in a bread line," he continued,

"I offer my services for room or board." He signed the letter only with his location: "Don Valley."[88] Another letter to the editor from a resident of the hobo jungle suggested, interestingly, that work could be created for the unemployed men of the valley by creating a project to straighten the river north of Bloor Street and to remove unnecessary weeds and trees from the valley.[89]

If pride was one reason these men chose the valley, the shrinking availability of other forms of relief was another. In June 1931 the *Star* counted 300 men in the valley "following [the] recent closing of all city missions and shelters, with the exception of the House of Industry." The brickworks population had expanded to 100 men; an additional 200 slept "on the banks of the muggy Don river with the sky as a blanket and the earth as a mattress."[90] Later that summer the jungle expanded again, with approximately 400 men camped along the flats of the Don River. As Reverend Bryce observed in a tour of the valley in August 1931, some men slept in boxcars and dugouts; others fashioned "most ingenious huts ... bivouacs of rushes ... bound together by striplings sewn through with thatch."[91] The photographs in figure 4.6 draw attention to the rich visual archive that exists for the Don Valley and the visible intersections between its social and environmental history.

The valley also offered material supports for transients who, out of necessity, travelled light. The river corridor provided natural amenities, such as water for drinking, cooking, and bathing, reeds and saplings for hut construction, and driftwood for campfires; it also yielded resources from the history of human settlement in the area. A local dump in the valley north of the Bloor Street Viaduct (the site of today's Chester Springs Marsh) provided a bounty of discarded objects that men used to furnish their makeshift homes: a picture frame, an old trunk, a radio antenna, and a semi-functioning kerosene lamp were some of the objects mentioned in a *Star* article of 20 August 1931. The most obvious attraction of the Don Valley site, however, beyond its proximity to the city centre, were the rail lines that ran through the valley. As former East York mayor True Davidson recalled in 1976, "the jungle became known amongst the fraternity of those riding the rods, and almost every freight that came down the Don brought more inhabitants to the area."[92]

As the Depression worsened and ever-increasing numbers of unemployed men from across the country congregated in the valley, mayors from Toronto and East York vowed to crack down on outsiders seeking relief within their city limits. Toronto police promised to "watch

4.6 (above and opposite) Makeshift dwellings in the Don Valley, 1930–1. (Courtesy of the East York Foundation Collection, Todmorden Mills Heritage Site, City of Toronto.)

every freight train" to "stop transients from forcing themselves on the municipality."[93] The coming winter's relief services would be provided to local residents only, and not transients from other areas, the mayors warned. The gap had widened for the men of the hobo camp. No longer the "respectable men" temporarily "down on their luck," the inhabitants of the jungle were increasingly portrayed by the press as an alien threat to the city's stability. They had become outsiders to mainstream society, rather than temporary transgressors.

The jungle, it seemed, had to go. In late September 1931 the province announced that 2,500 unemployed men would be drafted from congested southern Ontario centres for work on the Trans-Canada Highway project in northern Ontario.[94] Further work orders followed, and by the beginning of October the "peculiar and varied habitations" of the jungle had been demolished, their residents transferred to northern camps or removed to temporary shelters.[95] As the *Star* reported, the men of the Don Valley jungle had fared remarkably well for their ordeal: of 213 men examined by medical doctors prior to joining the first road-building contingent, only three were rejected as unfit for hard labour. No diseases were reported, and no cases of malnutrition. The men were more likely, in fact, to be overweight than underweight.[96]

These snapshots provided by newspaper accounts hint at the ways that both Roma families and Depression-era hoboes used the environment around them to enhance what must have been a fairly marginal existence. Both groups, it seems, chose the valley for access to certain amenities, such as water, firewood, and material scavenged from nearby landfill sites. Distance from authorities may also have been important, as the experience of Roma travellers in other parts of North America and the jungle residents' aversion to institutionalized shelter suggest. The brickworks manager's protests of the intrusion of plainclothesmen also implies a limited degree of protection afforded to homeless men under his roof. In its role as a semi-rural space on the edge of the city and, in its lower reaches, an industrial and heavily polluted space, the Don River Valley became a space on the margins. Devalued by more fortunate inhabitants of the city, it became a place for people pushed to the edges of society. Over the last forty years, infrastructure improvements have seen much of the valley "revalued" as a recreational landscape. But in some respects not much has changed: makeshift tents of the homeless can still be seen on the banks of the river in the lower valley, and each winter, the city uses the valley as a receptacle for huge amounts of filthy, salt-laced snow from Toronto's roads.

Conclusion

In this chapter the Don has emerged as an ambiguous borderland space that shifted and redefined itself in relation to the growing city beside it. It is perhaps best understood as a series of places in space and in time, all broadly definitive, in different ways, of the urban fringe. Moving north from the river mouth, Joseph Tyler's riverbank cave on the lower river near Queen Street, the woodland resort of the Brook's Bush Gang east of the river near Gerrard, the institutional landscape that straddled the river nearby, the hobo jungle on the river flats farther north at Pottery Road, and the camp sites of the Roma, farther north still, each in their time created pockets of possibility, retreat, and remove for people pushed for various reasons to the edges of society. As the lower valley became increasingly industrialized in the latter half of the nineteenth century, spaces with the capacity of providing shelter and retreat shifted farther north. It was in many respects the ambiguity of these spaces that made them attractive. Whether polluted by industrial uses or made undesirable by its difficult landscape of steep ravines and marshy lowlands, the valley was unattractive to residents of the centre. Here it was possible to step outside the regulating effects of the urban gaze and, as temporary campers or longer-term squatters, to feel removed from a discernible landowner.

The people who occupied these places were themselves diverse in their marginality. Where the members of the nineteenth-century Brook's Bush Gang or the early-twentieth-century Roma travellers were described within the terms of the "urban primitive," exotic and incomprehensible others incapable of participating in modern society, the Depression-era hoboes were described in markedly different terms, as "respectable men down on their luck." Temporarily fallen, they possessed in their familiar faces – predominantly white, male, and "willing to work" – the ability to reclaim their full status as productive members of society. A further divide separated those who were "placed" in the area as subjects of institutional reform and those who sought out the valley for the opportunities it offered. Still, as prisoners at the Don Jail, impoverished or mentally ill residents of the House of Refuge, unemployed transients, or ethnic "others," all possessed a degree of shared status as society's losers. Not the heroic rebels against the status quo that Eric Hobsbawn identified as social bandits,[97] they were instead more prosaic figures attempting to stay alive on the edges of a world they had lost or had never gained. In this way, the Don Valley operated (and continues to operate) as a place where various kinds of marginality – and by extension, various political economies – can be seen, from the familiar strategies of the outlaw and the squatter, to the more novel political economies of the Roma traveller and the Depression-era hobo. From this perspective, the valley becomes as much a borderland between rural and urban as a liminal space within which "old" and "new" political economies, modern and premodern lifeways, overlapped and asserted themselves.

Assessed as marginal by powerful groups in the urban centre, places like the Don River Valley, with its polluted waters and difficult-to-develop ravine banks, and populations like the Roma and the Depression-era hoboes, were among the unintended consequences of city building in early-twentieth-century Toronto. The ways the valley was imagined as a landscape of danger, disease, and deviance within the moral geography of the city both created and constrained opportunities for social belonging among the valley's residents, transient or otherwise. Unsuccessful or unwelcome in the city centre, the individuals who "resorted to Brook's Bush" in the 1850s or sought refuge in the wooded areas of the Don flats in the 1930s were nevertheless resilient, flexible, and creative actors in their own lives. They sought out the valley for the things it offered, as much as for the things they were denied in other parts of the city, and, for limited periods of time at least, it provided the refuge they sought.

5 Charles Sauriol and the Don Valley Conservation Movement

In the summer of 1983, Toronto conservationist Charles Sauriol sat down to capture some of his memories of the Don River Valley in the 1920s. He recalled a time before sewage fouled the waters of the upper river, before highway development sent a ribbon of pavement along the valley bottom – a time when the upper valley was still largely rural, and partly wild. "I remember," he wrote, "seeing the full moon break over the pines, spreading its beams ... over the misty shrouds that rose from the river ... Seated in front of the cottage, I could hear the water flowing over the river stones, and sometimes, just at dusk, the strident call of a whippoorwill."[1] For Sauriol, lived experience in the Don Valley led to a lifelong quest to protect it. Over the forty-one summers that he and his family spent in a cottage at the Forks of the Don, Sauriol evolved from a casual appreciator of "open spaces" to a fervent champion of the valley as a vital green space for wildlife and harried urban residents alike. Major events for the Don – including the construction of the Don Valley Parkway in the late 1950s and the protection of remaining floodplain lands in the early 1960s – would make themselves felt in deeply personal ways within Sauriol's own life history. Through Sauriol's experience, furthermore, we can chart the beginnings of the twentieth-century environmental movement, including the ideological shifts from private nature appreciation to nature as a public good, and, later in the century, from the sober tactics of postwar conservationists to the more playful and publicly engaged advocacy of the new environmentalism.

This chapter explores the intersections between Sauriol's life narrative and the history of the valley he loved, weaving from these interconnections a history of one individual's experience in place. Discernible in

5.1   Charles Sauriol, ca 1992. (City of Toronto Archives, fonds 4, series 101, file 14.)

Sauriol's life story is the history of the river itself, bending a serpentine and mutable path through some of the major events in his life. It was the river that drew his father Joseph to the city in 1886, when he relocated from eastern Ontario to take a job operating one of the dredges that straightened the Lower Don. Sauriol was born eighteen years later in 1904, the youngest of seven children in his francophone Catholic household. Less than two blocks from his childhood home near Toronto's Queen Street and Broadview Avenue, the canalized lower river appears to have been of little interest to Sauriol as a child. Instead it was the upper valley with its rolling "pine-clad" hills and deep swimming holes that captured his teenage imagination. When his family relocated to east Toronto in 1919, Sauriol joined other neighbourhood boys in the East Toronto 45th Boy Scouts Troop. The troop organized regular hikes and weekend camping expeditions to the East Don and Taylor-Massey Creek. Recalling his first camp-out in the valley at the age of sixteen, Sauriol wrote: "It was a wilderness at our door, an escape from home, school, discipline ... which held everything a red blooded nature loving boy could ask for."[2] Sauriol's time with the Scouts would rank among his fondest boyhood memories. The experience he gained constructing lean-tos and identifying plants and animals, and the values he absorbed, including core Scouting principles of self-reliance, civic leadership, and rational scientific judgment, shaped his later work as a conservationist and his lifelong passion for the outdoors.[3]

Through a Scouting contact Sauriol landed his first job in publishing, as a messenger with the *Saturday Night Press*. He later commuted this experience into a job with the Montreal publishing firm Poirier Bessette, accepting by the early 1930s the position of advertising manager that he would hold for thirty years. As his career in publishing began to take hold, positioning him within a distinctly urban and cosmopolitan milieu, Sauriol turned to the valley for release, occupying his time away from work with long solitary hikes in the upper valleys of the Don. In 1927, at the age of twenty-four, he arranged to lease a small farm worker's cottage near the Forks of the Don. The cottage would become the focal point for his experiences in the valley, a retreat from the pressures of urban life that he shared first with his father and brothers, and later with his wife Simonne and their four children.

Biography offers to studies of environmental history an alternate history of place, one informed by individual experience. It allows us to move from the macro-narrative of landscape change to the intimate territory of personal observation, memory, and response to changing circumstances. For environmental historians concerned with changing human expectations of and experiences in nature, it helps us to better comprehend the personal toll exacted by large-scale environmental change. More than this, too, it enables us to more evocatively imagine a landscape lost. While maps and archival images carry us some distance towards picturing the early-twentieth-century Don Valley, Sauriol's deep engagement with this place as a boy and later as a cottager breathes life into these renderings. Through his accounts of painstakingly replanting trees on a denuded slope, cavorting in the river with his children on a hot July afternoon, discovering the foundations of a former mill on a winter hike through the upper valley, he attaches stories to place. His loss of this storied landscape becomes, vicariously, our loss too. Thus, Sauriol's story is significant in part because it offers rare insight into the changing environments of the urban fringe in mid-twentieth-century Canada.

Most biographies in environmental history have taken as their subjects those prominent individuals whose influence shaped public consciousness or mapped the future of treasured national landscapes: John Muir, John Wesley Powell, Rachel Carson, Rosalie Edge.[4] Far fewer have explored the lives of less celebrated figures or those who dedicated themselves to efforts at the regional or local level.[5] This chapter joins a recent trend in biographical writing in exploring the lives of less prominent historical actors.[6] Here the interest rests not so much on individual achievement and influence as on the relationship between the individual and his or her social and political (and in this case, physical) milieu. As Alice Kessler-Harris notes, the importance of the individual rests not so much in "what she or he may have done, but [in] what her thoughts, language, and contests with the world reveal."[7] What I aim at here is not a fulsome narrative of Sauriol's life but rather a selective mapping of key events in his life onto the environmental history of the river – an overlaying of personal biography upon a biography of place. Through Sauriol's efforts to observe, record, and in many cases resist what he viewed as the unwelcome encroachments of urban development upon a remnant swathe of wilderness within the city, we can discern the influence of changing ideas about the environment through the twentieth century, and the ways those ideas, in turn, had concrete ramifications for the geography and environmental integrity of an urban river valley.[8]

Sauriol makes such a compelling subject for study in part because he left behind such a rich record of his life experiences. Author of six books about his experiences as a conservationist, an apiarist, and a cottager in the Don Valley, together with numerous unpublished manuscripts and regular diary entries throughout his life, he gathered meaning from the act of self-documenting. Executed with less elegance than the works of Muir or Leopold, Seton or Haig-Brown, and focused on a place perhaps less compelling than Yosemite or the wilds of British Columbia, his work never received the recognition that other conservationist-writers enjoyed in this period: most of his books are out of print, and his name is unknown to most Torontonians beyond local history and environmental advocacy circles. His influence survives, however, in the physical landscape of valley parklands, including the Charles Sauriol Conservation Reserve created in the East Valley in 1989, and in a number of other protected areas he had a hand in creating across the province.

While there is a growing body of work on the conservation movement in Canada, the urban open-space movement of the postwar years is a subject that has received only peripheral attention by Canadian scholars.[9] Focusing on the activities of grassroots conservationists at mid-century helps to demonstrate the endurance of conservationist thought beyond the movement's heyday in the 1910s. Changes in the approaches to protecting urban nature, I argue, are reflected in Sauriol's personal experience – the strategies he employed, the language he used, and the losses he suffered as a result of urban planning policies. Over his years as a rambler, a cottager, and later a campaigner for valley conservation, Sauriol's environmental consciousness shifted from a personal appreciation of nature on his private valley holdings to embrace the principles of rational management for the public good. Dramatic and unsettling change in a place that French historian Pierre Nora would identify as his *milieu de mémoire*, a setting "in which memory is a real part of everyday experience," also prompted acts of commemoration. Beginning in the 1940s, Sauriol produced a series of manuscripts reflecting on the character and history of a rapidly changing landscape. This personal archive of experience – including his five-volume "The Don Valley as I Knew It" and his 1945 manuscript "Fourteen Years on Four Acres" – became, in Nora's terms, a *lieu de mémoire*, a symbolic representation of a place transformed beyond recognition.[10] In this way the river valley remained a source of inspiration, and a seat for memory, throughout Sauriol's long twentieth-century life (1904–1995).

Summering in the Don

In his 1982 memoir *Remembering the Don*, Sauriol looked back on over forty summers spent with his family at a cottage on the East Don, recalling summers that "filled my time with the orchard, the garden, the apiary, the easy living by the then clean Don River."[11] Having first spotted the cottage on a weekend Scouting expedition at the age of sixteen, Sauriol arranged to lease the building and its surrounding four acres from the Canadian National Railway seven years later, in 1927. Constructed in 1899 by landowner John Taylor to house a farm hand, the cottage had been sold to the CNR along with a portion of the Taylor estate when railway construction divided the property in 1904.[12] It had seen a series of tenants in the intervening years and by 1927 was in a state of considerable disrepair. The "Lily of the Valley," as Sauriol came to call it, the cottage was a simple clapboarded structure consisting of a living room, a pantry, and three small bedrooms. Bounded by the Don on the east, north, and west, the property in 1927 was completely denuded of

5.2   Charles Sauriol in front of the original cottage at the Forks of the Don, July 1935. (City of Toronto Archives, series 80, file 8.)

trees, "save for two old apple trees ... [and] an ancient willow tree."[13] With the assistance of his father, and later his wife and children, Sauriol worked over the years to better the condition and comfort of the cottage, to expand and nurture his garden, and to reforest the property. He purchased the cottage from the railway company in 1930 and, after years of lobbying, finally purchased the land from them in 1939. Crucially for Sauriol in the years that followed, the land included a second, tenanted cottage (the former home of Philip de Grassi, a military officer who was first granted the land at the Forks in 1831) situated closer to Don Mills Road.

Sauriol's years at the cottage were guided by a closely held vision of self-sufficiency. In this wild place at the city's edge he aimed to pursue a "simple life" of discriminating consumption. "So indoctrinated was I in my love of simple things," he wrote in 1929, "that I was beset with remorse over the wiring of the cottage, which seemed as a desertion of my ideal towards country living."[14] A self-described "back-fence producer," he bottled honey from his apiary, made maple syrup from trees he had planted, fashioned preserves (presumably with his wife Simonne's assistance, though she is rarely mentioned in his writings) from the wide variety of fruits and berries he grew on site, and harvested the annual bounty from his vegetable garden to feed his family and friends.[15] In his writings, he made conscious comparisons to the families that worked the land before him. He and his father, he wrote in 1945, "were as pioneers, re-carving in this semi-wilderness a fine place to live."[16] While framing himself as a pioneer, Sauriol emphasized the divergence between his objectives and those of his forebears on the property. Philip de Grassi cleared the land of its trees to make it suitable for agricultural development. Sauriol, in contrast, worked to reforest the property as a "beautification" project: "I thought only to turn [my acres] into a place of beauty. Forest trees were planted by the thousands. Rich soil was wrested from sod and twitch grass ... [to become] a garden land in which fine fruits and vegetables grew."[17]

Sauriol's personal ethic of self-sufficiency, and the importance he placed upon the rehabilitation and "beautification" of degraded lands, demonstrate his connection with the diverse strains of conservationist thought that existed in Canada in the early decades of the twentieth century. A member of the rising professional middle class, Sauriol enjoyed a privilege inaccessible to many in the 1930s and 40s of owning not only a cottage property but a primary home within the city. Sufficient time away from work to enjoy and improve his holdings also characterized his position in society. As an urban advertising executive, Sauriol occupied the ambivalent position of promoting consumption while at the same time constructing a self-image of the discerning anti-consumerist. As such, he epitomized what T.J. Jackson Lears has identified as the ambivalence of anti-modernist dissent in early-twentieth-century America. Typically held by the urban educated elite, anti-modernist sentiment placed value in the hard but satisfying lives of rural premoderns. Its backward-looking impulses, however, often coincided with an enthusiasm for material progress and possessive individualism in a rapidly urbanizing, secularizing society.[18]

Sauriol's professed goals of self-sufficiency and his desire to seek solace in nature define him as a man of his times as much as they set him apart. While forging a summer home out the wilds of the city's Don Valley would have been considered an esoteric activity by most early-twentieth-century Torontonians, Sauriol's self-image in this period drew upon an established rhetoric of social and particularly urban reform. Between 1881 and 1921, the proportion of Canadians living in urban areas doubled from about 15 per cent to almost 50 per cent of the total population. In the same period, Toronto's population multiplied by six.[19] A wide range of problems, including poverty, crime, and a pervasive sense of anxiety, were thought to stem from the rapid industrialization and urban growth transforming Canadian centres. Social reformers in Canada, like their American counterparts, responded with a diverse array of movements to address the ills of urban life, among them what has generally been defined as a "back-to-nature" movement.[20] Distinctly urban and middle class in impetus, the movement promoted the benefits of outdoor life as an antidote to the hectic pace and corrupting influences of the city. Nature study in the schools, summer camps and Scouting organizations for boys, hiking clubs, and the proliferation of summer cottages among wealthy urbanites were among the outlets for a widespread desire to reconnect with nature in the early decades of the twentieth century.

Sauriol's writings reveal the influence of these ideas. In keeping with back-to-nature ideals, he saw the Don valley as "a realm of wild life that the city had not despoiled."[21] During the hard years of the Depression and the Second World War, the cottage provided solace for his "harassed mind." He wrote in 1945: "I went out to my place thousands of times ... Often an absent lover I wooed the place in fleeting moments. It may have been only to gather a basket of apples from the snug root cellar on a snowy evening, or to plant a seedling tree, or to gather an armful of wood ... but out I went, and as often as I went I cast overboard the debris of the day. Those pinched, sordid thoughts of wars, misery, consternation, and the woe of the world."[22] Like many Canadian men of his generation, he recalled that the works of nature writer and back-to-nature enthusiast Ernest Thompson Seton "kindled within me a dormant love for the outdoors." Works by Henry David Thoreau and American naturalist and writer John Burroughs also featured among his "perennial reads." Parallels with Thoreau are readily evident: both men found a meditative retreat from a rapidly changing society in a woodland cottage close to home; both sought a life of self-provisioning simplicity. No mention is made, perhaps surprisingly, of other conservationist-writers of the period, including John Muir, Aldo Leopold, and Canadian writers Roderick Haig-Brown and Grey Owl (Archibald Belaney). Unlike Muir and Haig-Brown, Sauriol seems to have professed little interest in testing himself in remote wilderness locations or engaging in manly wilderness activities such as fishing and hunting. It was perhaps the very domesticity of Seton's and Thoreau's projects that appealed to him: Thoreau, with his "experiment in simple living" a mile outside of Concord; Seton, who set his *Two Little Savages* in Sauriol's own Don Valley.

Sauriol's fascination with the valley was more than a summer cottager's desire for escape. His search for solace stemmed from a deeply held ethic of conservation. Efforts over many years to improve degraded areas in the valley through reforestation and bank stabilization reflected a belief in the rational management of nature's bounty. At the same time, in his writings and his later advocacy work, Sauriol expressed a passionately held conviction that the valley should be protected from urban encroachment, its "beauty spots" preserved as places for the physical and spiritual health of the city's residents. In Sauriol we can see the influence of early-twentieth-century conservationist thought, where a concern for pragmatic scientific management of natural resources was combined with a sense of moral duty to preserve nature's aesthetic beauty for future generations (conservation and preservation, in other words, were not mutually exclusive impulses).[23]

Threatened Paradise, 1940s

In the years following the Second World War, pressures from population growth and corresponding residential development were beginning to make themselves felt in Sauriol's beloved valley. More and more lands within the watershed were becoming earmarked for residential and industrial development. The growing expanse of paved surfaces, particularly in the lower valley, produced detrimental effects for the watershed's hydrological regime, including soil compaction, increased surface run-off, and corresponding declines in groundwater reserves. According to the Ontario Department of Planning and Development, by 1949 15 per cent of lands within the watershed had been urbanized. This figure would grow exponentially in the decades that followed.[24] "The city is expanding feverishly," Sauriol wrote in 1953. "Bulldozers are eliminating the beauty spots of centuries. Chain saws are heard all day long ... Once tranquil highways, including Don Mills Road, are crowded 'bumper to bumper' with traffic. The fields of yesteryear contain rows of houses. Expansion, we are told, will continue."[25] In the same year that Sauriol wrote, construction of Don Mills, Toronto's first modern suburb, began on the tablelands north of the Sauriol cottage. While the upper valley remained largely rural in the early 1950s, signs of change were, for Sauriol, unsettlingly present.

With population growth came increasing pollution. Storm sewer outlets carried herbicides, pesticides, road salt, and dog excrement from the city's ever-increasing paved surfaces into urban waterways. In the upper watershed, residential development quickly overtaxed a series of small and outdated sewage treatment plants, resulting in the discharge of partially treated effluents into the river.[26] Tests by the Provincial Board of Health in 1949 found a daily average of 6,500 pounds of suspended solids in the waters of the Don – almost double the normal summer flow of the river itself. Conditions became so bad that in 1950, a provincial conservation report described the Don as an 'open sewer' and ranked its water as the most heavily polluted in the province.[27]

River waters were not the only sink for wastes in the valley. Across the watershed, the steep slopes of valley ravines became convenient dumping areas for refuse. Until the introduction of sanitary landfill sites in the early 1950s, Toronto's ravines operated as receptacles – 'levelling-up places,' in the words of the city engineer – for household and industrial waste and street sweepings.[28] As many as forty-seven abandoned landfill sites have been identified throughout the Don watershed.[29] Land filling served the double purpose of storing wastes and removing the barriers to development posed by these yawning divides in the city's topography. Official dumping by the city was exacerbated by the common private practice of tossing unwanted materials – from the car window or by the truckload – in places where it quickly disappeared from sight. Sauriol wrote heatedly in a 1953 pamphlet: "It is not an uncommon sight to see garbage and refuse dumped indiscriminately in the ravine and along the roads of the Don Valley by people too stupid or selfish to realize they are destroying something that can never be replaced."[30]

Such environmental degradation was not confined to the Don. Across the province and in other parts of North America, farmers, naturalists, and foresters expressed growing alarm about the effects of deforestation, soil erosion, and flooding and their consequences for agriculture and forestry. In 1946, the province responded by passing the Conservation Authorities Act, which enabled local residents to request a conservation authority funded by the local and provincial government to manage and conserve resources in their watershed. Two years later, in 1948, the Don Valley Conservation Authority formed to address resource conservation throughout the Don watershed. Funded by the city of Toronto and the province, the Authority benefited from the technical expertise of the Ontario Department of Planning and Development (established in 1944), which published the comprehensive *Don Valley Conservation Report* as a background and guide for conservation activities in the watershed in 1950.

At the same time as these initiatives, grassroots activism was building upon local-level concerns. Ongoing encroachment by residential and commercial development onto valley lands led Sauriol and two conservation-minded colleagues to form the Don Valley Conservation Association (DVCA) in the spring of 1947. Attracting a membership of over 300 Toronto residents, the DVCA worked to protect valley resources and inform the public about a threatened wilderness at their doorsteps. Nature walks, annual tree planting days, and automobile tours of the watershed emphasized the still "wild and serene" Don Valley as a "green buttress" to the growing city below it. A contemporary of the better-resourced Don Valley Conservation Authority (which confusingly adopted the same acronym), the Association fuelled its activities almost entirely on the energies of its founders and the support of its membership.[31] Like the open-space campaigns of other North American centres in this period – notably American urbanist William Whyte's efforts to protect the Brandywine Valley outside of Philadelphia, and Congressman John Seiberling's campaign to protect the Cuyahoga Valley near Cleveland, Ohio – the DVCA emphasized conservation, aesthetic amenity, and outdoor recreation in their efforts to protect the Don.[32] While Sauriol makes no explicit reference to conservation initiatives elsewhere, he was well connected to conservation advocates locally, and clearly drew upon established tropes of conservation and wilderness preservation in advancing his campaign.

Some of the earliest initiatives of the DVCA involved efforts to control public behaviour in nature. Incensed by "despoilers of the beautiful," Sauriol and his colleagues set out to curb such "menaces to conservation" as "the shooting of songbirds, ducks [and] pheasants, the setting of grass fires, [and] the hacking of trees by juveniles." In 1947 they established a citizens' patrol of the valley to protect trees from the hatchets of young boys and rare wildflowers from the enthusiasm of their admirers. That same year, an Easter week "Save the Valley" campaign proved especially successful in "uproot[ing] vandalism." Visits to schools and Scout groups informed children about the benefits of non-intrusive nature study, while collaboration with local police saw the seizure of "18 axes, 7 bayonets and a few butcher knives" from would-be valley vandals.[33] As much as the DVCA aimed to cultivate respect for the non-human world, they also forwarded an understanding of nature as a place in which humans had no part, except as contemplative visitors or caring stewards. By proscribing certain behaviours and promoting others, they aligned themselves with their counterparts in wilderness conservation in constituting nature as a static entity that, bounded and regulated, could be protected from human interference.[34] In this ideological shift from private enjoyment to regulated public use of nature lay deeply personal consequences for Sauriol in the years to come.

In 1949 the DVCA reorganized into three regional branches within the Don watershed, Sauriol taking up the leadership of the East York branch (DVCA-EY). Two years later, Sauriol launched the DVCA-EY's quarterly magazine, *The Cardinal*. Written and produced entirely by Sauriol with modest financial assistance from the DVCA-EY, the magazine contained a mixture of short articles on valley history, fictional stories emphasizing the moral righteousness of nature stewardship, news about conservation activities, and educational "conversations" between the DVCA mascots, Canny and Candid Cardinal. Sauriol wrote in his inaugural Spring 1951 issue: "Persons residing in the Toronto metropolitan area have at their disposal a ... bower of natural beauty which is the envy of many other cities: *The Cardinal* will endeavour to make ... the streams, woodlands, birds and flowers at your door ... mean more to you than ever before."[35] Between 1951 and 1962, annual steam locomotive trips through the valley capitalized on a general public nostalgia for train touring.[36] These "Conservation Specials" brought considerable exposure to the DVCA cause, attracting an average of 800 passengers each year.[37] The DVCA continued to provide a grassroots voice for valley conservation into the early 1960s, when rapid environmental change and a shifting social-cultural landscape gave rise to new strategies.

Conservation activities in the valley received a boost from an unexpected source in the early morning of 16 October 1954. A tropical storm originally projected to dissipate over southern Ontario suddenly reintensified, pounding Toronto with winds that reached 110 kilometres per hour. From his home on Hillside Drive overlooking the valley, Sauriol watched through the night as heavy rain and winds transformed the Don into a rushing torrent with an astonishing capacity for destruction. "The quiet of the night," he wrote, "was shaken by the reverberations of huge floating trees pounding objects in their path; the water was littered with fast-moving objects scarcely discernible in the darkness."[38] In the space of forty-eight hours, Hurricane Hazel dumped 285

5.3 Unidentified Don Valley Conservation Association member with tree conservation signs, Don Valley, 1947. (City of Toronto Archives, fonds 4, series 81, file 73.)

5.4   Cover plate, *The Cardinal*, first edition, spring 1951. (City of Toronto Archives, fonds 4, series 104, file 14.)

millimetres of rain in the Toronto area, washing out bridges and roads across the city and taking eighty-one lives across southern Ontario. In Toronto alone, over 1,800 people were left homeless, and damage across the province was estimated at roughly $100 million (about $1 billion today). Although no lives were lost in the Don Valley, two cars and their occupants were swept into the river.[39] The storm and its consequences marked a turning point for conservation initiatives in the valley, and across the city; it also signalled a transition for Sauriol and his career as a conservation professional.

As the city rebuilt over the winter of 1954–5, it did so with a new awareness of the significance of valley lands as natural drainage channels for flood waters.[40] In 1957, four Toronto-area conservation authorities, including the Don, amalgamated to form the Metropolitan Toronto and Region Conservation Authority (MTRCA), which allowed for greater coordination between jurisdictions in regulating the use of urban watersheds. The MTRCA had the power to acquire valley lands for flood control and recreation purposes, a decision that would have important implications for the future of the Don Valley. Sauriol played a key role in these acquisitions as chairman of the MTRCA Conservation Areas Advisory Board from 1957 to 1971, and as the first executive director of the MTRCA Foundation – the fundraising arm of the MTRCA – from 1963 to 1966. Between 1957 and 1994, approximately 15 per cent of lands within the Don watershed were protected as part of the MTRCA flood plains protection program.[41] At the same time, the newly created Municipality of Metropolitan Toronto took up the massive task of overhauling the city's aging sewage infrastructure. Between 1956 and 1965, Metro removed five over-burdened sewage treatment plants from the Don watershed.

These developments had implications not only for river water quality, but also for the enjoyment of newly created valley parklands once made unbearable by the stench of sewage. The removal of upstream plants contributed to a change in the public perception of urban ravines. Once viewed as inaccessible wastelands and barriers to development – obstacles to be bridged or filled – these rugged valley landscapes were increasingly recognized as urban amenities, vital corridors of green space slicing through the heart of the city.[42]

While Hazel can be credited with tipping the balance towards watershed conservation in southern Ontario, and greatly accelerating plans for the acquisition of valley lands, flood plain protection had been a subject of discussion among conservation-minded planners and scientists for a number of years before the storm hit. The Toronto City Planning Board's 1943 *Master Plan for the City of Toronto and Environs*, for example, proposed to protect the Don and Humber river valleys and their tributary ravines from "encroachment and vandalism" by incorporating them within a greenbelt linked by a low-speed "drive-way."[43] The ODPD's 1950 *Don Valley Conservation Report* reiterated the need for a regional greenbelt as a means of protecting valley habitats and providing an outlet for recreation and respite for Toronto residents.[44] While the greenbelt as envisioned by city planners in 1943 would be abandoned, compromised considerably by the construction of two major expressways in the late 1950s, protection of valley lands by the MTRCA and the Metro Parks Department created a close approximation, stitching together into the proposed "U" shape of the greenbelt a patchwork of protected flood plain lands in the Don and Humber river valleys.[45]

In the protection of valley lands from private development and the removal of outdated sewage infrastructure, major milestones had been achieved in the conservation history of the Don. Flood control strategies that focused on large infrastructure developments such as dams and channel reinforcements, and parks that laid a uniform carpet of turf through valley lowlands, however, had their own consequences for valley habitats. Furthermore, large portions of valley ravine lands remained in private hands, providing sweeping vistas for Rosedale mansions and backyard play space for houses perched on the valley's edge. In the decades that followed, groups like the Toronto Field Naturalists pressed for more comprehensive ecological protection for urban valley lands, and a new generation of environmental activists began to lament the ongoing pollution of the river by stormwater runoff and riverside industries.

Heartbreak

In the late 1950s and early 1960s, dramatic changes in the landscape of the valley brought related upheavals in Sauriol's life. Foremost among these was the construction of the Don Valley Parkway (DVP) and the Bayview Avenue Extension through the valley. "I was standing in a pine grove of my own planting one day last June," Sauriol wrote in the spring of 1956, "when two men came along with maps in their hands. They were trying to locate the position of a roadway in relation to my acres. To any but my unbelieving eyes, the plan was clear enough; the road led across the meadows through my orchard, to the plateau on which stood the cottage. That road ... would wipe out the work of thirty years." Once again, the course of larger events in the history of the valley, and of the city more broadly, would have for Sauriol intensely personal ramifications. As Joy Parr has demonstrated so compellingly in her work on the destabilizing influences of megaprojects in people's daily lives in Canada, the massive environmental changes occasioned by such projects disrupted people's embodied understandings of the world – their daily sensory experience of place. As familiar places became unrecognizable, people lost established ways of knowing themselves.[46] Sauriol experienced something similar, endeavouring as he did to capture his own experience, and that of others before him, of a place in rapid flux.

Sauriol's shock notwithstanding, the parkway would have been a familiar topic of discussion for most Toronto residents through the 1940s and early 1950s. First proposed in 1943 as a scenic – and slow-moving – access route to future greenbelt lands, the parkway took on speed and width with Metro's plans for a network of expressways radiating outward from downtown Toronto in the early 1950s. Metro Chair Frederick Gardiner was a powerful advocate. He envisioned a modern multi-lane highway through the valley as a means of relieving congestion in the downtown core and carrying automobile traffic efficiently to the city's quickly expanding suburban districts. Rapid population growth in the postwar period created its own logic. Here Sauriol's appreciation of the valley as a *place*, for recreation, reflection, and restoration, met with Gardiner's reductive vision of the valley as a *corridor* through which to move automobiles and sewage pipelines.

Metro Council approved plans for the parkway in 1956; work began on the southern reaches of the highway two years later. In 1961, workmen pulled down the Sauriols' cherished cottage. The road right of way was surveyed, leaving Sauriol and his family with a portion of their original holdings, including the old de Grassi cottage on the west side of the river. Restored after Hurricane Hazel as the headquarters of Sauriol's Don Valley Conservation Association, the cottage provided an opportunity to regroup and start over. Demonstrating great pluck, Sauriol and his family packed their possessions and moved across the river. By 1964 construction was completed from the Gardiner Expressway north to Bloor Street; the parkway reached its end point at Highway 401 in 1967 (to be continued as Highway 404 in the 1970s and 80s).

For Sauriol, the loss of the cottage in the late 1950s coincided with a period of major transition in his working life. In December 1956, about

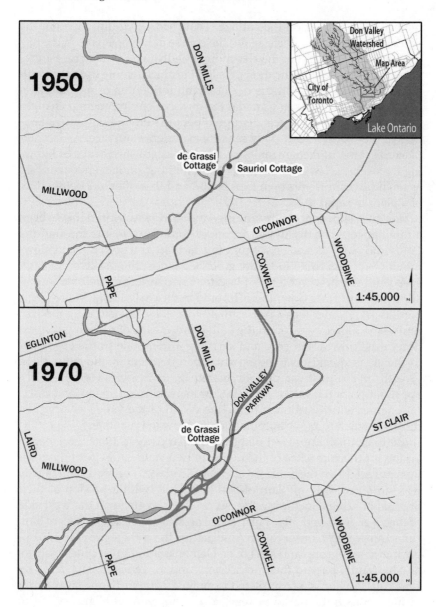

Map 4   Sauriol cottage locations, before and after the construction of the Don Valley Parkway, 1950 and 1970. (Map composed by Jordan Hale.)

a year before the cottage was torn down, he received a call from Frederick Gardiner asking if he would represent Metro on the future Metropolitan Toronto and Region Conservation Authority (MTRCA). Sauriol was stunned, and deeply honoured. "For years," he later recalled, "I had been humiliated, ignored, and put to one side, with no clout ... to do what I thought should be done."[47] Especially humiliating and perplexing for Sauriol was his exclusion from the MTRCA's predecessor, the Don Valley Conservation Authority. Sauriol accepted Gardiner's invitation, and in February 1957 took up the (unpaid) position of chair of the MTRCA's Conservation Areas Advisory Board. Working with an annual budget of $500,000, Sauriol was expected "to assemble land for conservation areas" across the Metropolitan Toronto region. "A more pleasant task could not have been handed to me," he recalled in 1991.[48] Sauriol held the position for fourteen years, stepping down in 1971.

Six years later, Sauriol faced change of a more destabilizing nature. Having worked for Poirier Bessette since the early 1930s, Sauriol left due to "changing fortunes" in 1963.[49] He found himself without an income for three years, a situation that in retrospect created the space for him to devote himself more fully to conservation initiatives. Later in 1963, Sauriol accepted a position as the first executive director of the MTRCA Foundation, the fundraising arm of the MTRCA. The position granted him travel expenses as well as a 5 per cent commission on monies raised. Three years later, Sauriol parlayed his experience with the MTRCA into a job with the newly established Nature Conservancy of Canada (NCC), where he remained for the next twenty-one years, taking up the role of executive director from 1982 to 1986 before his retirement in 1987.

These personal triumphs reflected a growing environmental awareness within Canadian society that built momentum, much like Sauriol's conservation career, through the 1960s. As Samuel Hays has concluded for the American context, a key difference between the environmental movement of the 1960s and 70s and its pre-war predecessors was the broad popular support it achieved.[50] Public concern for the environment stemmed in part from the gravity of ongoing problems, including, in the urban context, air and water pollution, issues of consumption and waste, and the shrinking availability of what was then termed "open space." In the loss of meadows, forests, and popular children's play areas close to home, American historian Adam Rome argues, lay the origins of postwar environmentalism. "The desire to preserve wilderness was ... [only] the most visible part of a much larger concern about the destructive sprawl of urban civilization."[51] For Torontonians, such concerns came to focus increasingly on the Don. By the late 1960s, the river had emerged as a potent symbol of environmental degradation and mismanagement.

Despite major improvements to sewage treatment and disposal following Hurricane Hazel, the Don remained dangerously polluted. Local industries continued to discharge harmful effluents into the sewage system, and combined sewers in the older parts of Toronto, including most of the Lower Don, continued to overflow during periods of heavy rain, sending raw sewage into the river. Faecal coliform levels soared as high as 61 million counts per 100 mL in the late 1960s, 25,000 times the safe swimming level of 2,400 counts.[52] The river had also become increasingly inaccessible to Toronto residents, especially in its lower reaches. The construction of the Don Valley Parkway and other arterial roads in the late 1950s and early 1960s had cemented the perception of the Lower Don as an urban wasteland criss-crossed with rail and road arteries and littered with abandoned industrial buildings, road salt storage sites, and equipment storage yards. Fences erected along the freeways made public access to the lower river valley very difficult, further sealing the fate of the Don as out of sight, out of mind.

Sauriol's approach to conservation, which combined public education about the wonders of Toronto's "back yard wilderness" with efforts to shame offenders, was joined in the late 1960s by a new and more playful brand of activism. In November 1969, an ad hoc group of University of Toronto professors and students organized under the name of Pollution Probe brought the plight of the Don to public attention.[53] Declaring the river "dead" as a result of years of pollution and detrimental development, Probe members led a one-hundred-car cavalcade, including a hearse, from the university grounds to a funeral ceremony on the river, north of the Bloor Street Viaduct. Funeral organizer Martin Daly detailed for a crowd of about two hundred the history of abuses to the river, while a student dressed as eighteenth-century writer and artist Elizabeth Simcoe played the role of the river's widow, weeping as she read excerpts from her diary describing a river once teeming with salmon and water fowl. As subway passengers looked on from the viaduct above, Daly concluded the event by tossing a wreath into the river. "And now," he announced to the mourners, "we await the resurrection."[54]

Pollution Probe's tactics were connected to larger trends in environmental activism in this period, when groups such as Greenpeace

5.5 Pollution Probe's Funeral for the Don, November 1969. (Courtesy of Tom Davey).

(established 1971) employed guerilla theatre, stunt work, and other unconventional techniques to capture public attention and bring a sense of urgency to their cause.[55] Close to mind for many observers would have been the June 1969 oil fire on the Cuyahoga River in Cleveland, brought to international attention by *Time* magazine in the summer of 1969.[56] The funeral for the Don received widespread media coverage and fuelled new demands from individuals and community-based organizations for a cleaner and more accessible Don River. Sauriol's response was dismissive: "All of my associations with the Don were reasonable and rational," he wrote in 1991, aligning himself with an earlier generation of sober conservationists. "I avoided such misfits in common sense as the burial held for the Don, complete with coffins and mourners."[57] Probe's message reiterated what long-established groups such as the Toronto Field Naturalists (and Sauriol's own DVCA, defunct since the early 1960s) had been saying for years: the Don had the potential to be a vibrant green space in the heart of the city, a refuge for wildlife and a destination for recreation, and it was worthy of protection. Unlike earlier groups, however, who struggled to deliver their message to a largely uninterested public, Pollution Probe spoke for a new generation that refused to accept the degradation of the environment as an inevitable consequence of development.

The 1969 funeral was followed by a brief surge of interest in the Don, and a 1971 campaign by the Ontario Water Resources Commission to reduce phosphates in Ontario waterways was successful in raising oxygen levels in the Don and improving aquatic habitat.[58] In the summer of the same year, college students hired for the MTRCA's "Don Patrol" removed more than 200 tons of litter from the river and surrounding valley. It wasn't until the late 1980s, however, that heightened public concern for the environment generated new and sustained visions for a restored river environment.

As the public awakened to deplorable conditions in environments close to home, Sauriol learned of a new threat to his holdings in the valley. Ironically, the threat would come from initiatives close to his own heart. "I am somewhat fearful for the cottage," he wrote in his diary for 19 September 1966. "Acquisition is in the [MTRCA's] 25 year plan." With his children grown, the de Grassi cottage (figure 5.6) had become more a place of solitary retreat and communion with friends than the active hub of family life it had once been. Nevertheless, he resolved to "put up a fight to keep the old place."[59] In January 1967, Sauriol received the expropriation papers for de Grassi. He was crushed. Still chair of the MTRCA Conservation Areas Advisory Board, he understood well

5.6   De Grassi cottage, winter 1955. (City of Toronto Archives, fonds 4, series 80, file 7.)

the Authority's policy of removing dwellings from risky flood plain areas in the aftermath of Hazel and of divorcing parklands from past signs of human occupation. He had held out hope, however, that his efforts in the valley would be celebrated rather than erased. "I would like to hold the dwelling's hands these next few years," he wrote on 25 January 1967, "watch the things I have planted grow, and take an interest in their affairs, so they are truly mine ... There will be a price [per] acre ... But the appraisal will not take into account the tiny pocket of bullrush that ... brought the swamp tree frogs ... nor the border where my herbs grow ... This is the value I place on it."[60] By the fall of 1967 Sauriol had purchased property in eastern Ontario's Hastings County, upon which he planned to rebuild a summer retreat. The MTRCA took possession of de Grassi in 1968, bringing to an end over forty years of summering in the Don Valley. Over those years, Sauriol had seen the valley change from a rural borderland of farms and woodlands to an increasingly threatened corridor of urban green space. In the ironic loss of the cottage to conservation initiatives of his own making lay a recurrent tension in Sauriol's life between private nature appreciation and the public good, and, for this newly created urban parkland, a tension frequently observed in parks historiography between the desire to create both a space for human recreation and a wilderness devoid of human influences. That this wilderness should exist just a few hundred metres from a major expressway, and within one of Canada's most urbanized watersheds, only heightened this irony.

Valley Remembered

In September 1989, Sauriol's beloved East Don Valley received protection as a nature reserve within the Toronto Parks system. Sauriol recalled the dedication as "the most rewarding, significant day in [his] long career as a conservationist."[61] Named in his honour, the Charles Sauriol Conservation Reserve stretched from the Forks northeast to Eglinton Avenue, encompassing sixty-seven hectares of signature valley lands. Fittingly, it commemorated both his lifelong commitment to valley conservation, and a valley landscape mostly lost. Later that fall, Sauriol received the Order of Canada for his life's work to protect natural spaces in Canada. That year also marked a turning point in citizen efforts to revitalize the Don. In February, Toronto City Council responded to concerns from local residents' associations by endorsing a recommendation "that the Don River and its related recreation and wildlife areas be made fully useable, accessible and safe for the people of Toronto no later than the year 2001."[62] Two months later, *Toronto* magazine hosted a day-long public forum on the future of the Don at the Ontario Science Centre. Attended by about 500 people, the forum represented a watershed in public awareness about the Don. Later that spring, the newly created Task Force to Bring Back the Don presented a vision for a clean, green, and accessible Don – a resurrection, of sorts, of a long-neglected urban river. Since its establishment, some 10,000 Task Force volunteers have planted tens of thousands of trees, shrubs, and wildflowers in the Lower Don Valley, removed many tons of garbage and debris, and thrown their muscle behind forty restoration projects throughout the central and lower valley.[63] The slow process of deindustrialization had created space for new possibilities. By the time of Sauriol's death in 1995, the river had re-emerged as a symbol of urban health – specifically, the health of the relationship between urban residents and the natural environment upon which they depend.

Looking back on Sauriol's remarkable life, and on the parallel history of the river in this period, one can discern the impressions of key moments in the environmental and cultural history of twentieth-century North America. As Sauriol planted trees to reforest his holdings and restore his land to health, he did so within the context of the early 1930s Dust Bowl in prairie Canada and the midwestern United States, and of the conservationist ideologies of Aldo Leopold and others that emerged in response to such disasters. In the 1940s, when Sauriol spearheaded a campaign to protect the Don Valley from urban encroachment and to kindle in Torontonians a sense of respect for the "wilderness at their doorsteps," he benefited from (and contributed to) the shift towards watershed-level management of natural resources in Ontario. The construction of the Don Valley Parkway, with its huge reverberations in Sauriol's life, had larger consequences still for the ecology of the watershed – the parkway constituting the largest single piece of infrastructure in the river valley. The turn towards flood plain protection following Hurricane Hazel and its consequences for Sauriol's remaining holdings on the Don transformed remaining valley-bottom lands into public recreational amenities, reflecting at the same time an established trend in parks management of erasing signs of past habitation from the landscape. Finally, in Sauriol's trajectory from conservationist-practitioner on his valley holdings to local activist to "conservation professional," we can chart the parallel development of the environmental movement in Canada, with its deeply pragmatic farmer-scientist roots.

Historical participants in Toronto's tumultuous twentieth century, both Sauriol and the Don emerged as hybrid entities: glancing backward to a rural, premodern past while moving inevitably towards an urban, modern future. Inasmuch as Sauriol's "paradise" was itself a hybrid landscape, part natural system and part cultural artefact, Sauriol himself personified this hybridity in his identity as part urban professional, part "back-fence producer." This ambivalence also emerged in his choice to live out his dream of the "simple life" not in the wilds of Algonquin Park, but within a threatened rural landscape on the urban periphery. Witness to so much dramatic change through his long twentieth-century life, Sauriol gave voice to a profound sense of loss in his reflections about the river and its past. "One by one I have seen the landmarks of my day and of my surroundings disappear …

The farmlands, the trails, the trees, buried in, covered over or chopped down," he wrote in 1981.[64] Facing the loss of this *milieu de mémoire*, Sauriol drew comfort from his personal archive of experience – the documents, photo albums, books, and decades of diaries that comprised, in Nora's terms, a personal *lieu de mémoire*, a symbolic representation of lived past experience. "I need but go to any one of them," Sauriol wrote in 1991, to "relive ... those days when, as a young fellow, I ... hefted a pack on a trek up the Don."[65]

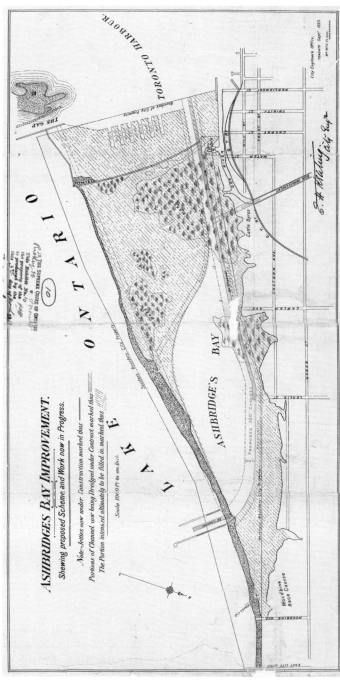

Plate 1. Keating's Proposed Ashbridge's Bay Improvement Plan, 1893. (Note: south is at the top of the map.) The Government Breakwater, constructed in 1885, runs south from the foot of Cherry Street (third street from the right), separating the marsh from the harbour. An east-west sandbar divides Ashbridge's Bay and the lake. Gooderham and Worts cattle sheds are noted immediately east of the bend in the river. (E.H. Keating, *Ashbridge's Bay Improvement Shewing proposed Scheme and Work now in Progress* [Toronto: City Engineer's Office, 1893]. City of Toronto Archives, fonds 200, series 725, file 7, MT95.)

Plate 2. MVVA Port Lands Estuary Proposal, 2007. (Rendering by Michael Van Valkenburgh Associates, Inc. Courtesy of Waterfront Toronto.)

Plate 3. Keating Channel Neighbourhood, MVVA *Port Lands Estuary Proposal*. (Rendering by Michael Van Valkenburgh Associates, Inc. Courtesy of Waterfront Toronto.)

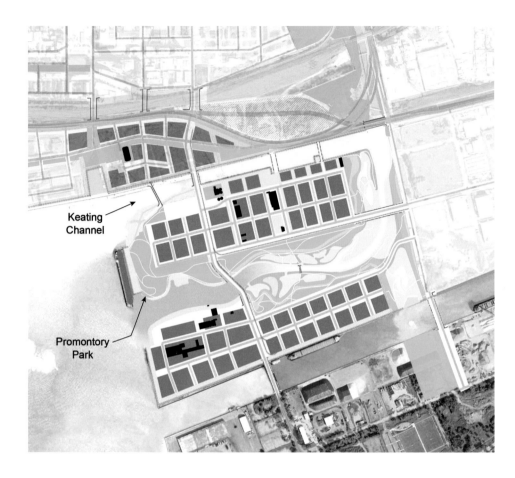

Keating
Channel

Promontory
Park

Plate 4. Amended design for river mouth, 2012. Note the hardened western edge of Promontory Park, south of the entrance to Keating Channel. The Lafarge Cement Plant is represented by the small black square on the south bank of the river mouth across from the park. (Rendering by Michael Van Valkenburgh Associates, Inc. Courtesy of Waterfront Toronto.)

6 Metro Toronto and the Don Valley Parkway

The construction of the Don Valley Parkway (DVP) between 1958 and 1966 marked a turning point in the history of the valley. With it, the significance of the valley shifted, from a polluted periphery of the nineteenth-century city to a vital transportation corridor in the centre of a larger metropolitan region. The valley's historical role as a corridor for the movement of people and goods, by water and later by rail, pre-ordained its transformation. The DVP became, in effect, the grandest elaboration of this persistent theme in the history of the relationship between the river, the valley, and the evolving city. Following the line of least geographical resistance, it was a "friction-free" development in more ways than one: few homes stood in the way of the proposed road; few existing roads required incorporation; and few people objected.

The largest piece of infrastructure to occupy the watershed, the road had long-term consequences for valley ecologies. First and foremost, it brought people to the valley in unprecedented numbers, and with them, the noise, wastes, and related environmental effects associated with highway developments. Heavy truck and automobile traffic, together with the road itself, altered hydrological cycles, displaced and destroyed animals, and introduced new sources of contaminants to valley air and waters.

Just as the road development shaped the history of the valley, so the valley – its geography, hydrology, and its history of human uses – came to bear upon the history of the DVP. Valley landscapes both supported and constrained the developing roadway. Existing geological contours and historical water flow patterns provided the gentle curves and gradual grades that define the "parkway character" of the road, while valley slopes and hillocks supplied fill for lowland sections. As the road developed, valley topographies necessitated additional work and expenditure in some places; steep slopes and established hydrological patterns resulted in mudslides and flash floods in the years after the parkway was opened to the public. Existing human infrastructure in the valley, such as the CN and CP rail lines, and the network of existing bridges, also played a role in the development of the road, alternately constraining and facilitating alignment options.

Transformative as it was for the valley, the DVP was also a ground-breaking development in the history of Canadian cities. A product of the growth-friendly, capital-rich atmosphere of the early years of Toronto's experiment with metropolitan governance, it was among the first urban expressways in Canada. The Gardiner Expressway and Montreal's Laurentian Autoroute, both of which opened partial routes in 1958, counted among the few urban expressways in operation when the DVP opened its first segment in August 1961. The road signalled Toronto's status in this period as an aspirational city. Billed as a modern solution to Toronto's congestion problems, it was from the outset a hybrid roadway in format and function. The nature of its design – a scenic, winding parkway flanked by an urban greenbelt – and the audacity of its construction through narrow ravine lands and a valley bottom already criss-crossed by a river and two rail lines, reflected at once optimism for the future and nostalgia for a slower-moving, more familiar past.

As much as the DVP was a signature development of North America's first metropolitan government, it was also the vision of a man synonymous with that government from 1953 to 1962: Metro's founding chair, Frederick Gardiner. Possessed with what his biographer called an "unalloyed fascination" with the thought of building modern multi-lane highways, Gardiner was a tenacious promoter of the DVP as a vital component of a larger network of urban expressways serving the metropolitan region.[1] The DVP presented an ideal flagship project for the metropolitan government as an enabler of efficient traffic circulation, suburban growth, and intra-municipal cooperation. Gardiner's impressive influence within the metropolitan government and his role as the public face for major Metro infrastructure developments in this period make him an essential part of this story.

This chapter examines the history of the parkway development and the unique political conditions that shaped its development. It explores the often-conflicting experiences of the parkway by Toronto residents: as a corridor and a barrier; an inhibitor and a facilitator of valley experiences; a long-sought-after solution to Toronto traffic problems; and, from the perspective of urban ecologists, among the most intransigent of problems facing the Don Valley, and the city, today.

The Metropolitan Concept

Like so many North American centres in the years following the close of the Second World War, Toronto grew explosively, outpacing the efforts of overstretched municipal bodies to regulate and provision that growth. By the late 1940s, the city and its surrounding municipalities struggled under the weight of a ballooning suburban population and outdated, inadequate municipal infrastructure. A 1949 report by consulting engineers Gore and Storrie warned that water and sewerage infrastructure was dangerously overtaxed across the region, resulting in regular overflows of raw sewage into area streams and inadequate supplies of clean drinking water.[2]

Traffic congestion provided a daily reminder of the effects of rapid growth and changing transportation habits on the city's outdated infrastructure. Traffic volumes in the downtown core doubled between 1945 and 1955, making Toronto one of North America's most congested cities. By the late 1940s, 130,000 vehicles squeezed into the downtown core every weekday. Traffic congestion became so unbearable, and parking so scarce, that the area south of Dundas earned a reputation as the "suffering acres."[3] Vehicle registrations, however, only continued to increase. By 1955, 340,000 passenger vehicles had been registered across the metropolitan region (one car for every 3.7 people, a ratio exceeded in North America only by Detroit and Los Angeles), and planners projected a ratio of one car for every 1.4 people by 1980.[4]

Efforts to address these problems were hampered by a political context of fractured municipal jurisdictions and sizeable financial disparities between the city and its suburban municipalities. Drawing upon a healthy assessment base of industrial, commercial, and residential properties, the city of Toronto had relatively little difficulty provisioning its residents with municipal services. Its twelve surrounding municipalities, however, faced the opposite circumstances: an inadequate tax base characterized by few industrial and commercial properties, and rapidly expanding residential districts that required costly municipal services.[5] Attempts to address region-wide needs in this environment, such as sewage and roads infrastructure, met with repeated failure through the late 1940s and early 1950s. Despite the presence of two municipal planning bodies – the Toronto City Planning Board (CPB), established in 1942, and the regionally focused Toronto and Suburban Planning Board, established in 1946 (and renamed the Toronto and York Planning Board [TYPB] the following year) – region-wide planning was stymied by the difficulties of securing cost-sharing arrangements across municipalities with divergent priorities and disparate revenue bases. Some important ideas emerged from these planning bodies, such as the concept of a suburban "greenbelt" to contain growth, an interconnected single public transit system, and a network of urban expressways; however, with the bodies' limited access to funds and the authority only to commission studies and make recommendations, these ideas failed to gain the necessary support from the region's municipal councils.

In response to this urgent need for infrastructure development across the metropolitan region and the need for a well-resourced coordinating body to oversee such developments, the provincial government of Leslie Frost passed legislation in April 1953 to create the Municipality of Metropolitan Toronto. Comprising twelve councillors from Toronto, including the mayor, and one representative from each of the city's twelve surrounding municipalities, "Metro" assumed planning authority over a vast metropolitan region, including over 800 square kilometres of land in the adjacent townships of Vaughan and Markham. More powerful than the municipalities it encompassed, it had the ability to tax real estate and borrow funds. While the municipalities retained their individual fire and police departments, public health facilities, and libraries, Metro took on responsibility for major infrastructure functions such as arterial roads, major sewage and water facilities, regional planning, public transportation, and metropolitan parks. These powers allowed Metro to exert unprecedented influence over the development of the region.

Metro's founding chair, Frederick Gardiner, was a central figure in these developments. A promoter from the early 1940s of major infrastructure projects to facilitate the region's growth, he was also an important voice in the push to create a federated municipal body in the early 1950s. As reeve of the tiny, affluent village of Forest Hill from 1937 to 1949, Gardiner had initially been "unswervingly hostile to any scheme under which his constituency would cede all or any of its autonomy to a metropolitan regime."[6] His experience with several region-wide planning bodies in the 1940s, including his appointment and later chairmanship of the Toronto and York Planning Board (1946–53), slowly warmed him to the idea of a federated metropolitan region. An advocate, and in many cases an author, of the TYPB's most ambitious plans, he witnessed their successive failure with mounting frustration. As TYPB chair in 1949, Gardiner led board members to resolve in camera that "nothing short of a unified municipality" could address the problems facing the metropolis.[7] His personal friendship with Ontario Premier Leslie Frost, and his growing influence in the metropolitan region, helped to shepherd through the establishment of the metropolitan government – the first of its kind in North America – in 1953.

Gardiner was a logical choice to chair the nascent council. His professional background as a highly successful lawyer and a businessman with diverse interests across the country lent him an entrepreneurial edge befitting his role and positioned him to draw support from powerful players among the city's elite. A deep familiarity with the metropolitan region and proven leadership in municipal politics further recommended him. The creation of Metro, with Gardiner at its helm, created the conditions for major infrastructure development across the region.

Parkway or Expressway?

Gardiner didn't waste any time getting expressways onto the Metro agenda. In 1953 and 1954, Metro's road engineers worked to sketch out a network of arterial highways for the expanding metropolis. Their plan called for five new expressways to facilitate automobile movement throughout the region. The proposed Lakeshore Expressway ran along the waterfront, extending the province's existing Queen Elizabeth Way into the city. Four radial expressways stretched out from the downtown core: from west to east, the Humber Expressway (Highway 400 extension), Spadina Expressway, Don Valley Parkway, and the Scarborough Expressway (Lakeshore Extension) along the abandoned CNR right of way in the east (see figure 6.1). Subsequent plans would include the Crosstown Expressway running parallel to Davenport Road from the DVP to the Highway 400 extension in the west; and the Richview Expressway running along Eglinton Avenue through Etobicoke. Within these plans, the Lakeshore Expressway was to receive first priority, followed by the Spadina Expressway and then the Don Valley Parkway. For a number of reasons that will emerge as the story unfolds, the DVP became Metro's second, and last, expressway project seen through to completion. In the fall of 1955, consulting engineers FENCO-Harris completed their functional plans for the parkway. The plans were approved by Metro Council in 1956, and construction began on the

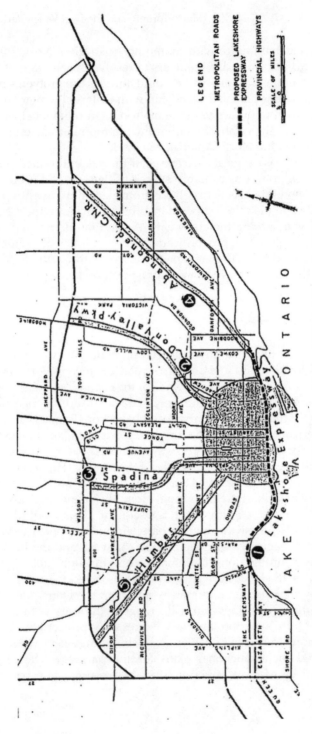

6.1 Metropolitan Toronto Transportation Plan, 1955. (Source: *Globe and Mail*, 1 December 1955.)

mid-section of the parkway, from Bloor Street to Eglinton Avenue, in 1958. By 1964 construction was completed from the Gardiner Expressway north to Lawrence Avenue; the parkway reached its end point at Highway 401 in 1966 (continued as Highway 404 in the 1970s and 80s).

The choice of the name "parkway" was not a casual one. With it, Gardiner and his planners envisioned the gentle curves, pleasing vistas, and relatively slower speeds of the suburban and regional parkways constructed in the eastern United States and Canada in the 1920s and 30s. The name had connotations not only for the nature of the road itself, but for the landscape that surrounded it. In naming the roadway as they did, Metro planners signalled that the adjacent river valley lands would be protected from residential and commercial development. Drawing as they did upon successful examples from the United States, they also drew upon examples that were, for the most part, three decades old.

From the mid-1910s to the mid-1930s, parkways enjoyed widespread popularity as safer and more efficient alternatives to conventional roads, which, in addition to seasonal challenges of mud and dust, suffered from "poorly designed intersections, hazardous road alignments, and rampant ... commercial development."[8] The term "parkway" was first used in the late 1860s by landscape architect Frederick Law Olmsted and his partner Calvert Vaux to describe the landscaped boulevards they incorporated into plans for Brooklyn's Prospect Park. Designed to connect urban parklands with other parts of the city, these "pre-automobile" parkways functioned simultaneously as low-speed transportation corridors and recreation areas. In subsequent projects in New York City, Buffalo, and Boston, Olmsted and Vaux replicated the concept of "[weaving] nature into the urban fabric," separating pedestrians from vehicle riders and presenting "scenic views of the landscape without interrupting traffic flow."[9]

By the early twentieth century, as access to automobiles increased, the parkway concept migrated to the suburbs. Olmsted's Bronx River Parkway (BRP), with its limited-access design and its curving course through the Bronx River valley, provided a ready analogue for planners of the DVP. Connecting the suburban borough of the Bronx with the Taconic State Parkway in Westchester County to the north, the BRP, like the future DVP, facilitated suburban development along its length and contributed to significant increases in the property values of adjacent lands. Its construction, ironically, also helped to protect against riverside development. By the 1890s, ad hoc development along the Bronx River had resulted in severe erosion of the riverbanks. Olmsted's

1895 proposal for the parkway conceived of the road in part as a form
of landscape rehabilitation: road construction would not only "[shore]
up the river bank" but "simultaneously [prevent] further riverside
development."[10] When the parkway was completed in 1925, it moved
through the Bronx River Reservation, a corridor of protected land that
became New York's first linear park.

Built for the automobile rather than the horse and buggy, this new
generation of parkways adapted traditional parkway design features,
including wide, tree-lined borders, graceful S-curves, and grade-
separated intersections, to accommodate the higher speeds and longer
distances of automobile travel. Rather than bringing nature (however
reconfigured) into the city, suburban parkways allowed "the urban
built environment to penetrate the yet-to-be-settled countryside."[11] The
success of the Bronx River Parkway as both a scenic pleasure drive and
a commuter thoroughfare between New York City and Westchester
County, and the real-estate boom it generated in these newly accessible
parkway suburbs, led to an explosion of parkways development in New
York State and across the continent in the late 1920s and early 30s. In
Canada, the Niagara Parkway was constructed in this period, together
with a number of scenic "drive-ways" in the Ottawa area. Championed by engineers, landscape architects, and planners alike, parkways
expanded across North America as agents of urban renewal, boosters
of suburban property values, and connective corridors between metropolitan areas and distant suburbs and recreational areas.

By the late 1930s, however, a combination of factors, including larger
traffic volumes, demands for higher speeds, and the perceived extrava-
gance of expenditures on scenic and recreational improvements, led to
the demise of the parkway in favour of more specialized roadways.
High-speed urban expressways, divided interstate freeways, and scenic wilderness parkways came to replace the multi-purpose parkway
in the postwar years. As John Van Nostrand has shown for Ontario's
Queen Elizabeth Way, a growing cultural proclivity for efficiency over
aesthetics, coupled with the marginalization of landscape architects by a
new generation of highway engineers, gave rise to the wider, straighter
form of the freeway and the urban expressway.[12] In some cases, such
as Connecticut's Merritt Parkway, the parkway concept survived only
in name. In others, such as Los Angeles's Pasadena Freeway, original
plans for a parkway were abandoned in favour of the freeway model.

Traditional winding, scenic parkways were still constructed in the
United States and Canada into the 1940s and 50s, but they tended to

serve more distinctly recreational interests, such as the US National Park Service's Blue Ridge Parkway in Virginia, Alberta's Icefields Parkway, and the Gatineau and Champlain parkways in Canada's capital region. Others, such as the Taconic and Garden State parkways, adopted a hybrid approach that "combine[d] reasonably high speeds and safety with varied and attractive landscape design."[13] But the golden age of parkway development was over, and many celebrated parkways were undergoing retrofits in the name of safety and efficiency. Close to home, the Queen Elizabeth Way between Toronto and Buffalo, originally constructed to incorporate majestic architectural and landscape features, was being rebuilt to accommodate faster and safer movement.[14]

Established with the operative to construct modern, state-of-the-art infrastructure across the metropolitan region, why did Metro Council, with Gardiner as its chair, endorse an unfashionable and largely discredited road design? The answer lies partly in the landscape: the choice of the river valley route beckoned the adoption of a traditional parkway design with adjacent recreational areas. It also lies in the nature of Toronto in this period. Not yet the metropolis of New York or even Montreal, it was a second-tier Canadian city, an aspirational place. The principles of efficiency, aesthetic improvement, and modern design caught up in the parkway concept would doubtless have appealed to civic officials and politicians planning the city of the future.

Like the 1950s-era regional parkways in the US, the DVP was from its outset a hybrid roadway, reaching back to the romantic ideals of a scenic parkland corridor while attempting to serve present and future demands for a high-speed commuter highway linking developing suburbs with the downtown core. Metro planners used the parkway term interchangeably with the neutral "Don Valley Roadway" and the seemingly oppositional "Don Valley Expressway" in their 1955 preliminary planning documents. This ambivalence about the nature of the roadway itself suggests a certain looseness in the final parkway designation. The tendency to stretch the parkway moniker to accommodate changing priorities, rather than to discard it entirely, signals the persistence of conflicting ideas about modernity in this period.

The concept of a parkway up the Don Valley, furthermore, was not a new one: Metro inherited an idea that had been circulating for over forty years. From 1914 to 1945, a series of "Don roadway" plans sought to make use of the valley as a natural corridor for north-south traffic. These schemes can be loosely grouped into two categories: those motivated by aesthetic or conservation ideals, which envisioned a slow-moving "park-way" or boulevard through a protected recreational landscape; and those motivated by ideals of efficiency, which saw the valley as a natural route for a high-speed roadway and placed little emphasis on the function of surrounding valley lands. The tension between these ideals would persist in the planning of the actual DVP development at mid-century.

The first of these Don roadway plans took shape in 1914, when Toronto City Council appointed Conservative MP Sir Edmund Osler to chair a citizens' committee charged with assisting council in planning a proposed system of boulevards encircling the city. The circuit would widen existing roadways in the south, west, and north, connected in the east by a "parkway" through the Don Valley.[15] Influenced by Garden City models of suburban development, the plan sought to create landscaped boulevards as a form of public space and a mechanism of civic beautification. After two years of work the committee succeeded in securing land donations to support the right of ways of more than half of the proposed thirty-four miles of boulevards. Only Lake Shore Boulevard was completed, however, before war forced a realignment of the city's priorities.

Eighteen years later, in 1932, a more comprehensive vision emerged to use valley topography to support a network of roadways along the city's eastern boundary. Conceived in part as an unemployment relief project, the plan differed from its predecessor in proposing a series of "high speed roadways" through the valley. A "trunk traffic-way" would run along the Lower Don from Keating Street to Don Mills Road, continuing from there along the West Don to terminate just east of the city limits. From this, three branches – one westerly and two easterly – connected the driveways with existing road infrastructure in the city's northeast (figure 6.2).[16] Championed by Toronto mayor William Stewart and Conservative MPP Wilfrid Heighington, chair of the short-lived Toronto and York Parkways committee, the plan received support from the provincial legislature as part of a broader act to empower local municipalities to construct a range of improvements to the Don Valley, from public walks and bridle paths to arterial roads and "general suburban development."[17] East York ratepayers, however, objected to the proportion of the project price tag (over 60 per cent) they would be forced to carry and to the nature of a bill that allowed municipalities to impose costly projects on ratepayers without consultation. A smaller number of residents expressed concern about roadways themselves and their consequences for the character of the valley. In a letter dated 23

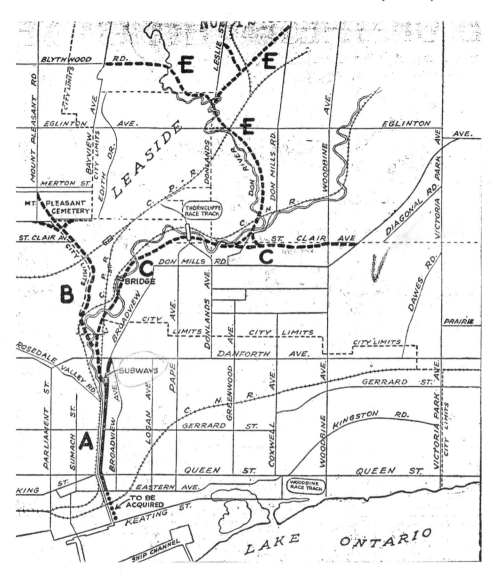

6.2 Don Driveways Plan, 1932. (Reprinted from "Don Valley Roadway Planned as Relief Work," *Toronto Board of Trade Journal* [November 1932].)

February 1933, artist Fred H. Brigden implored Premier George Henry, member for York East, to "prevent the construction of a road of any kind up the valley of the Don ... Surely we can preserve one sanctuary of Peace and Quiet where the good old pastime of walking can be exercised and children can have an outing without fear of destruction ... What ever is done I hope that no effort will be made to 'improve' it." Like its predecessor, the proposal eventually floundered on the failure of some area landowners to dedicate necessary lands for the road right of way.[18]

Plans for a high-speed roadway of varying routes and dimensions through the Don Valley continued to surface through the 1930s, including the January 1938 Belt Line plan, which envisioned a ring of "speedways" around the city using existing right of ways and undeveloped lands in the Don Valley as an eastern connector.[19] These competing visions for the valley – a slow-moving "parkway" or boulevard, versus an efficient, single-purpose "speedway" – came together in the Toronto City Planning Board (CPB)'s 1943 *Master Plan for the City of Toronto and Environs*. Prepared within an environment of optimism for the city's prospects, and drawing inspiration from models of regional planning in the UK and the US, the 1943 *Master Plan* represented the first attempt by the city to engage in comprehensive planning for the wider region surrounding Toronto.[20] The plan contained the seeds of many future metropolitan initiatives. Produced by Italian-trained architect Eugene Faludi for a citizen board of planning professionals and prominent businessmen, it proposed a network of superhighways and rapid transit lines to move commuters between new suburban developments and the downtown core. An outer "agricultural belt" would prevent haphazard residential development beyond metropolitan limits, while an "inner green belt" encompassing the city's two main river valleys – the Don and the Humber – would protect valley lands "from encroachment and vandalism" and provide recreational opportunities for "active sports or passive relaxation in unspoiled natural scenery" (figure 6.3).[21]

Unlike the plans of the 1930s, which viewed the Don Valley principally as a traffic corridor, the 1943 proposal placed the valley within a wider planning framework that considered multiple uses of city spaces. A proposed superhighway would take advantage of the river's straightened and industrialized lower reaches; further north, the upper valleys would receive protection as a "priceless heritage" for the metropolitan area. Reaching back to the 1914 boulevards proposal, Faludi drew a low-speed recreational parkway through this greenbelt space,

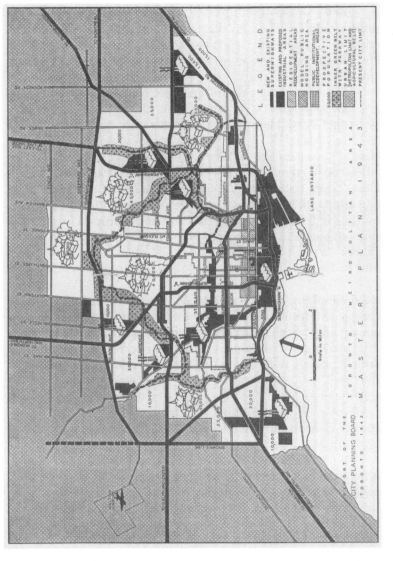

6.3 City Planning Board of Toronto, *Master Plan for the City of Toronto and Environs*, 1943. (City of Toronto Archives, fonds 2, series 60, item 510.)

as a means of viewing and accessing valley parklands. Running east from Yonge Street and up the lower and west branches of the Don, the parkway would cast a loop around the city's existing built-up areas, connecting with the proposed 401 bypass highway in the north before moving south along the Humber River to the lakeshore. The CPB plan was endorsed by Toronto City Council in 1944, but it was not received enthusiastically, and council soon set about designing their own, more practical plan for the city. While some of the CPB's ideas, including the outer and inner greenbelt, would find their way into later plans, the master plan itself "quietly disappeared" in the shift towards professional planning conducted by government rather than citizen-led bodies.[22]

When Toronto City Council resurrected an earlier vision of a high-speed roadway through the Don Valley in the fall of 1945, they received support from 75 per cent of the electorate.[23] Challenges surrounding cost-sharing and land acquisition, however, sent the 1945 plan to the same fate as its predecessors: an imagined future that inspired considerable public support, but little action, and no road.

If You Build It, They Will Come

In planning and building the DVP, Metro mobilized an imagined future of suburban growth in the northeast quadrant of the metropolis. The road would not only service development, it would drive it. For Metro officials, the challenge lay in balancing these longer-term objectives with pressing demands to relieve traffic congestion in the downtown core. Finding an alignment that would meet these objectives and contain costs, while preserving the "parkway character" of the road, was the central objective of early planning activities for the DVP.

In October 1955, consulting engineers FENCO-Harris[24] submitted to the Metro government their plans "for a limited access parkway in the Don Valley following the Don River and the East Branch where feasible."[25] After considering several routes, they recommended an alignment along the east bank of the Lower Don from the proposed Lakeshore Expressway north to the intersection with Don Mills Road near the Forks. From here, the parkway would continue along the river's east branch, rising out of the valley to occupy the tableland north of Lawrence Avenue and continuing along the former Woodbine Avenue right of way north to Highway 401 (figure 6.4). In keeping with Metro Planning Board recommendations, FENCO-Harris recommended a parallel roadway running along the west bank of the Lower Don (the future

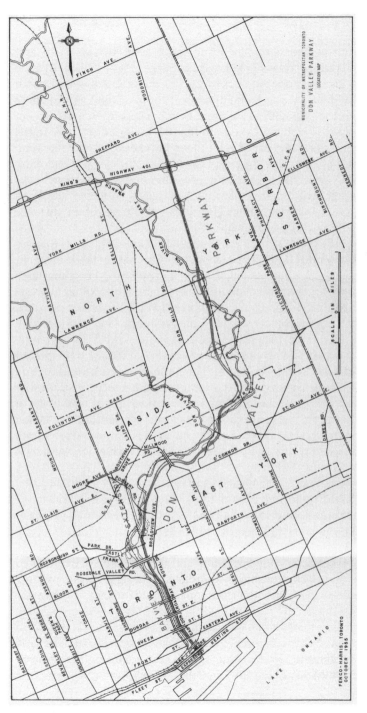

6.4 Proposed Don Valley Parkway alignment, 1955. (FENCO-Harris, *Functional Report on the Proposed Don Valley Parkway to the Municipality of Metropolitan Toronto*, October 1955, City of Toronto Archives, fonds 220, series 10, item 683, p. 9.)

Bayview Extension) to relieve congestion on Mount Pleasant Road, and the extension of Lawrence Avenue westerly from Victoria Park Avenue to connect with the proposed parkway. Comprising three lanes in each direction separated by a grass median, the proposed road would allow "for safe travel at sixty miles per hour." Seven major interchanges from the Lakeshore to Sheppard Avenue in the north would facilitate traffic movement in areas slated for development. In response to the planning board's desire to integrate the expressway with the city's developing rapid transit system, FENCO-Harris recommended the construction of three commuter parking sites near the parkway's southern terminus; from here, planners hoped, motorists might ride the rest of the distance into the downtown core on transit.

In aligning the road as they did, consultants capitalized on the valley's function as a kind of "frictionless corridor" within the metropolitan region. The parkway's valley location meant it could be completed more efficiently, and with considerably less expense, than other expressways in Metro's proposed transportation network. Wherever possible, the consulting engineers located the route on public lands, minimizing the expense of private property expropriations. Areas with potential for future commercial development were also avoided, with preference given instead to greenbelt land. The parkway route would occupy existing road right of ways in two locations: the East Don Roadway along the lower river; and the Woodbine Avenue right of way north of Lawrence. Locating the route on mostly undeveloped lands enabled rapid construction at a number of locations simultaneously without disrupting present traffic flow. It also provided a convenient parkland setting for the road with minimal additional expense. The "parkway character" of the road, consultants explained, would be enhanced by "round[ing] and mold[ing] slopes to existing ravines and tableland" and constructing "low crib walls" in lieu of cutting slopes in places "where retention of existing stands of trees is desirable." The route, furthermore, "would be landscaped to blend into the existing expanse of Greenbelt and suburban development" and the centre median widened to thirty feet in selected locations in order to "preserve … the existing flora." A lack of roadside advertisements would further enhance the parkway experience: the road flowed through Metro-owned greenbelt lands, precluding the erection of roadside billboards.

Construction could be completed, the consultants estimated, as early as 1958, at a total estimated cost of $28,674,000, including the connecting roads at Bayview, Lawrence, and the Lakeshore Expressway.[26] In

May 1958, Metro Council approved construction of the first segment of the DVP from Bloor Street to Eglinton Avenue. Work had begun the previous year on the companion Bayview Extension, running parallel to the parkway on the west bank of the Lower Don, and was scheduled for completion in 1959. Construction would be completed in segments, beginning with the Bloor to Eglinton stretch and followed by Eglinton to Lawrence Avenue, Lakeshore Avenue to Bloor, and Lawrence to Sheppard Avenue (immediately north of Highway 401), respectively.

The parkway would transform the valley from a barrier to east-west movement and eastward development, to a corridor that facilitated this movement. In establishing their rationale for the project, Metro planners positioned the DVP as a response both to existing problems of traffic circulation in the city and its suburban municipalities, and to future needs. They identified the valley itself as one of the city's most formidable obstacles to efficient vehicle movement. North of Bloor Street, none of the region's major east-west thoroughfares crossed the valley, including St Clair, Eglinton, and Lawrence Avenues, forcing vehicles to reroute north or south to navigate around valley topography.

The chosen alignment for the road, however, mobilized the valley corridor as a driver of future growth. It was intended to address anticipated, rather than existing, congestion. Unlike earlier Don Roadway plans, which had routed the roadway north and west to accommodate existing development, Metro's preferred alignment took a different path, extending north and east into what was, in 1955, mostly undeveloped farmland. As DVP project engineer Murray Douglas recalled in a 1992 interview, "We wondered where the traffic was going to come from, literally. Once you got past Don Mills Rd., where were you going? There was nowhere to go, there was no development up there.'[27] A "road to nowhere," it epitomized the aspirational outlook of Toronto in this period: not yet a "great city," it was a place in the process of becoming.

Within this context, the importance of developers in shaping the alignment of the roadway and the placement of its interchanges is not surprising. Foremost among these within the history of the DVP was E.P. Taylor's Don Mills Development Company (DMDC). Holders of over 2,000 acres of farmland around the intersection of Don Mills Road and Lawrence Avenue East, DMDC presented their vision for a planned community of residential, commercial, and industrial sub-districts at the first meeting of the Metro Planning Board in September 1953 (see figure 6.5). At the same time, the Metro Roads Committee

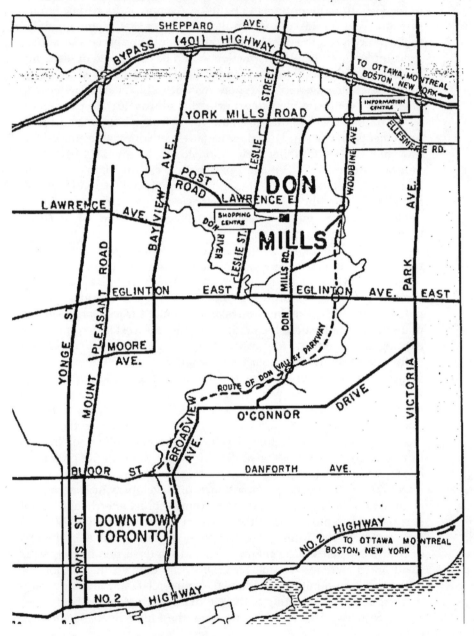

6.5   Don Mills Development Company, *Plan for Don Mills*, ca 1954. (City of Toronto Archives, fonds 2, series 112, file 150.)

was reviewing plans for the DVP inherited from Toronto City Council, including an alignment running northerly and easterly from Keating Street to connect with Don Mills Road.[28] Eager to avoid a six-lane highway through the heart of his firm's development, DMDC's vice-president Angus McClaskey made an offer to the Metro Planning Board at its December 1953 meeting: DMDC would dedicate "for highway purposes a diversionary road leading north-easterly from the Don Mills Road to Woodbine Avenue"; in exchange, it would be relieved of the requirement to widen Don Mills Road to 120 feet through its proposed development at Lawrence Avenue.[29] Although McClaskey's proposed diversionary road was never incorporated into plans for the DVP, the developers had made their point. In the fall of 1954, the Metro Planning Board abandoned the Don Mills alignment, proposing as an alternative the Woodbine Avenue right of way to the east.[30]

Metro's relationship with developers can best be understood as a symbiotic one. For Gardiner, the DVP was not simply a corridor for efficient traffic movement; it was a catalyst and an enabler of suburban growth. As it reached into the blank spaces of Metro's land use maps, it would create the conditions for new private development along its length. Just as the road attracted development, development would pull the road. And from this logic, places like Don Mills and infrastructure developments like the DVP were inextricably linked and mutually supporting. That developers stood to benefit enormously from the construction of the parkway is evident in the text of their advertisements for prospective developments. The Don Mills Development Company, already reaping Metro investments in the 1955–6 extension of Eglinton Avenue over the east and west Don valleys, used future road construction to promote the convenience of their holdings. "Don Mills is easy to reach from any direction," a 15 September 1955 ad read in the *Toronto Daily Star*, "and it will be even easier to get to when new roads are finished … The proposed Don Valley Parkway will cut in half the present driving time of 25 minutes to downtown Toronto."[31]

But Metro also stood to gain, at times, from consultations with developers. In the fall of 1955, for example, less than an hour after FENCO-Harris had presented their plans for the DVP, the Don Mills developers requested a realignment of the interchange at York Mills Road and the Woodbine Avenue right of way sixty feet to the east and the construction of an underpass to link two sections of their development (Parkway East and Parkway West) divided by the parkway alignment. They offered to offset the cost of the underpass with a donation of twenty-six acres required for parkway development, and an offer of thirty-six acres of greenbelt lands in the valley at a highly discounted price. Legally obliged to provide through access or compensation to properties severed by the parkway, Metro agreed to the changes. In the end, the realignment actually resulted in considerable construction savings for Metro, and council profited from the arrangement.[32] Here, as before, Gardiner's belief in the role of private sector development as a fundamental driver of urban growth saw him balance a willingness to accommodate business interests with a desire to see his visions for modern infrastructure implemented. Visible in these negotiations is the degree to which the parkway, as it was laid out in the 1955 FENCO-Harris report, was a malleable construct subject to adjustments in both the alignment of the route and the character of the future roadway. Development, and developers, drove the road.

Provisions for public transit connections slipped into the background as the project progressed. Plans for three commuter parking lots in the lower valley were quashed in 1955 when Metro learned it lacked the legal authority to establish parking lots; suggestions that the roadway should accommodate express buses and transfer facilities were relegated to an uncertain future at the discretion of the Toronto Transit Commission.[33]

The parkway development also placed in relief the question of expressways versus public transit as a solution to the city's transportation problems. Unlike most transportation plans in the United States, Toronto's vision for modernizing its transportation network had long included provisions for rapid public transit in addition to a network of expressways. Gardiner was among the early advocates for a "balanced system" that included public transit. Constructing subway and expressway projects simultaneously, however, threatened Metro with an enormous financial burden. An expressways advocate first and foremost, Gardiner pressured council to push ahead with plans for the DVP, placing on indefinite hold plans for an east-west subway line.

The subway-expressway debate was one of the few occasions when Gardiner encountered trenchant opposition from his technical staff. In January 1955, Metro Planning Board director Murray Jones urged council to step back their plans for the DVP. Referencing the dramatic population growth anticipated for the east end of the city and Scarborough, he warned that a six-lane expressway "would be full the minute you opened it." A combination of "transit and commuter lines," he concluded, is "the only answer to the mass movement of people." Jones's warnings were rebuffed as more talk, less action. "The whole east end of the city will be on your shoulders like three tons of bricks," Gardiner thundered in response, "if you tell them they must wait six months before the engineers can start." Council ordered an immediate start on functional plans for the parkway, and Jones's concerns were effectively dismissed. When questioned as to why he chose to ignore the advice of his experts, Gardiner responded characteristically: "The recommendation of our experts is that we stop, look and listen, that it is foolhardy to go ahead with [the parkway project]. That may be good advice but the administration finds itself in a position of having to get along. The work cannot be delayed."[34]

Gardiner's impatience with his technical staff also emerged in debates about the road's alignment. While planning staff and other Metro agencies were in general agreement about the route from the Lakeshore to Don Mills Road, and further north, from Lawrence Avenue to the interchange with Highway 401, the steep ravinelands between Don Mills Road and Lawrence Avenue posed significant challenges to road construction. A traffic analysis for the Don Valley area weighed the options of running the roadway up the west bank of the East Don, with its required double crossings of the CP rail line and the river, and an alignment that ran east of the rail line, crossing the rail line just once north of Lawrence.[35] Gardiner conducted his own investigations. According to Timothy Colton's 1980 biography, Gardiner spent many weekends tramping through the valley with Metro Planning Chair J.P. Maher in tow, determined to find a way to do what his engineers said was impossible. "The engineers were saying you couldn't put a six-lane highway in [the valley]," he recalled in a 1961 interview with the *Toronto Daily Star*. "So we'd have a look at [it and] say: We'll move the railway over a piece. We'll tear down the hill. We'll shift the river over a piece, then we can have the highway through there. That's what was done years later."[36] Gardiner's can-do attitude was in the end triumphant: significant alteration of the river channel and surrounding landscape, between Don Mills and Lawrence and in a number of other places along the length of the parkway, enabled the preferred alignment along the east branch of the river.

In the larger story of the Don River, it is tempting to cast Gardiner in the role of the high-modernist technocrat imposing his bird's-eye vision on the landscape. As James C. Scott has observed, urban planning initiatives of the 1940s and 50s – the height of modernist faith in scientific and technical progress – sought to create administrative order through the imposition of uniform, geometric grids upon the landscape, an order most evident from above.[37] And yet to see Gardiner in these terms is to strip him of his complexity. Gardiner was a man who straddled a mid-century moment when high-modernist ideals coexisted with older, more traditional ways of doing things. Almost sixty years of age when he took up the position of Metro chair in 1953, he was very much a product of another time. In his former role as reeve of the tiny village of Forest Hill, a position he held for twelve years (1937–49), Gardiner operated in a milieu "of intimate scale and face-to-face relations."[38] His reappointment as reeve through three election campaigns and his formidable record of influence on the floor demonstrated his success in this affluent, deeply conservative community, despite his reputation as a promoter of often unpopular residential and commercial developments.

He was also, as we have seen, the product of another milieu. A highly successful trial lawyer and promoter of diverse commercial enterprises in his early career, Gardiner saw himself and his role as Metro chair as an entrepreneur and a promoter – a businessman more than a politician. A fascination with modernity's promises of growth and bigness, and an unwavering faith in technology, coexisted in Gardiner with the more timeless skills of the salesman and promoter. He brought these influences together to strategic effect in council, his tone "alternat[ing] between a studied world-weariness and urbanity and a kind of disarming rusticity."[39] His willingness, furthermore, to scramble down ravine banks in pursuit of his vision, and his aversion to the slow, deliberative methods of the professional planner, make Scott's characterization of the powerful technocrat removed from the landscape a still more awkward fit.

Instead, Gardiner's refusal to accommodate any delay in proceeding with the parkway plans can be seen as a product of both his character and his past experience. In his first public address as Metro chairman, to the Ontario Insurance Adjusters' Association in the spring of 1953, Gardiner referenced his "bitter experience as chairman of the [Toronto and York] planning board," which led him to believe that only a federated council could solve the problems facing the region. During his tenure on the planning board, suburban municipalities repeatedly blocked the board's efforts to push through arterial roads and water and sewer mains. Some of the projects the board recommended could never be carried out in 1953, he lamented, because the land required to complete them had been developed while the municipalities deliberated. Other projects could still be done, but at much greater expense. He cited by way of example the eastern branch of the proposed Don Valley Parkway, which in its 1945 iteration was to follow the valley northeast and link with O'Connor Drive to relieve traffic congestion in East York. The township of East York blocked these plans, and the land required for the eastern branch was developed. To pursue an eastern extension, Gardiner explained, we would "have to go out further, to Eglinton or Victoria Park Avenue." He listed parkland in the Humber Valley as another lost hope, developed in the intervening years for residential housing and apartments. The "inter-municipal haggling" of the 1940s and early 1950s, he concluded, had limited the city's options. Only now, with the formation of Metro, can we "get off the shackles that have bound this city for 40 years. Now we can get to work and straighten out the kinks."[40]

Unlike the other expressways in Metro's transportation scheme, the Don Valley Parkway aroused almost no public opposition. As the consulting engineers predicted, the location of the roadway through largely undeveloped valley lands meant the project required only limited expropriations of private lands and posed little threat to property values. Furthermore, the general popularity of cars and expressways in this period guaranteed the project a good reception. Although the shine was just beginning to come off expressway projects in the United States at this time (San Francisco's freeway revolt of the late 1950s being perhaps the most notable example), traffic congestion in Toronto and the city's relative lack of experience with urban expressway development created favourable conditions for public support. Rather than questioning the project, public sentiment seems to have largely revolved around getting it done sooner. For residents in the city's east end, the noise of heavy transport vehicles on city streets and mounting congestion problems on major thoroughfares prompted demands to expedite plans for a limited-access highway through the valley.[41] Suburban development in the northern reaches of the city only compounded these problems. North York's Don Mills development, already supporting a population of 7,000 in 1955, planned to accommodate another 25,000 people over the next five years, threatening to strain heavily congested traffic arteries still further.[42] Parkway planners estimated the road would reduce travel time from the proposed suburbs northeast of the city from sixty to twenty minutes.

Rhetoric around the parkway development promised not only to solve these congestion problems, but to do so cheaply. As *Globe and*

Mail columnist Ron Haggart commented when construction of the parkway was announced in June 1958, the DVP "will probably be the most road, in terms of service, for the least money– that the taxpayers of Metropolitan Toronto will ever get." With less than twenty-five properties requiring expropriation, and the majority of the parkway falling on public lands, land acquisition would be relatively inexpensive. The routing of the parkway through the valley, which Haggart advertised as an "almost ideal superhighway route," also brought cost savings. Because the valley lands already ran underneath existing obstacles such as railway lines and roads, "the fantastic cost of many overpasses [would] be avoided." Passing neatly under four existing bridges and the CPR trestle in the lower valley, the DVP made efficient use of a river valley which "political leaders have in the past been too lacklustre to exploit."[43] Further cost savings would be achieved by the method of construction: like the nineteenth-century rail lines that preceded it, the DVP would be built as much as possible using "cut and fill" methods, which minimized hauling expenses by using materials cut away from slopes to fill the roadbed.[44]

The DVP is generally remembered for its minimal damage to existing neighbourhoods. But some people did lose their homes, and many of those homes were located in some of the city's poorest districts. In the early 1960s, for example, a number of homes and other structures in Corktown, an Irish immigrant community located east of Parliament Street and south of Queen, were demolished to make way for the DVP's Richmond Street off-ramp and the Eastern Avenue overpass. Among the more noteworthy buildings lost was the House of Providence, established by the Sisters of St Joseph in 1857 to care for orphans and the elderly poor. Executed at a time when urban renewal projects were rolling out across the continent, the Corktown demolitions generated little discernible public opposition and almost no attention in the press.

The first section of the parkway, a two-kilometre stretch between Bloor Street and Eglinton Avenue, opened to traffic in August 1961. Subsequent sections were completed and opened to traffic over the next five years: Eglinton to Lawrence in October 1963, the Gardiner (formerly Lakeshore) Expressway to Bloor in November 1964, and Lawrence Avenue to Highway 401 in November 1966. Delays in constructing the Sheppard Avenue bridge immediately to the north pushed the final completion date to March 1967. In the end, the highway was constructed without the three commuter parking lots proposed in the 1955 plan and without the express bus lanes that the planning board had recommended.[45] The final tally for the parkway and its connector roads (the Bayview and Lawrence Avenue extensions and the connection with the Gardiner Expressway) was $46.5 million, roughly $20 million over original estimates. Additional charges for haulage of soils from unstable valley slopes and higher-than-anticipated expropriation fees accounted for most of the difference. By today's standards, $46.5 million was still a bargain for such a major piece of infrastructure, constructed through difficult terrain. Over the space of just twelve years, from planning to completion, the DVP had radically transformed the ecology and the human experience of an iconic city landscape.

Ecology of a Parkway

In choosing to construct a "parkway" through the Don River Valley, Metro signalled a roadway that would be in harmony with surrounding landscapes. Unlike conventional roadways, with their intrusive cuts and fills, parkways typically followed existing contours, allowing the road to "lie more naturally upon the land."[46] The rhetoric of traditional parkway design sought to balance aesthetic considerations with safety and economy. Designers placed emphasis on the experience of driving, noting the value of broad, landscaped borders in screening out garish roadside commerce and the effect of graceful curves, grade-separated exits, and undulating terrain in eliminating blind spots, softening hazardous curves, and reducing the probability of accidents. These design features made both economic and environmental sense. Gently sloped banks resisted erosion better than the steep raw cuts created by standard construction methods; conserving topsoil and replanting roadsides with native vegetation reduced costs and produced a more stable environment that required less maintenance.[47] Highly constructed landscapes, they succeeded nevertheless in creating the illusion of a "natural" roadway – one that, in fitting the surrounding landscape, was somehow meant to be there.

Yet, as we have seen, parkway design principles were only loosely apprehended by Metro planners and politicians. "Parkway" was a malleable concept used interchangeably with other terms, flexible enough to accommodate different political priorities at different times. Evidently, Metro felt little public pressure to present the road as a benign influence on the landscape. Notably absent, for example, in the rhetoric around the parkway is an emphasis on its scenic value or its potential to attract tourists – qualities celebrated by proponents of more remote parkway landscapes. Nor would roadside pullouts encourage drivers to take in the valley scenery; this was not, after all, Stanley Park.

Instead, the DVP was widely perceived as a welcome development for a blighted space. Addressing the inaugural meeting of Metro Council in January 1960, Gardiner asked, "Who remembers the Don Valley north of ... the Prince Edward Viaduct which so recently was a swale and a jungle until the bulldozers tore the whole countryside apart and put it together again into what in a few months will be the Don Valley Parkway and the Bayview Extension?"[48] In conjunction with plans to transform the surrounding valley lands into landscaped parks and recreational amenities, the road would act as a civilizing force to convert an unruly, dangerous landscape into a pleasing scenic backdrop. For Gardiner, and for many Toronto residents in this period, the DVP represented the best use of a natural corridor through the city. The history of the valley as a corridor for the movement of people and goods, by water and later by rail, preordained its transformation as a modern transportation corridor.

Construction of the parkway brought dramatic changes to the look and character of the valley. Hills were levelled, valley slopes deforested, railway lines relocated, and the river bed straightened and rerouted in at least six places over the length of the road. For the lower river, already straitjacketed by a railway line along its western bank, the highway further cemented its future as a canal bolstered by steel piling and divorced from its floodplain. A series of check dams further altered the river's hydrology by controlling the speed and direction of the river's flow near the diversion points.[49] More noticeable to Toronto residents would have been the removal and alteration of significant valley landmarks. Losses included the unusual conical form of Sugar Loaf Hill, which stood alone in the lower valley immediately north of the Prince Edward Viaduct. The hill was razed to accommodate the Bayview Extension. Immediately north of the Don Mills interchange near the forks of the river, the thirty-six metre Tumper's Hill, remembered by Don Valley conservationist Charles Sauriol as "a gorgeous place for hiking and rambling," was levelled and used for fill. By the time the parkway was completed in 1966, billions of cubic metres of earth had been excavated and shifted, and fill had reduced the width of the lower valley by almost a third.[50]

The DVP had massive implications for the ecology of the watershed. At a basic level, it brought people into the valley in unprecedented numbers. People and their vehicles introduced noise, waste, and contaminants into the watershed, including motor oil, toxic chemicals,

6.6   Grading on the Don Valley Parkway at Don Mills Road, facing east, November 1959. The remains of Tumper's Hill are visible in the background. (City of Toronto Archives, fonds 220, series 3, file 116, item ES13-187.)

animal faeces, and road salt in winter. The road itself carried its own consequences. As scientists in the relatively new field of road ecology have shown, hardened road surfaces prevent the absorption of rain and snowmelt, speeding run-off rates to local streams and increasing the risk of flash floods. Hard surfaces also absorb considerable solar energy, adding warmth to the toxic cocktail released as stormwater into local waterways.[51] The effects on aquatic plant and animal life are well documented, and the Don is no exception. Identified as Ontario's most polluted river (and Canada's third most polluted) in a 2007 Environment Canada survey, the river currently supports only the hardiest of fish species.[52]

The highway also erected a formidable barrier to animal movement. From the earliest recorded observations to the notes of twentieth-century naturalists, the valley has been understood as a vital corridor for animal movement: a migration route for passenger pigeons, bats, and salmon, and a pathway for resident species such as deer, wolves, and coyote. According to area naturalists, highway construction displaced many small animals, including foxes, ground hogs, and raccoons, pushing them into neighbourhoods to the east.[53] Others were, and continue to be, killed on the road itself.

Despite the magnitude of these changes, and the cumulative effects of running a high-speed roadway up a river valley, there is little evidence of public demand for protection of its natural features. Charles Sauriol recalled being "a voice in the wilderness" against the parkway project in a 1992 interview with the *Toronto Star*. "There just weren't many people arguing against it, but in building it, they took ... away some irreplaceable things."[54] *Toronto Daily Star* columnist Ron Haggart was among the few who commented on the changes wrought by the parkway construction. Writing a day before the first section of the parkway opened on 31 August 1961, he lamented the loss of Sugar Loaf Hill, once the inspiration for Ernest Thompson Seton's 1898 children's classic, *Wild Animals I Have Known*. In reducing the hill to 1.25 million cubic metres of earth, the dump trucks carried with them a place known and beloved by "three generations of schoolboys."[55] Gardiner dismissed such minority sentiment with characteristic terseness. "I'll tell you what the Don Valley was," he reputedly told a Metro Council member who lamented the loss of the Don woods near Castle Frank. "The Don Valley was a place to murder little boys, that's what it was."[56]

Concern for the effects of the parkway construction on valley environments was also mitigated by Metro's companion initiative to acquire and protect lands surrounding the parkway as part of an "inner greenbelt." One of few surviving concepts from the city planning board's 1943 *Master Plan*, greenbelt lands would be acquired from area municipalities and developed into landscaped parklands by the Metro Parks Commission. This arrangement was hard-won: just as construction was set to begin in June 1958, Toronto City Council threatened to deny Metro construction crews access to undeveloped city parklands on the path of the proposed parkway. Stung by the loss of portions of the CNE grounds to accommodate the Gardiner Expressway, city council insisted that fair compensation be paid to surrender parklands to expressway development. Some twelve hectares of undeveloped city parklands lay in the proposed path of the DVP, north of the Bloor Street Viaduct. Gardiner agreed to assume the valley parklands and to develop (in accordance with the original vision for the parkway) any surplus lands remaining after parkway construction as Metro parkland. South of the viaduct, he agreed to restore any city recreational properties or parkland damaged by construction activities – namely, the city's playing fields at Riverdale Park.[57] The agreement set the tone for future land acquisition arrangements with other municipalities as the parkway proceeded.

Shortly after the issue was resolved, *Star* reporter Douglas Blanchard toured the proposed "inner greenbelt" lands with Metro Parks Commissioner Tom Thompson. Their discussion sheds some light on the practice of urban park making in mid-twentieth-century Canada, and perceptions of nature that guided this practice. Driving overland through the valley with Blanchard at his side, Thompson pointed to the treed slopes along the valley walls. These "tree lands," he noted, "are being carefully preserved." When the roadway is completed, "all available land will be landscaped and made into park." As if to counteract the scene of graders and bulldozers "[churning] up the valley" before them, Thompson added, "even when the parkway is completed the natural setting will be little changed. Anyone driving down to work will feel pretty close to nature."[58] Thompson's equation of a "landscaped park" with a "natural setting ... little changed" recalls established tropes of improvement in parks historiography and the need for parks to "better" nature for human enjoyment. In July 1958, Metro commissioned a plan for the design of the greenbelt lands from the same engineering firm that designed the parkway; the plans were approved by Metro council the following summer.

From the Windshield

At 2:30 p.m. on 3 August 1961, Gardiner and Premier Leslie Frost officially opened the first section of the parkway from Bloor Street to Eglinton Avenue. Several hours later, the parkway experienced its first traffic jam. With only two interchanges, at Bloor in the south and Eglinton in the north (the intermediary Don Mills interchange was not approved by Metro Council until 1964), the two-kilometre stretch of roadway backed up quickly in periods of heavy traffic. Narrowing from three lanes to one at its northern terminus, traffic had nowhere to go but onto busy Eglinton Avenue, already congested with its own rush-hour traffic. In the words of one reporter, it was "a five-minute trip from Dreamsville to Nightmare Junction."[59] Drivers reported waits of over twenty minutes at Eglinton, and urged Metro to alleviate the problem by hastening construction of the parkway north to Lawrence – not anticipated to be completed until 1966. Metro's considerable capital, however, was stretched over a number of projects, including the Bloor-Danforth subway line. As Metro Traffic Engineer Sam Cass commented, "We just can't build everything at once."[60]

For all the rhetoric about the valley as an "ideal route" for the road, sweeping curves through ravine lands presented some problems for drivers. In the first five months of 1965, the roadway saw 139 accidents, resulting in eighty-six injuries and four deaths. In response to these fatalities, Metro's chief coroner Dr Morton Shulman released a report criticizing the neglect of "basic safety features" in the DVP's construction. Many of the accidents on the DVP, Shulman concluded, were the result of "unnecessary hazards." Steep roadside slopes that threatened to "flip ... a car striking them at high speed" and exposed concrete light standards were among the "death-dealing roadside obstacles" Shulman itemized.[61] Metro Roads Commissioner G.O. Grant countered defensively, and to little effect, noting that the accident rate on the DVP compared favourably with other highways in the region. At an average of 1.2 accidents per million vehicle miles (apvm) between 1962 and 1965, the DVP was safer, he concluded, than Highway 401 with its rate of 3.0 apvm, and considerably safer than urban expressways in the United States, with rates of up to 5.5 apvm.[62] Delivered at a time when traditional parkways in the United States and Canada were facing their own costly retrofits in the name of safety and efficiency, Shulman's report was part of a larger movement away from aesthetics in highway design. His report raised considerable public alarm and eventually resulted in significant alterations by the Metro Roads Department, including the placement of guard rails in front of light standards and exposed slopes, the installation of emergency call boxes along the length of the parkway, and the paving of the centre grass median – originally seen as an important component of the road's "parkway character" – to accommodate accidents and breakdowns.[63]

The valley's steep ravine walls brought problems of a different kind for motorists. In April 1969, the slope below Davies Crescent, just west of Don Mills Road, gave way in heavy rain, covering the northbound and part of the southbound lanes with three feet of mud and debris. The slide hit in the height of the evening rush, causing one driver to swerve into a guard rail. Only minor injuries were reported, but the slide backed up northbound traffic from the entry ramps of the DVP to Don Mills and clogged alternate routes in every direction. The combination of heavy rains and the spring thaw were cited among the reasons for the slide, which brought down roughly 1,000 square metres of mud and sod that had been staked to the hillside the previous year. Commenting on the slide, residents of Davies Crescent pointed to a longer history of problems. Ten years earlier, a smaller slide had occurred on the same embankment after trees were removed to facilitate parkway construction. Although a drainage system had been installed to address the problem, the failure to replant the slope with trees suggested that slides would continue to be a problem.[64]

Today, the DVP has become synonymous with the valley itself. References to "the Don Valley" on the radio are shorthand for the DVP: the place has become the road. The parkway imposed a new way of experiencing the valley. For most Torontonians, the view from the windshield on their daily commute is their only contact with the river valley. As Gabrielle Barnett argues in her work on the changing experience of nature in California's redwood forests, this practice of "drive-by viewing" shapes the way people perceive and experience nature in the valley.[65] Early-twentieth-century automobile travel, Barnett proposes, with its relatively slow speeds and narrow, unsurfaced roads, recreated a "premodern way of seeing" for motorists familiar with the blurred, flattened landscapes produced by modern train travel. Automobile tourists described their experience of distant wilderness landscapes in the language of the sublime, awed by the unmediated experiences of landscape permitted from their ultra-modern vehicles. Early proponents of vehicle access to wilderness parks argued that the more people who saw and experienced these parks, the more they would value and seek to protect them. As automobile speeds increased and roads improved in the postwar period, the detail and depth of vision celebrated by earlier automobile tourists were replaced, Barnett argues, by a modernized, industrial vision "incompatible with seeing scenery."[66] Wilderness preservationists came to see roads as a threat rather than a means of protecting nature.

That the designers of the DVP attempted to blend the expectations of a commuter highway with the scenic surroundings of the traditional parkway places it somewhere in the middle of these extremes: a modern roadway that sought at once to convey a utopian vision of the future while generating nostalgia for a premodern way of experiencing landscape. While the parkway's modern vision feels dated today, an experience of the parkway "at its best" – driving southbound on a Sunday morning along the roadway's final sweeping curves into the city – still affords dramatic views of the valley that, while falling short of the sublime, are at least highly picturesque. The visual pleasure of moving through valley landscapes is especially pronounced in comparison with Metro's other expressway, the Gardiner – a high-speed thoroughfare lined with billboards that moves through the thoroughly urban and industrialized space of the Toronto waterfront. For most motorists on the DVP, however, the slow weekday creep down the valley in bumper-to-bumper traffic inspires something less than exultation.

The DVP not only created new ways of experiencing the valley, it also dramatically altered older ways of experiencing it. Walking along the Lower Don River one is struck by how much the parkway dominates the landscape. It occupies a place above the riverbed, bridging it or capping a steep gravel embankment along the valley wall. It is present, as a distant hum, through much of the lower valley, and on stretches of the Lower Don Trail that border the roadway, the sound of the speeding traffic is overwhelming. With it, too, comes the dust, the litter, and the oil-slicked run-off common to all highways. The sounds of the valley that Sauriol celebrated – "the frogs in the pond with their steady trill"; "the rush of the wind in the tree tops"; "the gurgling of the water as the river flows over [the stone] dam"[67] – have become, in the presence of the highway, historical sounds, difficult to experience without the hum of the traffic in the background. Limited crossing points for walkers and cyclists in the valley further assert the dominance of the road. The new transportation corridor, like the river itself initially, and the railway lines that followed, erected barriers east-west, just as it facilitated access north-south. Once a favourite location, as Sauriol remembered, for "hiking and rambling," hikers today can walk the river only upon segments of paved trail. Fencing along the lower reaches of the river further constrains public access, and those seeking to follow the river corridor beyond established trails face an obstacle course of steep ravine walls, narrow rail trestles, and overlapping highway and rail infrastructure. In these ways the DVP has had significant ramifications for human experience in the valley, forever altering the capacity for what Sauriol, or Ernest Thompson Seton before him, would have described as moral and physical rejuvenation achieved through experience in an "unspoiled place."[68]

Conclusion

Today, the DVP is the only north-south expressway leading into Toronto's downtown – a role, as Gardiner and his engineers would remind us, that the parkway was never designed to support. Always intended to function as part of a larger transportation network, including the never-realized Scarborough, Crosstown, and Spadina Expressways, and a closely-linked system of public transit, the DVP's chronic traffic congestion (inspiring drivers to nickname it the "Don Valley Parking Lot") was entirely predictable. By the time the parkway was completed in 1966, it was already the continent's busiest artery during peak traffic periods.[69] Traffic volumes exceeded capacity by the early 1980s, and by 2001, the DVP carried 160,000 vehicles a day on a roadway designed to carry 60,000. Traffic is routinely heaviest, both north and southbound, between Eglinton Avenue and Highway 401. Multiple lanes merging from highways 401 and 404 slow southbound traffic in this stretch, while northbound traffic often backs up behind heavy trucks struggling up the valley's steep grades. The DVP is today a much more dangerous road than it should be. For such a short stretch of road, the parkway sees an average of 1,100 collisions per year. Ironically, the majority of these collisions occur north of Eglinton, where the road climbs out of the valley and straightens along the developed tableland, leaving its traditional "parkway" features behind.[70]

For Gardiner, however, who viewed the completion of the road- way from retirement, the DVP was a monumental achievement and an essential component of a network of infrastructure supporting the development of the metropolitan region. Gardiner stepped down from his role as Metro Chair in January 1962. He would live to see the rest of his proposed network of expressways discredited and abandoned. Opposition from ratepayers in tony Rosedale put an end to plans for the Crosstown Expressway in the early 1960s. Plans for the Spadina Expressway, commissioned immediately before Gardiner's retirement, launched a whirlwind of public opposition before being halted by Pre- mier William Davis in 1971. In 1974, Metro Council finally agreed to abandon the Scarborough Expressway.

Considered within the history of human relationships with the val- ley, the DVP realized, in twentieth-century terms, a series of earlier attempts to capitalize on the valley as a natural transportation corridor. In doing so, it transformed the geographical significance of the valley from a dumping ground at the old city's edge, to a vital corridor of movement through the centre of a larger metropolitan region. With the completion of an east-west subway line in 1966, the valley eclipsed Yonge Street as the city's most distinct east-west divide. From seat of the fledgling town of York in the 1790s, to polluted eastern periphery from the mid-nineteenth to the mid-twentieth century, the valley moved once again to the centre of the lived experience of the city in the early 1960s as an important driver of economic development and suburban growth.

The construction of the DVP also foreclosed other futures, especially for the lower valley. For urban ecologists seeking to revitalize a neglected urban green space, for example, the presence of a six-lane concrete thoroughfare running alongside the river places firm limits upon restoration efforts. As we shall see, twenty-first-century plans to "naturalize" the area around the river mouth halt abruptly at the Narrows, where possibilities are circumscribed by the straitjacket of a rail corridor on the river's east bank, and an expressway on the west. No amount of shoreline vegetation can soften the hard edges here; nor can sinuous curves be reinscribed along a river bed canalized with concrete piling.

For all its problems, the parkway must be considered, within the constraints of its time, as something of a success. In kinaesthetic terms, it captures the essence of the parkway model as a scenic roadway. With its great sweeping turns and valley vistas, it offers some of the most pleasant views of the city. Deep-red roadside sumacs in fall and lush green expanses in spring make it a place to connect with the seasons. Unlike the other highways of the metropolitan region, it is a place from which to catch glimpses of an urban nature that only few Toronto residents experience directly. In this review of the history of plans for a "Don Roadway," it is clear that things could have been much different. Engineers and planners could have been more destructive of valley environments, seeking straight lines for high-speed travel rather than heeding existing valley topography. Here parkway design principles, however diluted, played a discernible role in creating the road we live with today. Finally, the DVP, and the valley that supported it, enabled the northeastern expansion of the city. As DVP project engineer Murray Douglas observed in a 1992 interview, "People love to hate the Parkway ... but Metro would not have developed nearly to the extent that it has if that hadn't have been available. You can't imagine the city without that road."[71]

7 Remembering the Don

In recent years, the Don has been the subject of renewed interest as a place of possibility within the Toronto landscape. On the river flats north of the Prince Edward Viaduct, the environmental non-profit group Evergreen has transformed the site of the former Don Valley Brick Works into Canada's first environmental discovery centre.[1] Further south, plans are underway to re-route the mouth of the Don through the Port Lands, approximating its historical course. It is to this project and the implications it has for the public memory of the river that I turn to now. As we have seen, the Don has inspired a series of imagined futures over the past 200 years, from the dreams of individual millers who hoped the stream's flow would be sufficient and predictable, to the grand vision of future industry and prosperity put forward by the Don Improvement Plan of the 1880s, to visions of a rapid-transportation corridor and a catalyst for suburban development in the 1950s and 60s. The proposed Lower Don Lands plan (LDL) aims to replace what has become an obsolete industrial landscape with a new imagined future for the Lower Don River and the Port Lands, one that emphasizes sustainability and connectivity in urban design.

The latest in a long history of improvements for the lower river and its mouth, the Lower Don Lands plan promises to be a massive undertaking. Proposed by Waterfront Toronto, the city's lead waterfront development corporation, within the context of a broader mandate to revitalize Toronto's neglected waterfront, the plan aims to transform the 125-hectare area surrounding the river mouth into new mixed-use residential neighbourhoods and parklands. At the centre of these plans is the rerouting and naturalization of the mouth of the Don River.[2] The debates these plans have generated around how the river should look, how it should relate to the city around it, and what aspects of its history should be incorporated, are the subject of discussion here. To what extent, I ask, has the public memory of the river – the history of human relationships with the river and the lessons people have taken from it over time – been incorporated into plans for the river's transformation? How, and to what extent, does the past weigh upon and shape efforts to revitalize languishing urban districts and degraded environments?

Over the past thirty years, memory studies have positioned landscape among a range of sites, including place names, folklore, autobiographies, and television, in which "history is embedded or a dialectic of past-present relations is rehearsed."[3] According to Pierre Nora, dramatically altered landscapes eliminate opportunities for spontaneous memory in that they remove the sensory cues of past experience.[4] One might take issue with the unconditionality of Nora's assertion: to the observant eye, elements of the past persist even in the most radically altered environments; these clues might also be perceived in entirely different ways by a new generation. Nevertheless, he identifies something very real here in human responses to changing landscapes.[5] In sites like the Lower Don Lands, the combined impacts of industrialization and past improvement schemes have so transformed the landscape as to make it difficult to imagine any other reality. As Nora would argue, such acts of erasure invite "sites of memory" to replace the living memories they obliterated.

Projects like the LDL plan, with its intentional references to past landscape features, can be interpreted within this vein. And yet, the same industrial artefacts that obliterated what came before are themselves cues to a different way of perceiving and valuing past environments. If memory in the sense of remembered past landscapes has been mostly erased in the Lower Don Lands, opportunities still exist to appreciate the complex ways in which the past informs the present. Historical geographer D.W. Meinig and landscape historian J.B. Jackson dedicated their careers to transforming the way we look at ordinary landscapes, encouraging their students to see them not as snapshots of the present but as accumulations of complex past decisions and processes.[6] An appreciation of present environments as complex mosaics deeply contingent upon past decisions, values, and relationships guides my analysis here.

This chapter looks at the ways the past informs twenty-first-century plans for the mouth of the Don, focusing on three overlapping "sites of memory": the physical realities of the site (the ways in which the past, in the form of contaminated soils or concrete structures, places demands upon the present); processes and methods informed by past experience; and references within the planning documents to past landscapes and the outcomes of past planning processes. It compares the current plans for the river mouth with the 1880s Don Improvement Plan, paying particular attention to the political and economic contexts within which they were created and the territories they sought to transform. Insights developed in reviewing the 1880s plan are mobilized to assess this most recent improvement scheme for the mouth of the Don.

The Lower Don Lands Project

In February 2007, Waterfront Toronto[7] announced an international design competition intended to secure a world-class plan for redeveloping the lands surrounding the mouth of the Don River.[8] The task given to firms selected for the competition was an ambitious one: they were to envision the revitalization and "renaturalizing" of an area that had been marginalized for years. Waterfront Toronto sought a plan that would create "an iconic identity for the Don River" while addressing flood protection and habitat restoration needs in the Lower Don Lands, the 125-hectare industrial area located south of the rail corridor at the east end of Toronto harbour (a portion of the former Port Industrial District).[9] Twelve weeks later, a consortium headed by Michael Van Valkenburgh was announced as the winner of the competition. The design competition jury agreed that Michael Van Valkenburgh and Associates (MVVA)'s *Port Lands Estuary* proposal created "a spectacular and compelling vision for the area" by "balancing and integrating urban and naturalized environments."[10]

The mouth of the Don River is the centrepiece of the MVVA design (colour plate 2). Here, the team proposed to create a new kind of territory where "the city, lake, and river interact in a dynamic and balanced relationship": an urban estuary.[11] The design concept shifted the river's mouth so that it would wind south of its current right-angle turn at the Keating Channel, moving through the Port Lands to empty directly into the harbour. Keating Channel would remain intact as a functioning waterway and alternate outfall for the river. By relocating the river mouth further south, MVVA argued, they would produce for it the "iconic identity" sought by Waterfront Toronto: centred in the Port Lands, the river mouth would enjoy greater visibility from other points along the Toronto harbour, "reasserting the presence of the river in the city and allowing it to become a symbol of the Lower Don Lands as a whole."[12] Surrounding the river, a newly created landscape would be devoted to parkland. Serving as a floodway as well as a recreation space, this central parkland would anchor several mixed-use neighbourhoods, each of which would combine spaces for living, working, recreation, and entertainment with access to transit and pedestrian routes.[13]

Unlike Charles Sauriol's desire to create a natural retreat *from* the city, here nature and culture would purportedly come together as both destination and extension of the urban fabric. While much of the design concept's focus is devoted to urban revitalization through built form, ecological restoration receives considerable attention in plans for the river corridor itself. Here, MVVA proposed to reference the lower Don's historic wetlands and native forests by constructing pockets of marsh and woodland habitat around the new river mouth. Access to nature – as aesthetic environment and, to a limited extent, as functional ecosystem – would be a key factor in the district's marketability.[14]

The MVVA team and the board members at Waterfront Toronto who solicited their involvement were not the first to imagine a different future for the Lower Don Lands. Visions for the restoration of the river mouth were first forwarded by the Task Force to Bring Back the Don in 1991. Noting the natural tendency of the Lower Don to fill with sediments, they recommended allowing "the natural delta-building processes in the lower valley to be accommodated at the [river] mouth," recreating over time "a delta and productive marsh habitat" that would "once again [link] the river biologically and physically with Lake Ontario." Such a plan would require changes to the Lower Don channel and the repurposing of a portion of the harbourlands as a sedimentation basin and marsh. The recreated marsh, they speculated, would greatly reduce annual dredging costs in Keating Channel and provide habitat for fish, waterfowl, and other aquatic species. Furthermore, a revitalized industrial area would "create an appropriate setting for new waterfront development."[15] In 1992, the Task Force vision was incorporated into the recommendations set out by the Royal Commission on the Future of the Toronto Waterfront, which outlined the benefits of "[regenerating] a marshland delta" and surrounding greenspace.[16] Subsequent planning bodies for the waterfront also recognized the opportunity presented by "large areas of mostly public-owned, underused or vacant land" in the Port Lands.[17] In March 2000, the Toronto Waterfront Revitalization Task Force recommended "a naturalized river mouth, bordered by park spaces" as part of a larger strategic plan to redevelop the waterfront.[18]

Over ten years of general recommendations were finally given concrete form in the City of Toronto's 2001 Central Waterfront Secondary Plan, *Making Waves*. Building upon the 1991 work of the Task Force to Bring Back the Don, and the legacy of subsequent waterfront planning bodies, the award-winning document established the planning context for the Lower Don Lands project and related redevelopment initiatives in the Port Lands.[19] Key aspects of subsequent projects, including flood protection for the West Don Lands and the transformation of the Port Lands into a number of new urban districts, received elaboration, together with plans to "renaturalize" the river mouth as "a key open space and recreational link to the Don Valley, West Don Lands … and waterfront park system … [and] a gateway to the new urban communities in the Port Lands."[20]

When the Toronto Waterfront Revitalization Corporation (later renamed Waterfront Toronto) was created by federal, provincial, and municipal governments in 2001, it identified the naturalization of the mouth of the Don River as one of its four priority projects.[21] It selected the Toronto and Region Conservation Authority (TRCA) as the lead agency to conduct the naturalization and flood protection work in the Lower Don Lands. Together, Waterfront Toronto and the TRCA then embarked on a series of closely intertwined environmental assessment processes to explore alternatives for the Lower Don Lands.[22] The 2007 design competition occurred within the context of these developing plans for the area. In the years that have followed, the detailed planning associated with the environmental assessment process has seen MVVA's winning *Port Lands Estuary* proposal modified and refined in order to create a viable plan for the site's redevelopment.

Flood protection, and the development it will enable, form the central rationale for the Lower Don Lands plan. A massive area south, west, and east of the lower river, including much of the Port Lands, falls within the floodplain of the Don River. Existing infrastructure provides insufficient protection in the event of a major flood, and these circumstances, together with the presence of contaminated soils throughout the Port Lands, have been the main obstacles to redevelopment of the area to date. Without reliable and sustainable mechanisms for flood control, no significant development can occur in the Port Lands. The relocation of the mouth of the Don River emerged primarily from this flood control imperative.[23] Design features such as the greenway between the relocated river channel and the Ship Channel, and the maintenance of Keating Channel as an alternate outfall, satisfy flood protection requirements first and foremost. The project's corollary objectives of naturalization (creating new wildlife habitat) and city building (creating new residential and commercial districts) are both connected with, and dependent upon, the removal of flood risk from development lands.

Landscape and Memory

Incorporating aspects of the river's past has been an important part of these efforts to reimagine the lower river and its relationship with the city. Artefacts of past improvement schemes work their way into the plans, together with remnants of the area's industrial history. The river's natural history also finds space here, in infrastructure designed to accommodate ongoing ecological processes such as seasonal flooding. This referencing of the past was to some extent unavoidable, demanded by the physical realities of the site: the existence of monolithic structures such as the Gardiner Expressway and the Keating Channel; the annual accumulation of sediments near the river mouth; and the presence throughout the Port Lands of contaminated soils left behind by over a century of industrial activity. As D.W. Meinig wrote, "every landscape is an accumulation": both a "rich store of data about the peoples and societies which have created it" and "a great exhibit of consequences."[24] In the Lower Don Lands, the past presses upon and constrains the present in multiple ways.

In this chapter I treat the MVVA design concept for the Lower Don Lands as an artefact in itself: like the other imagined futures detailed in this study, the initial concept has been, and continues to be, subject to considerable manipulation as it moves through various political and technical planning channels, and again as it meets with the land itself, with all of its particularities and potentially unforeseen responses. The possibility that the scheme will not be implemented at all must also be enumerated among the range of potential outcomes.

"It is neither possible nor desirable to erase the past," MVVA asserted in the opening paragraph of its 2007 *Port Lands Estuary* proposal; "likewise, it is neither possible nor desirable to replicate what nature had placed here before."[25] Characteristic of the team's approach throughout its proposal, this statement has important implications for the role of public memory in the site's reconstitution. Geographer David Lowenthal has observed that while the past sustains us as a source of identity, it also constrains us by becoming a burden that "cripples innovation" and options for the future: "We preserve because the pace of change and development has attenuated a legacy integral to our identity and well-being. But we also preserve … because we are no longer intimate enough with our legacy to rework it creatively."[26] The MVVA proposal presented this kind of "creative reworking" of the past, proposing to "[weave] … several heritage structures … into the new urban fabric" in order to "[speak] to the physical past of the site."[27]

Most significant among these structures is the Keating Channel. Constructed in the 1910s, this concrete channel runs east-west from the harbour, intersecting the river outlet at a ninety-degree angle. Unlike earlier visions for the river mouth, which proposed the demolition of Keating Channel to make way for a new, naturalized outlet to the lake, MVVA proposed to retain Keating Channel as a "significant urban arte-fact of the Port Lands." As colour plate 2 illustrates, the main channel of the river would be routed farther south through the Port Lands, with Keating Channel serving as a smaller, secondary outlet. Repurposed as an "urban amenity" lined with "retail-oriented promenades," it would serve simultaneously as a "flood channel, gateway, and connective tis-sue between adjacent neighbourhoods" (see colour plate 3).[28]

This recasting of a formerly derelict space as an urban amenity has significant implications for the site's social composition. An area that had become by the 1860s a refuge for society's outcasts is here radi-cally reworked as a space for upwardly mobile members of the knowl-edge economy. As geographer David Harvey has shown, capitalism continually produces new strategies of accumulation and, with them, new landscapes to replace those that have become obsolete.[29] Just as industrial capital reshaped the area surrounding the river mouth in the latter half of the nineteenth century, here urban nature is again recon-figured as a strategy of accumulation, wherein access to the waterfront and naturalized environments serves to heighten property values. In this way, the LDL plan exemplifies what Harvey has identified as a pro-cess of "creative destruction": an imagined landscape of consumption comes to replace an obsolete landscape of production.

In addressing the river's natural processes, the MVVA proposal and subsequent planning documents show evidence of learning from past experience. Flexibility and adaptability are terms that appear fre-quently throughout the planning documents. In its initial vision for the project, MVVA stated:

We want to restore the interaction between lake, river and land by design-ing around the dynamics of nature: changing lake levels, river flows and climate. We will allow the design to be flexible, dynamic, and fluid so that change is anticipated, expected, and a valued part of the experience of living with nature, rather than a point of vulnerability and a threat to the city.[30]

Flood protection features alone, with their emphasis on anticipating, and planning for, the reception of floodwaters in the event of a major flood, are indicative of this new approach. Recognizing, for example, that "the hydrology of the Don River is characterized by extreme fluctuations in water flow and floating debris," the MVVA design team proposed that the river channel be cut to different depths and surrounded by park or "spillway" lands in order to "accept and deliver varying volumes of water, from low to moderate to severe flood events."[31] Keating Channel would operate as an alternate outfall to the Inner Harbour, with the Ship Channel further south as an additional spillway for floodwaters.

This approach differs markedly from the character of nineteenth-century improvement projects for the lower river, which tended to work against rather than with the river's hydrological cycles. Rather than an evolving relationship between built and natural features on the ground, nineteenth-century planners seemed to expect an instant fix to long-established problems. The result was a rigid system of infrastructure unable to accommodate the shifting ecological processes it sought to control: the cedar piling that divorced the straightened river channel from its floodplain failed to contain rising waters in times of flood, while river sediments accumulated unabated along the river's lower reaches, negating the potential for "flushing action" in the channel. The degree to which the LDL plan can reverse this will be an important consideration for its success.

In other aspects of the design, however, natural processes have been less successfully accommodated. Plans for the management of river sediments, for example, have been modified considerably as the planning process has progressed. While the original MVVA design concept proposed to collect, cleanse, and reuse river sediments within the project to create landforms such as flood protection berms, this idea was later rejected as unviable, in part due to its anticipated expense. Current plans propose to trap sediments north of Keating Channel. These deposits would then be dredged, dewatered, and transported to the Leslie Street Spit for disposal, much as they have been for decades.[32]

More innovative solutions have been proposed for the treatment of contaminated soils throughout the Lower Don Lands. In July 2010, Waterfront Toronto established a pilot soil recycling facility in the Port Lands to determine the feasibility of treating and reusing contaminated soils on site. The success of the pilot in cleansing soils for reuse have led to plans for a permanent facility in the Port Lands.[33]

References within the design concept to the historical ecology of the river are another way the past informs this imagined future for the river mouth. The proposed routing of the river channel in a winding southerly course through a naturalized wetland environment reflects the river's historical course before it was straightened and channelized in the 1880s. Using Joseph Bouchette's 1815 *Plan of York Harbour* and other early-nineteenth-century sources as a reference, the MVVA team sketched in broad strokes the historical ecology of the harbour (figure 7.1).[34] Based on their assessment, the lower river wound through a lowland savannah before curving west through a marsh formed jointly by the effects of river and lake. In its final reach, the river moved south through the marsh, slicing through the narrow sandbar to slip into the harbour about midway along the marsh's western edge. By roughly mirroring this historical course, MVVA professed to release the river "where it wants to be," at the shore of Lake Ontario.[35] Pockets of wetland habitat throughout the design, they note, reference the extensive marshlands surrounding the nineteenth-century river mouth, while creating viable habitat for wildlife. Here, nature is a deliberate and acknowledged construction.

Waterfront Toronto and the TRCA's careful distinction between *naturalization* and *restoration* warrants some discussion here. While the MVVA proposal makes deliberate references to the river's multiple pasts, and employs the phrase "ecological restoration" to describe aspects of their concept design, restoration refers to the establishment of selected wetland habitat features (to the restoration of ecological function) rather than the recreation of a historical landscape.[36] As TRCA project manager Ken Dion emphasizes,

nothing is being restored through this [project]. We are trying to establish a sustainable green river mouth that is resistant to the new environmental realities being located at the mouth of one of the most urbanized rivers in Canada. It will be nothing like the original marshes that occurred here 150 years ago; as such, [restoration] is not an appropriate term.[37]

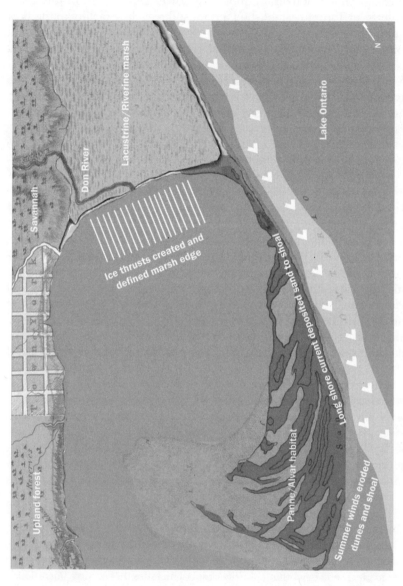

Labels within image: Savannah; Upland forest; Don River; Lacustrine/Riverine marsh; Ice thrusts created and defined marsh edge; Long shore current deposited sand to shoal; Panne/Alvar habitat; Summer winds eroded dunes and shoal; Lake Ontario; N

7.1 Historical ecology of the Lower Don Lands, MVVA Port Lands Estuary Proposal. (Rendering by Michael Van Valkenburgh Associates, Inc. Courtesy of Waterfront Toronto.)

Acknowledging the misperceptions introduced by the term "restoration," Waterfront Toronto and the TRCA have adopted the term "naturalization" instead.[38] "Natural features" such as flexible channels, aquatic grasses, and reeds typical of riverine marshes are built into the site's design, with no expectation of reproducing the full range of historical ecosystem features. Such an approach reflects long-established restoration practices in Europe, where practitioners seek to "renature historic conditions" rather than embrace the fallacy of reproducing pristine landscapes devoid of human intervention.[39]

The term also creates space for the inclusion of references to multiple pasts. Whereas "restoration" suggests the reconstruction of a single period in time, "naturalization" is devoid of these temporal connotations. The plan incorporates artefacts from a continuum of time, rather than a single "historical reference landscape." Thus an approximation of the river's early-nineteenth-century outlet to the lake can exist alongside late-nineteenth-century industrial structures and the early-twentieth-century Keating Channel. Rather than attempting to recreate some kind of pre-settlement landscape (fraught on many levels, not least the monumental task of removing artefacts of settlement), then, project proponents are free to reference the past through specific landscape forms and to juxtapose these referents with elements reflective of present sensibilities. In effect, they aspire to create a postmodern landscape, shot through with internal references to the site's history, forward and backward looking at the same time.[40]

Another Imagined Future?

Since 2007, Waterfront Toronto and the TRCA have conducted public and stakeholder consultations in order to assess a series of alternative designs for the river mouth as required by the environmental assessment process. Consensus centred on a river mouth alignment that reaffirmed the features of the MVVA concept design. The future of the project, however, is less than certain. Costs for the naturalization component of the Lower Don Lands project are estimated at anywhere from $300 to $400 million, with expenditures for transit, trail networks, and other public infrastructure bringing the total closer to $650 million.[41] With funds only to cover the planning and not the implementation of the project, Waterfront Toronto must create partnerships with private developers and senior governments in order to realize its vision. Its success in other waterfront revitalization projects such as Sugar Beach and Sherbourne Common stands them in good stead. The scale and complexity of the LDL project, however, create challenges of a larger order.

As Waterfront Toronto itself acknowledges, the LDL plan is "one of the largest and most complex public infrastructure projects ever undertaken in the City of Toronto."[42] The complexity of the plan is apparent on several levels. Staged over three decades, the plans have been developed in conjunction with no less than seven active environmental assessments[43] and are dependent upon major infrastructure upgrades. Waterfront Toronto also faces considerable challenges related to its governance structure. Unlike the organizations that have revitalized waterfronts in other cities, Waterfront Toronto lacks the power to borrow money and expropriate land. Instead, it must leverage its public capital to partner with private developers, who buy the land for development. It must also gain approvals, project by project, from each of the three levels of government that supply its funding and consult with as many as fifty public agencies and corporations, each of which has a stake in the future of the waterfront.[44]

The vulnerability of the project to shifting political priorities was demonstrated as recently as August 2011, when Toronto Councillor Doug Ford attempted to usurp Waterfront Toronto's authority by replacing the Lower Don Lands plan with his own vision for the area, one that involved the construction of a monorail, megamall, and giant Ferris wheel. The resulting public outrage largely affirmed Waterfront Toronto's mandate and its plans for the Lower Don Lands.[45] Pressure from the city to accelerate the plans and to trim costs, however, resulted in the reopening of the planning process. The resulting amendments reduced the proposed area for naturalization from thirty-three to twenty-two hectares. In response to the concerns of the Toronto Port Authority and several Port Lands industries, the plans were further revised to reduce the reach of proposed parkland (Promontory Park) into the inner harbour and harden its western edge in order to preserve existing dock walls (see colour plate 4).

Phasing for the project was also completely overhauled to make public expenditures for infrastructure and naturalization work more contingent upon development revenue. The revised plan divides flood protection works into more cost-efficient segments, removing flood risk from a successive series of lands with each phase and freeing them for development. Under this new phasing the naturalized river mouth would likely be constructed last. The naturalization of the south side of the river mouth would proceed only upon the voluntary relocation of the Lafarge cement plant, which has occupied the south side of Polson Slip for over eighty years.[46]

While political wrangling at the local level has hindered project progress, the plan for the Lower Don Lands has been the subject of considerable international attention. In addition to several design awards, the project was selected by the Clinton Climate Initiative in 2009 as one of the urban projects it will support in helping to demonstrate that cities can develop in ways that are "climate positive."[47] The award celebrated the project's emphasis on sustainability in urban design, including energy-efficient building design, carbon-reduction measures to reduce greenhouse gas emissions, and high levels of transit servicing.[48]

Despite the recognition the plan has received, the uncertainty surrounding project implementation indicates that it may well join the long line of other imagined futures proposed for the Lower Don Lands and never realized. We have been here before: recall the nineteenth-century equivalent of the Waterfront Toronto design competition – the call for "the three best reports on the means to be adopted for the preservation and improvement of the Harbour of Toronto" issued by the Toronto Harbour Commissioners in 1854, which asked expert contestants to turn their attention specifically to the relationship between the Don, the harbour, and Ashbridge's Bay.[49] Although the winning entries were much celebrated, and reprinted for wider distribution in the *Canadian Journal* of that year, no action was taken on contestants' recommendations until almost twenty years later, and even then the construction of the Government Breakwater represented only a partial (and ultimately unsuccessful) remedy to "the Don problem."

Like past plans, the Lower Don Lands project has been, and will continue to be, subject to change. Like its 1880s predecessor, the search for cost efficiencies and fluctuations in political will have already resulted in the omission or alteration of key design elements that may have produced better results. All aspects of the revised plan remain subject not only to the vagaries of the environmental assessment process, but also to the uncertainties of the economic climate – uncertainties that are closer to us all following the 2008 collapse of global financial markets. To its credit, Waterfront Toronto has managed the jurisdictional and political hurdles associated with the project with creativity and tenacity. The breadth of its vision and its demonstrated commitment to public engagement throughout the planning process have earned the agency considerable public support.[50] The limits of its power, and ultimately of its purse, however, mean that further compromises will likely be necessary in order to realize what is an extremely complex multi-year initiative.

Should the Lower Don Lands project proceed in the years to come, the extent to which it will "undo" the legacy of nineteenth-century improvement initiatives will be necessarily limited. The 1880s Don Improvement Plan transformed the area from the CN rail crossing at Eastern Avenue north to Riverdale Park. The Don Narrows, as this area is referred to today, falls outside the area designated for revitalization by Waterfront Toronto. The formidable physical constraints of the site, bounded as it is by a rail corridor on the west and the Don Valley Parkway on the east, greatly limit the possibilities for naturalization. And yet efforts are being made. Recommendations from the Task Force to Bring Back the Don and other citizens' groups to extend naturalization initiatives to the Don Narrows led the TRCA to include the area in their environmental assessment for the naturalization of the river mouth. As part of this process, the TRCA worked with consultants and community members to identify and evaluate opportunities to improve stream habitat in the Narrows without exacerbating the potential for flooding that is such a central concern of the Lower Don Lands initiative.[51] Like the Lower Don Lands plan, proposed naturalization initiatives in this section of the river are dependent upon the availability of funds for implementation, together with considerable cooperation among jurisdictional authorities – in this case, between the TRCA and the city of Toronto, which holds responsibility for maintaining the corridor of the Don Valley Parkway and the sheet piling that bounds the river.

If, as Pierre Nora suggests, we require the creation of "sites of memory" to illuminate past environments and past sensibilities, the LDL plan aims to provide those cues. As we have seen, the past informs the project in subtle and overlapping ways, through referents to past landscapes and past planning outcomes, processes and methods informed by past experience, and finally, through the physical realities of the site itself – the ways in which the past, in the form of contaminated soils or concrete structures, places demands upon the present. On paper, the project challenges the public, as David Lowenthal has proposed, to become "intimate enough with our legacy to rework it creatively," to attempt not to recreate the past but to recognize it and incorporate it within a new and different vision for the future.[52]

The uncertain future of the LDL plan compels us to consider the Lower Don as a place still open to future possibilities. As the efforts of the Task Force to Bring Back the Don and other citizen groups have shown us, there are multiple ways to envision the future of this space. Not to be elided here, either, are the ways the Don is appreciated in the present. For many Torontonians, the neglected spaces along the lower river provide a welcome place for recreation and reflection, and an escape from the monotony of the city streets. Here, the relics of former industrial establishments and the presence of railway tracks and highway overpasses may do more to signal the area's layered past than would any designated heritage features within an aesthetically recalibrated landscape. The opportunities for informal experiences afforded by this marginal space within the city present an important contrast to the elite civic vision embodied by the LDL plan. Will it be possible to "get lost" in the redesigned Lower Don Lands? What will the likelihood be of unexpected discoveries in such a carefully constructed landscape? Any redevelopment plan of this size requires us to think about what will be lost or swept aside when the bulldozers arrive to effect another tabula rasa. If the 1880s improvement plan has taught us anything, it is to weigh carefully what will be lost in preparing for the next imagined future for the Lower Don.

We might wonder what Jane Jacobs, Toronto's celebrated opponent of urban renewal initatives, would have thought. While the project proposes to revitalize what is essentially an industrial brownfield,[53] its size and scope will inevitably obliterate or at least significantly disrupt the pollution-tolerant organisms that have gained a foothold on this site in the years since the industries moved out. "Renaturalization," in this sense, has been occurring for years. If the adjacent Leslie Street Spit serves as any indication, time may prove the best strategy for renaturalizing heavily disturbed sites. The five-kilometre long peninsula, constructed by incremental lakefilling initiated in the late 1950s, is today one of the city's most cherished "wild" spaces, and one of few places in the city barred to automobile traffic.[54] Over 400 plant species have been identified on the peninsula, along with a wide range of bird and butterfly species. Volunteers have also reported occasional sightings of beavers, otters, red foxes, and coyotes.[55]

For a range of reasons, the Lower Don Lands is unlikely to see the same future as the Leslie Street Spit. Perhaps most powerful among these is the site's proximity to and visibility from the city centre. Too valuable to let sit as unoccupied brownfield (or, as in the case of Leslie Spit, as "urban wilderness"), the site also serves as a constant reminder to civic leaders of the failure of past development schemes. From the dubious gains of the Don Improvement Project in the 1880s, to the harbour expansion projects initiated in response to the 1959 opening of the St Lawrence Seaway, and subsequently abandoned,[56] the area has consistently failed to meet expectations. Ongoing and substantial dredging expenses incurred to maintain clear passage in the area around the mouth of the Don reinforce this sense of the area as a blight on the city's image. For these reasons, and for the revenues to be reaped from new taxable properties, the Lower Don Lands is likely to emerge, in ways comparable to Vancouver's False Creek, as another sought-after residential district for wealthy urban professionals. As the most recent revisions to the plans show us, the naturalization of the river mouth has already been relegated to the final phases of the project. Whether and to what extent the naturalization features of the plan will be developed will depend, in large part, on Waterfront Toronto's ability to defend the plan against encroachment, and its nimbleness in fostering private-sector partnerships and raising funds.

Conclusion

Looking back on the over 200 years of human experience with the Don documented in this study, we can sift several findings from the layers of detail that have accumulated. Most striking in the narrative arc of this book was the Don's slippage in the eyes of Toronto's civic leaders from a place of relative importance – a place fit enough to host the province's first parliament buildings – to a place widely perceived, by the mid-nineteenth century, as polluted, dangerous, and disease-ridden. As we have seen, the foul odours and polluted waters resulting from the Lower Don's designation as a "space apart" were for many observers the price of prosperity and the cost of keeping other parts of the city more habitable. Less appreciated as a source of natural resources, the river valley nevertheless continued to serve as a vital component of the city's economy in its role as a sink for municipal and industrial wastes. The "re-centring" of the valley in the mid-twentieth century as a metropolitan corridor running through the middle of a larger region, rather than the edge of the old city, contributed to a shift in perception once again. More Torontonians than ever before experienced the valley on their daily commute to the city centre. Viewed through the windshield, the valley's brilliant fall foliage and lush greenery in summer helped put to rest associations of the valley as a dangerous, polluted underworld. Efforts by local conservationists to protect valley environments and improve public awareness further fuelled this transition. Still polluted and neglected in its lower reaches, the river valley today is nevertheless valued as one of Toronto's most iconic landscapes.

By bringing together approaches from social and environmental history, this study reveals some of the connections between places and populations constructed as marginal by privileged observers and decision makers. As we have seen, the processes that identified certain individuals as deficient "others" mirrored similar imperatives at work in classifying difficult or unpredictable environments as "waste spaces." Marginality was not an inherent characteristic of landscapes or of human populations; it was actively produced. Just as the valley emerged as an ambiguous borderland space redefined in relation to the evolving city, the people who turned to the river flats and forested ravines for refuge also demonstrated diverse circumstances and strategies that underscored their marginality, from the familiar strategies of the squatter to the novel practices of the Roma traveller. From this perspective, the valley occupied a borderland in both space and time, as much an intermediary zone between rural and urban as a liminal space within which "old" and "new" political economies, self-provisioning and capitalist lifeways overlapped and asserted themselves.

The urban fringe appears in this book as a useful place from which to study the city's historical relationship with its environment. By focusing on the edges, this study has illuminated the social and environmental consequences of urban development processes and decisions. A slippery "in-between" space neither fully urban nor fully rural, the Don River Valley emerged as a space worthy of our attention. Developments in the periphery, as Richard Harris has shown so compellingly in his work on blue-collar suburbs in Toronto, interacted in complicated and reciprocal ways with varied forces at work in the centre. Approaching urban history from the vantage point of the periphery opens up, in Harris's words, "new vistas" and allows "familiar urban landmarks [to] take on a new aspect."[1] Other cities have had (and continue to have) similar spaces, and they deserve more attention. In the histories of places like Vancouver's False Creek, Halifax's waterfront, or Minneapolis's Bohemian Flats, we might locate evidence of alternate strategies of "getting by" within the context of the modern city.[2] As this study has shown, these liminal spaces at the city's edge provided opportunities for refuge, for self-provisioning, and for pursuing what David Shi has called "the simple life."[3] As such, they exemplify places where modern capitalist political economies overlapped with older economic strategies. How these "empty spaces" on the urban fringe were reconceived by proponents of various development schemes through time, and the effects of these redevelopments upon the human and non-human ecologies they displaced, warrant greater attention by urban historians.

Returning to the story of Princess Margaret's 1958 visit to the city, and the city's last-minute efforts to cleanse the river before her arrival, we are reminded of the steadily worsening pollution and inadequate, belated response that characterized the city's relationship with the Don through the nineteenth and much of the twentieth centuries. Revisiting this narrative also places into relief the history of the Lower Don as a landscape of progress. The city's choice of Riverdale Park on the Lower Don as the location for the Princess's visit and, by extension, the setting from which to put the city "on show" was a mid-twentieth-century expression of a larger and remarkably persistent tendency to showcase the Lower Don as a landscape imbued with future possibilities. From Simcoe's choice of the marshy lowlands west of the river as the site for the province's parliament buildings, to the medical and reformatory institutions located above the banks of the lower river in the 1860s, to the grand visions that accompanied the Don Improvement of the 1880s, to the construction of the DVP in the 1960s, and finally the current plans for the naturalization of the river mouth, the Don has expressed in material ways a succession of imagined futures for the city and the particular ideological, political, and economic contexts within which these visions were created.

Imaginings for the river reached outward, modelling their designs upon the perceived success of improvement projects in other river cities and situating their objectives and methods within the rapidly industrializing political and economic imperatives of their times. As we have seen, the tendency of these plans to fail or "underdeliver" reflected the realities of budget shortfalls and fluctuating political will, together with shifting and unforeseen environmental conditions. The rationalization of design plans to accommodate these changing circumstances constrained their potential for success, omitting features that may have produced better results. Cyclical processes such as seasonal flooding and sediment deposition also impinged upon the probability of project success. Here, the river emerged as an autonomous and causal force in the city's history. Despite its small size, the Don played a considerable role in shaping the development of the city and in conditioning the relationship between urban residents and their environment, from the attempts of early harbour masters to corral the debris it jettisoned each spring into Toronto harbour, to the devastating impact of Hurricane Hazel in 1954.

And yet, as much as we can read the history of the river, the valley, and the city as a story of unintended consequences and environmental decline, we must also recall the flip side to this story, in which the river features as an economic success story. An important source of raw materials for bricks and lumber, and the site of valuable industries, the Don helped to build modern Toronto. Its function as a sink for wastes was no less important, enabling as it did the city's residential and industrial expansion. Finally, and perhaps most significantly, was the valley's role as a transportation corridor. In the 1880s the valley facilitated the development of an eastern rail entrance to the city. Seventy years later, civic leaders took advantage of the same natural corridor in constructing the Don Valley Parkway, a major artery of commodity circulation and mobility in the region. In both periods, these developments fuelled economic growth and contributed in important ways to the city's expansion. From this perspective, then, a neglected and polluted river was the consequence of building a functioning city of 2.5 million people.

In the dialectic between cultural and material change that has been in play throughout this study, the Don by the late twentieth century moved from being a blighted and neglected place to become a degraded but ultimately salvageable natural system, and in this transformation it took on symbolic significance as an indicator of urban health. Efforts by municipal, regional, and citizen groups to protect and promote the river and to remove obstacles to citizen access opened possibilities for new relationships with the Don. With access to the river valley came opportunities to see the Don not simply as a landscape defiled, but rather as a place where natural processes – however compromised – continued to function. As Jenny Price notes in her work on the Los Angeles River, the recognition of nature as existing in the places where we live, and not just in some more pristine form outside the city, brings with it a compelling rationale for sustainability in the practices of our daily lives.[4] The attempts of citizen-activists to grapple with the potential of the Don for restoration within the constraints of the existing built environment have yielded, over the last two decades, a newfound appreciation for the hybridity of urban landscapes that are neither fully constructed nor fully "natural," but some combination of the two. Observers of the Don have taken from their experiences with the river and its history the lessons of ecology: the concept of carrying capacity, that ecological systems have limits in the amount of wastes they can assimilate; and the concept of connectivity, that watersheds must be understood as a connected whole, rather than a series of component parts.

Today, the river is cleaner than it has been for almost a century, but still polluted enough to rank among Canada's most polluted rivers in a 2007 Environment Canada study.[5] The bulk of this pollution comes not from industry or single-source polluters but from the everyday activities of urban and suburban life – flushing toilets, driving to the grocery store, salting driveways in winter. Run-off from streets and parking lots carries oil, road salt, animal wastes, and other harmful substances into the storm sewer system, and from there directly into the Don. Almost 1,200 storm sewer outfalls dump into the Don and its tributaries, and after heavy rains stormwater makes up over 70 per cent of the river's flow. Existing pollution makes the river unsafe for people to wade or swim in, but for wildlife, the consequences are life-threatening. According to the Toronto and Region Conservation Authority, chloride from road salt is harmful to aquatic wildlife at 240 milligrams per litre of water. Levels in the Don River are consistently much higher than this, reaching a high of 3,920 milligrams in samples taken between 2002 and 2005.[6] Runoff from streets also raises the water temperature of the river to levels only the most adaptable species can tolerate. White sucker, emerald shiner, fathead minnow, and blacknose dace are among the few fish species that have adapted to the toxic conditions in the Lower Don.[7]

In a watershed that was once almost entirely forested, only 7 per cent of forest cover remains. Almost all of the watershed's original wetlands have been filled or paved over, and 85 per cent of its lands have been developed for residential or industrial purposes.[8] Throughout the watershed, soil compaction, vegetation removal, and the growing expanse of paved surfaces have resulted in dangerous increases in surface run-off and corresponding declines in groundwater reserves.[9] For the river, these changes have produced consistently low flows under normal conditions and sudden flash floods in times of heavy rainfall. In August 2005, for example, surface run-off from a severe rainstorm caused the Don to swell to record highs in some reaches, flooding adjacent roadways and buildings and eroding fragile stream banks. The Ontario insurance industry later ranked this storm as the most expensive natural disaster in the province's history.[10]

Over the last twenty years, restoration initiatives have recreated a very small percentage of the lower valley's once extensive wetlands, providing important habitat for moisture-seeking plants and animals. Dedicated groups of volunteers have pulled on rubber boots on Sunday afternoons and trudged through the neglected lands of the lower valley to sink shovels into gravel, haul topsoil, and nurture seedlings. In the valley bottoms, the TRCA has invested considerable funds into improving ecological diversity by restoring native vegetation alongside grassy recreation corridors.[11] These efforts represent only small pockets, however, in a landscape dominated by urban networks of transportation, waste disposal, and power provision. In short, the best restoration initiatives cannot alter the fact that the Don flows through Canada's most urbanized watershed. Placed in juxtaposition with the long history of grand visions for the river – the few that were realized remembered largely for their shortcomings – these small restoration projects can be distinguished for their humble expectations, modest size, and relatively rapid implementation. Realized with little funding and less fanfare, these projects have demonstrated that at least limited ecological function can be restored to even intensely manipulated environments. Anyone who has visited the Weston Quarry Garden at the former Don Valley Brick Works has experienced the wonder of a place transformed, from abandoned clay quarry to vibrant wetland. The extent to which the river has become a symbol of this potential for redemption ("bringing back" the Don being the rallying cry of the river's acclaimed citizens' organization)[12] suggests that something deeper than the rehabilitation of isolated micro-environments is at work. For many Toronto residents, the potential of the Don lies in the depth of its decline. Small recoveries become, in this wider context, emblems of hope for a renewed relationship not just with a beleaguered urban river, but with the planet as a whole.

Notes

Introduction

1 "Princess' Touring Time Spurs Row, Nate Objects," *Toronto Daily Star*, 28 May 1958; "Toronto Public to See Margaret 95 Minutes," *Toronto Daily Star*, 13 June 1958.

2 "Our Perfumed Don," *Toronto Daily Star*, 31 July 1958.

3 David Crombie, *Regeneration: Toronto's Waterfront and the Sustainable City. Final Report, Royal Commission on the Future of the Toronto Waterfront* (Ottawa: Minister of Supply and Services Canada, 1992), 238.

4 Review of Charles Sauriol, *Remembering the Don: A Rare Record of Earlier Times within the Don River Valley* (Toronto: Consolidated Amethyst Communications, 1981), *Toronto Star*, 31 January 1982, C10.

5 Letter from Dorothy B. Lewis, of York Pioneer and Historical Society, 5 February 1982, in Charles Sauriol, "Remembering the Don, 1981–83," General Subject Files of Charles Sauriol, ca 1970–1995, file 26, series 103, fonds 5, City of Toronto Archives (hereafter CTA).

6 Queen Elizabeth and King George VI did visit Riverdale Park in 1939. Newspaper coverage of the royal visit on 22 May highlighted opportunities for children to view Their Majesties at Riverdale Park. "Thousands, Tired but Happy Reach Home Late at Night: Suburban Children Saw King and Queen in Toronto Parks," *Toronto Daily Star*, 23 May 1969, 6.

7 "Princess' Second Home Mayor Offers Castle," *Toronto Daily Star*, 31 July 1958.

8 Ontario Department of Planning and Development (hereafter ODPD), *Don Valley Conservation Report* (Toronto: Ontario Department of Planning and Development, 1950), Part VI, 15.

9 The others being, from west to east, Etobicoke Creek, Mimico Creek, the Humber River, Highland Creek, and the Rouge River.

10 These included Castle Frank Brook (also known as Brewery Creek or Severn Creek), Yellow Creek (also known as Rosedale Brook, Silver or Sylvan Creek), Mud Creek (also known as Mount Pleasant Brook), and Cudmore Creek (also known as Burns Creek). Each of these tributaries entered the Lower Don from the northwest in the area roughly bounded by Pottery Road and Winchester Street. Two smaller tributaries, Sumac Creek and Crookshank Creek, entered the river from the northwest between Eastern Avenue and Front Street.

11 Carolyn Merchant, *Reinventing Eden: The Fate of Nature in Western Culture* (London and New York: Routledge, 2003).

12 Joel A. Tarr, *Devastation and Renewal* (Pittsburgh, PA: University of Pittsburgh Press, 2005); Ari Kelman, *A River and Its City: The Nature of Landscape in New Orleans* (Berkeley: University of California Press, 2003); Christopher Armstrong, Matthew Evenden, and H.V. Nelles, *The River Returns: An Environmental History of the Bow* (McGill-Queen's University Press, 2009); Matthew Evenden, *Fish versus Power: An Environmental History of the Fraser* (Cambridge: Cambridge University Press, 2004); Michèle Dagenais, *Montréal et l'eau* (Montreal: Boréal, 2011).

13 Statistics for 2011 indicate that the watershed was 26 per cent urbanized. Rural lands constituted 40 per cent of the watershed, and natural cover or parkland, 32 per cent. "Humber River Watershed Features," Toronto and Region Conservation Authority, http://www.trca.on.ca/protect/water sheds/humber-river/watershed-features.dot (accessed 6 January 2012).

14 Joy Parr, *Sensing Changes: Technologies, Environments, and the Everyday, 1953–2003* (Vancouver: UBC Press, 2009).

15 Pierre Nora, *Realms of Memory: Rethinking the French Past*, trans. Arthur Goldhammer (New York: Columbia University Press, 1996).

16 John R. Stilgoe, *Borderland: Origins of the American Suburb, 1820–1939* (New Haven and London: Yale University Press, 1988), 10.

17 I refer here to Richard White's classic *The Middle Ground: Indians, Empires and Republics in the Great Lakes Region 1650–1815* (New York: Cambridge University Press, 1991).

18 Ignasi de Solà-Morales, "Terrain Vague," in *Anyplace*, ed. Cynthia C. Davidson (Cambridge, MA: MIT Press, 1995).

19 Matthew Gandy, *Concrete and Clay: Reworking Nature in New York City* (Cambridge, MA: MIT Press, 2002); Matthew Gandy, "Rethinking Urban Metabolism: Water, Space and the Modern City," *City* 8, no. 3 (2004): 363–79, doi:10.1080/1360481042000313509.

20 Rob Shields, *Places on the Margin: Alternative Geographies of Modernity* (London and New York: Routledge, 1991).

1. The Colonial River

1 Mary Quayle Innis, *Mrs. Simcoe's Diary* (Toronto: MacMillan, 1965), 104.

2 Ibid., 106.

3 Robert I. MacDonald, "Toronto's Natural History," in *Toronto: An Illustrated History of Its First 12,000 Years*, ed. Ronald F. Williamson (Toronto: James Lorimer, 2008), 16.

4 Several excellent accounts exist of the geology and natural history of the region. See Nick Eyles, *Toronto Rocks: The Geological Legacy of the Toronto Region* (Toronto: Fitzhenry and Whiteside, 2004); MacDonald, "Toronto's Natural History"; Betty I. Roots, Donald A. Chant, and Conrad E. Heidenreich, *Special Places: The Changing Ecosystems of the Toronto Region* (Vancouver: UBC Press, 1999).

5 Edith G. Firth, *The Town of York, 1793–1815: A Collection of Documents of Early Toronto* (Toronto: Champlain Society, 1962), 4.

6 Graeme Mercer Adam, Charles Pelham Mulvany, and Christopher Blackett Robinson, *History of Toronto and County of York* (Toronto: C. Blackett Robinson, 1885), 211.

7 J.M.S. Careless, *Toronto to 1918: An Illustrated History* (Toronto: James Lorimer, 1984), 9.

8 Albert Boime, *The Magisterial Gaze: Manifest Destiny and American Landscape Painting C.1830–1865* (Washington and London: Smithsonian Institution Press, 1991), 21.

9 Carolyn Merchant, *Reinventing Eden: The Fate of Nature in Western Culture* (London and New York: Routledge, 2003), 89.

10 E.A. Cruikshank, ed., *The Correspondence of Lieut. Governor John Graves Simcoe* (Toronto: Ontario Historical Society, 1923–31), vol. 1, 19 October 1793.

11 Ontario Department of Planning and Development, *Don Valley Conservation Report*, part 1: 42–3.

12 Joseph Bouchette, *The British Dominions in North America* (1831), cited in Adam, Mulvany, and Robinson, *History of Toronto and County of York*, 206.

13 Victoria Freeman, "'Toronto Has No History!' Indigeneity, Settler Colonialism and Historical Memory in Canada's Largest City," *Urban History Review* 38, no. 2 (Spring 2010): 21–35.

14 Colin M. Coates, "The Colonial Landscapes of the Early Town," in *Metropolitan Natures: Environmental Histories of Montreal*, ed. Stéphane Castonguay and Michèle Dagenais (Pittsburgh, PA: University of Pittsburgh Press, 2011), 21.

15 Legitimate claims to ownership, Locke purported, saw human labour married with the land to transform and "improve" it. *The Second Treatise of Government*, ed. Thomas P. Peardon (New York: Macmillan, 1952).

16 Coll Thrush makes a similar observation about the Aboriginal history of Seattle, noting the tendency among settler populations to view the area's first peoples as "shades of the past, linked almost mythically to a lost nature." Stories of the city's Aboriginal past, he finds, reflect the widespread assumption that "native history and urban history – and, indeed, Indians and cities – cannot coexist, and one must necessarily be eclipsed by the other." *Native Seattle: Histories from the Crossing-Over Place* (Seattle: University of Washington Press, 2008), 9. On the colonial project of displacement of Aboriginal peoples and repossession of land more generally, see Cole Harris, *Making Native Space: Colonialism, Resistance, and Reserves in British Columbia* (Vancouver: UBC Press, 2002).

17 For further detail on the history of pre-contact Aboriginal settlement in the Toronto area, see Edward S. Rogers and Donald B. Smith, eds, *Aboriginal Ontario: Historical Perspectives on the First Nations* (Toronto: Dundurn Press, 1994); Donald B. Smith, "Who Are the Mississauga?" *Ontario History* 67, no. 4 (1975): 211–22; Donald B. Smith, "The Dispossession of the Mississauga Indians: A Missing Chapter in the Early History of Upper Canada," *Ontario History* 73, no. 2 (1981): 67–87; Bruce G. Trigger, ed., *Handbook of North American Indians*, vol. 15: *Northeast* (Washington, DC: Smithsonian Institution, 1978); and Ronald F. Williamson, "Before the Visitors," in *Toronto: An Illustrated History of Its First 12,000 Years*, ed. Ronald F. Williamson (Toronto: James Lorimer, 2008), 25–52.

18 John Ross Robertson, *The Diary of Mrs. John Graves Simcoe, Wife of the First Lieutenant-Governor of the Province of Upper Canada, 1792–6* (Toronto: W. Briggs, 1911), 214–15, https://archive.org/details/diaryofmrs johngr00simcuoft (accessed 23 June 2014).

19 The name *Nechenquakekonk* appears without translation on surveyor Alexander Aitken's 1788 map of the Toronto area. The translation for *Wonscotonach* appears in Augustus Jones, "Names of the Rivers, and Creeks, as they are called by the Mississaugas," 4 July 1796, Surveyors' Letters, vol. 28, pp. 103–5, RG 1-61-0-6, Archives of Ontario, cited in Henry Scadding, *Toronto of Old: Collections and Recollections Illustrative of the Early Settlement and Social Life of the Capital of Ontario* (Toronto: Adam, Stevenson, 1873), 233. Donald B. Smith interviewed Basil Johnson in 1986; the translation appears in his *Sacred Feathers: The Reverend Peter Jones (Kahkewaquonaby) and the Mississauga Indians* (Toronto: University of Toronto Press, 1987), 256. Thanks to John P. Wilson for drawing this to my attention.

20 Freeman, "Toronto Has No History."
21 In 1805 the colonial administration attempted to resolve the uncertainty surrounding the 1787 purchase. The 1805 Toronto Purchase, signed by eight Mississauga chiefs, affirmed the boundaries of the 1787 surrender. It is doubtful the terms of the treaty were fully understood, however, as the Mississauga chiefs accepted just ten shillings in exchange for ratifying the surrender and relinquished rights to the same lands they had previously insisted were outside the 1787 treaty (among these the Toronto Islands, long considered sacred territory by the Mississauga). The Mississauga maintain that they were unfairly compensated for lands in the Toronto Purchase and that the boundaries of the 1805 treaty were misrepresented. In 2010, they settled a land claim with the Canadian government for $145 million.
22 The Task Force to Bring Back the Don (TFBBD), *Bringing Back the Don* (Toronto: City of Toronto Planning and Development Department, August 1991), 26; Williamson, "Before the Visitors," 41–2.
23 Evidence of lakeshore camps from this period has been discovered along the former shore of Lake Iroquois, remnants of which still exist in the elevated ridge along Davenport Road in Toronto (Williamson, "Before the Visitors," 28).
24 Ibid., 33.
25 Artefacts recovered from the site have been dated at 2,500 to 6,700 years old.
26 Williamson, "Before the Visitors," 45.
27 Ibid., 26.
28 Ontario Department of Planning and Development (ODPD), *Don Valley Conservation Report* (Toronto: Ontario Department of Planning and Development, 1950), part 1: 34.
29 In these early years, time limits for settlement duties were not strictly enforced, allowing for many absentee landowners. John Ross Robertson, *Robertson's Landmarks of Toronto: A Collection of Historical Sketches of the Old Town of York from 1792 until 1833, and of Toronto from 1834 to 1893* (Toronto: J. Ross Robertson, 1894), vol. 6: 194–5.
30 Maria Tippett and Douglas Cole, *From Desolation to Splendour: Changing Perceptions of the British Columbia Landscape* (Toronto: Clarke, Irwin, 1977), 26.
31 Innis, *Mrs. Simcoe's Diary*, 186.
32 ODPD, *Don Valley Conservation Report*, part 4: 1.
33 William Henry Smith, *Canada, Past, Present and Future: Being a Historical Geographical, Geological and Statistical Account of Canada West* (Toronto: Thomas Maclear, 1851), 19–20.

34 Innis, *Mrs. Simcoe's Diary*, 110.

35 Ibid., 170.

36 Ibid., 177.

37 Eleanor Darke, *"A Mill Should Be Built Thereon": An Early History of Todmorden Mills* (Toronto: East York Historical Society, 1995), 22.

38 Smith, *Canada, Past, Present and Future*, 19–20. During the same winter that the Skinner brothers constructed their mill at Todmorden (on Lot 19, Concession II from the bay), William Berczy and a group of German immigrants from New York State established another sawmill (subsequently known as the "German Mills") further north, along a tributary of the east branch of the Don in Markham. It is difficult to say which mill was constructed first. ODPD, *Don Valley Conservation Report*, part 1: 70.

39 E.A Cruikshank, ed., "Simcoe Papers," *Ontario History* 26 (1930): 331, cited in Darke, *A Mill Should Be Built Thereon*, 28. Aaron Skinner sold his share in the mills to Isaiah and returned to Niagara in the summer of 1797. Darke, *A Mill Should Be Built Thereon*, 34.

40 Ian Wheal to A.E. Skinner, 25 January 1983, Skinner Family Records, Mixed Media Materials Relating to Toronto, file 3, series 1243, fonds 2, City of Toronto Archives (hereafter CTA).

41 William Lea, "The Valley of the Don," *Toronto Evening Telegram*, 4 February 1881.

42 Wheal to Skinner.

43 ODPD, *Don Valley Conservation Report*, part 1: 150.

44 Gary Miedema, "When the Rivers Really Ran: Water-Powered Industry in Toronto," in *HtO: Toronto's Water from Lake Iroquois to Lost Rivers to Low-Flow Toilets*, ed. Wayne Reeves and Christina Palassio (Toronto: Coach House Books, 2008), 68.

45 ODPD, *Don Valley Conservation Report*, part 1: 74; Adam, Mulvany, and Robinson, *History of Toronto and County of York*, 94.

46 Adam, Mulvany, and Robinson, *History of Toronto and County of York*, 94.

47 Most farmers followed customary practices of leaving small copses of trees on their holdings, particularly on hillsides, ravines, and along watercourses.

48 ODPD, *Don Valley Conservation Report*, part 1: 76–7, 165. Farmers typically cleared only one-third to one-half of their holdings in the 1840s and 50s; after 1865, they often cleared up to two-thirds of their land. By the end of the century, many properties in the watershed had been entirely cleared of their forest cover.

49 J. David Wood, *Making Ontario: Agricultural Colonization and Landscape Re-creation before the Railway* (Montreal and Kingston: McGill-Queen's University Press, 2000), 158.

50 ODPD, *Don Valley Conservation Report*, part 4: 3–4.

51 Robertson, *Robertson's Landmarks*, vol. 6: 212.

52 Scadding, *Toronto of Old*, 227.

53 Innis, *Mrs. Simcoe's Diary*, 111.

54 On the nostalgia associated with nineteenth-century mill sites, see Miedema, "When the Rivers Really Ran."

55 R. Peter Gillis, "Rivers of Sawdust: The Battle over Industrial Pollution in Canada, 1865–1903," *Journal of Canadian Studies* 21, no. 1 (1986): 85. See also Gilbert Allardyce, "'The Vexed Question of Sawdust': River Pollution in Nineteenth Century New Brunswick," *Dalhousie Review* 52, no. 2 (1972): 177–90.

56 Smith, *Canada, Past, Present and Future*, 20.

57 David Crombie, *Regeneration: Toronto's Waterfront and the Sustainable City. Final Report, Royal Commission on the Future of the Toronto Waterfront* (Ottawa: Minister of Supply and Services Canada, 1992), 234; C.R. Nash, Provincial biologist, Address to the Toronto Field Naturalists Club, 1924, cited in Charles Sauriol, *Remembering the Don: A Rare Record of Earlier Times within the Don River Valley* (Toronto: Consolidated Amethyst Communications, 1981), 92. By 1896, the native "land-locked" Atlantic salmon had completely disappeared from Lake Ontario and its tributary rivers and streams. See Margaret Beattie Bogue, *Fishing the Great Lakes: An Environmental History, 1783–1933* (Madison: University of Wisconsin Press, 2000).

58 Although steam was in use in both saw and grist mills by 1850, steam grist mills were still very rare until the 1870s. In sawmills, steam use was common by 1880. ODPD, *Don Valley Conservation Report*, part 1: 158–9.

59 Samuel Wilmot, letter 112, 12 February 1811, Correspondence and memoranda relating to surveys received by the Surveyor General, arranged by correspondent, vol. 35, RG 1-2-1, Archives of Ontario, cited in Isobel K. Ganton, "Development between Parliament Street and the Don River, 1793–1884," unpublished ms, 1974, p. 35, item 347, fonds 92, Papers and Theses Collection, CTA.

60 The park reserve was one of several government properties granted the trustees for capital-generating purposes. The trustees had the power to sell or lease portions of the land and direct the profits to the construction and maintenance of the York General Hospital. See C.K. Clarke, *A History of the Toronto General Hospital: Including an Account of the Medal of the Loyal and Patriotic Society of 1812* (Toronto: William Briggs, 1913), 34–5.

61 Ganton, "Development between Parliament Street and the Don River," 12; Clarke, *History of the Toronto General Hospital*.

62 Lots along King and Parliament Streets were quickest to sell. The only other major land purchase before 1830 was the Roman Catholic Church's

purchase in 1822 of two five-acre blocks east of Power Street and north of the first rank of lots on King Street. St Paul's Church, the first Roman Catholic Church in Toronto, was established on the site in the same year.

63 Justice William Dummer Powell, "Appeal for York General Hospital" [1824], reprinted in Firth, *The Town of York, 1815–1834*, 228–9.

64 Reprinted in Edith G. Firth, *The Town of York, 1793–1815: A Collection of Documents of Early Toronto* (Toronto: Champlain Society, 1962), 230.

65 The strain of malaria prevalent in early-nineteenth-century southern Ontario was less deadly than its tropical counterparts. As James L.A. Webb concludes, malaria lasted only a few generations in North America. The "principal and characteristic disease of the North American agricultural frontier," malarial infections receded as crop cover stabilized disturbed, logged-over soils and habitats for mosquito breeding decreased. *Humanity's Burden: A Global History of Malaria* (Cambridge and New York: Cambridge University Press, 2009), 5–6; 88–9.

66 Firth, *The Town of York, 1793–1815*, 242. In 1911, for example, the *Encyclopedia Britannica* defined malaria as "an Italian colloquial word (from mala, bad, and aria, air), introduced into English medical literature by MacCulloch (1827) as a substitute for the more restricted 'marsh miasm.'" The term was "generally applied to the definite unhealthy condition of body known by a variety of names, such as ague, intermittent (and remittent) fever, marsh fever, jungle fever, hill fever, 'fever of the country' and 'fever and ague.'" "Malaria," *Encyclopedia Britannica* (1911), vol. 17, p. 461, https://archive.org/details/EncyclopaediaBritannica1911HQDJVU (accessed 30 January 2014).

67 Sir Isaac Brock to James Green, 29 July 1803, reprinted in Firth, *The Town of York, 1793–1815*, 72.

68 Petition of Inhabitants of York, 11 February 1830, reprinted in Firth, *The Town of York, 1793–1815*, 30–1.

69 Conevery Bolton Valencius, *The Health of the Country: How American Settlers Understood Themselves and Their Land* (New York: Basic Books, 2002), 12.

70 Ibid., 89–90.

71 Ibid., 110–14. See also Martin V. Melosi, *The Sanitary City: Urban Infrastructure in America from Colonial Times to the Present* (Baltimore: Johns Hopkins University Press, 2000); Melosi, *Effluent America: Cities, Industry, Energy, and the Environment* (Pittsburgh, PA: University of Pittsburgh Press, 2001), 225–37; and Joel Tarr, *The Search for the Ultimate Sink: Urban Pollution in Historical Perspective* (Akron, OH: University of Akron Press, 1996), 342–3.

72 See also "Toronto General Hospital," *Upper Canada Journal of Medical, Surgical, and Physical Science* 3, no. 2 (1853): 69–77.

73 Lieutenant-Governor John Colborne to Viscount Goderich, 23 January 1833, reprinted in Firth, *The Town of York, 1793–1815*, 31–3.

74 Frederick H. Armstrong, *A City in the Making: Progress, People and Perils in Victorian Toronto* (Toronto: Dundurn, 1988), 17.

75 Ganton, "Development between Parliament Street and the Don River, 1793–1884," 35. The liberties stretched east of the river in a thin band from Queen Street south to the lakeshore all the way east to the east end of Ashbridge's Bay. Only by satisfying certain population and assessed property qualifications could areas within the liberties receive full city membership as annexations to existing wards or as wards of their own. In 1859 the liberties were abolished entirely, bringing full city rights and responsibilities to the suburban area west of the Don and east of the river south of Queen. Interestingly, the area of the "Don marshes" – south of King Street and west of the river – was left out of the 1859 incorporations, likely because of the area's long-established reputation for insalubriousness.

76 Property owners in the liberty east of Parliament enjoyed lower taxes from 1834 until the liberties were abolished in 1859. Properties east of the river north of Queen Street fell within county jurisdiction, with its lower taxes and fewer services, until Riverdale was annexed to the city in 1884.

77 Ontario Department of Planning and Development, *Don Valley Conservation Report*, part 1: 137.

78 Careless, *Toronto to 1918*, 138. Aggregate data from assessment rolls corroborate Careless's conclusions. Data compiled for the decades between 1870 and 1910 show that property values within the wards on either side of the river (St David's Ward, parts of St Lawrence's Ward, and, after 1884, St Matthew's Ward on the east side of the river) were consistently lower than wards with comparable populations in other parts of the city.

79 Ibid., 89–94.

2. Making an Industrial Margin

1 "Eastern Smells," anonymous letter to the editor, *Toronto Daily Globe*, 16 June 1874, 2.

2 City engineer E.H. Keating reported in 1892 that "the sewage discharged into [Ashbridge's] bay from a population of 9,500 persons comes in at the foot of Blong, Logan, Morse, Carlaw, Pape, Leslie, and like streets." *Rickey v. City of Toronto, Schofield-Holden Machine Co. v. City of Toronto* (1914), 30 OLR 523, 553.

3 Originally located on the west side of the river east of Trinity Street, the cattle sheds were relocated to vacant land east of the river and south of the

GTR line as part of an expansion of the distillery operations in 1866. Inge- .
nious in their efficiency, company owners constructed a pipeline alongside
the railway track to convey the grain swill from their Trinity Street distillery to the cattle sheds east of the river. Dianne Newell and Ralph Greenhill, *Survivals: Aspects of Industrial Archaeology in Ontario* (Erin, ON: Boston
Mills Press, 1989), 92.

4 Gene Desfor, "Planning Urban Waterfront Industrial Districts: Toronto's
Ashbridge's Bay, 1889–1910," *Urban History Review* 17, no. 2 (1988): 80.
Profits from cattle were derived from the lease of space, rather than from
the cattle themselves. Gooderham and Worts charged $20 per head per
season to feed and house cattle owned by various drovers between the
months of November and June. With space to accommodate 4,000 cows,
they produced an annual income of roughly $80,000. "The Smell at the
Don," *Toronto World*, 8 May 1884.

5 Gooderham and Worts, "Eastern Smells," letter to the editor, *Toronto Daily
Globe*, 10 June 1874, 2.

6 "Eastern Smells," anonymous letter to the editor, *Toronto Daily Globe*,
16 June 1874, 2. Signed, "Another 'Sufferer' who cannot go to a quiet
Watering-Place."

7 "Fragrance from the Don," *Grip*, 20 June 1874, reprinted in Isobel K. Ganton, "Development between Parliament Street and the Don River, 1793–
1884," unpublished ms, 1974, p. 56, item 347, fonds 92, Papers and Theses
Collection, CTA.

8 "Eastern Smells," 2.

9 Andrew Hurley, *Environmental Inequalities: Class, Race, and Industrial
Pollution in Gary, Indiana, 1945–1980* (Chapel Hill: University of North
Carolina Press, 1995); Ken Cruikshank and Nancy B. Bouchier, "Blighted
Areas and Obnoxious Industries: Constructing Environmental Inequality
on an Industrial Waterfront, Hamilton, Ontario, 1890–1960," *Environ-
mental History* 9, no. 3 (2004): 464–96; Martin V. Melosi, *Pollution and Reform
in American Cities, 1870–1930* (Austin and London: University of Texas
Press, 1980).

10 George H. Rust-D'Eye, *Cabbagetown Remembered* (Erin, ON: Boston Mills
Press, 1984).

11 Martin Melosi attributes this focus on smells to the equation of filth with
nuisance that persisted before widespread acceptance of bacteriological
theories of disease in the late nineteenth century. At a time when miasmas
and other sources of filth were perceived as sources of illness, pungent-
smelling or "bad air" carried for observers the direct threat of disease.
The Sanitary City: Urban Infrastructure in America from Colonial Times to the

Present (Baltimore: Johns Hopkins University Press, 2000), 77. See also Andrew Hurley, "Creating Ecological Wastelands: Oil Pollution in New York City, 1870–1900," *Journal of Urban History* 20, no. 3 (May 1994): 340–4.

12 Michèle Dagenais and Caroline Durand, "Cleansing, Draining and Sanitizing the City: Conceptions and Uses of Water in the Montreal Region," *Canadian Historical Review* 87, no. 4 (2006): 624. See also Arn Keeling, "Sink or Swim: Water Pollution and Environmental Politics in Vancouver, 1889–1975," *BC Studies* 142/143 (Summer/Autumn 2004): 72; Christopher Otter, "Cleansing and Clarifying: Technology and Perception in Nineteenth-Century London," *Journal of British Studies* 43, no. 1 (2004): 40–64.

13 Robert Lewis, *Manufacturing Montreal: The Making of an Industrial Landscape, 1850 to 1930* (Baltimore and London: Johns Hopkins University Press, 2000), 15.

14 W.S. and H.C. Boulton, *Atlas of the City of Toronto and Vicinity, 1858*, Toronto Reference Library Atlas Collection.

15 Lewis, *Manufacturing Montreal*, 261; Raphael Fischler, "Development Controls in Toronto in the Nineteenth Century," *Urban History Review* 36, no. 1 (2007): 16–31.

16 Fischler cites City of Toronto Bylaw No. 432 (1866), which prohibited the storage of more than ten barrels of petroleum and one barrel of benzine in the city centre. South of Front, east of Berkeley, west of Simcoe, and north of Bloor Street, these restrictions did not apply. *Bylaws of the City of Toronto, from the Date of its Incorporation in 1834, to the 13th January, 1890, Inclusive* (Toronto: Roswell and Hutchison, 1890), cited in Fischler, "Development Controls," 30n54.

17 The move was partly initiated due to pressure from the city, which purchased the former refinery site for the construction of the high-level rail bridge through the valley. Toronto City Council Proceedings (hereafter TCCP), 1890, Appendix, pp. 468–9. In 1927 the company merged with Frontenac Oil Refineries to become McColl-Frontenac Oil Company. It was later purchased by Texaco.

18 TCCP, 1852, Minute 17.

19 Lewis, *Manufacturing Montreal*, 20.

20 *Toronto Daily Globe*, 12 February 1866, 24 January 1867, cited in Susan Smith, "Industrial Development along the Banks of the Don River South of the Present Bloor-Danforth Thoroughfare from 1793–1911," course paper (Department of Geography, University of Toronto, 1994), 28; Toronto Historical Association, *A Glimpse of Toronto's History: Opportunities for the Commemoration of Lost Historic Sites* (Toronto: Toronto Historical Association, 2002), site no. 182.

21 Toronto Historical Association, *A Glimpse of Toronto's History*, site no. 188. In 1927, Davies's company amalgamated with the Harris Abbatoir Company to form Canada Packers. Operations were relocated to the two Harris abattoirs in West Toronto; the Davies plant on Front Street was sold and most of it demolished.

22 Theodore Steinberg, *Nature Incorporated: Industrialization and the Waters of New England* (Cambridge and New York: Cambridge University Press, 1991), 209.

23 In his inaugural address to council on 16 January 1888, Mayor Edward F. Clarke referred to the "projected construction" of the Rosedale Creek Sewer running from Tannery Hollow on Yonge Street into the Don River. Toronto City Council Proceedings (hereafter TCCP), 1888, Appendix, p. 1.

24 W.T. Jennings, city engineer, *Report on the Disposal of the Sewage of the City of Toronto* (Toronto: J.Y. Reid, 1890), 5; *Two Reports on Sewage and Garbage in the City of Toronto*, file 72, series 654, fonds 70, Larry Becker Fonds, CTA.

25 Between 1871 and 1881, Toronto's population increased from 56,092 to 86,415. By the end of the following decade, immigration and the annexation of adjacent areas more than doubled the city's population to 181,120. Heather A. MacDougall, "Public Health in Toronto's Municipal Politics: The Canniff Years, 1883–1890," *Bulletin of the History of Medicine* 55, no. 2 (1981): 187.

26 Catherine Brace notes that typhoid fever persisted through the 1880s and 90s, with an average of 200–300 cases per year. Typhoid incidence rose dramatically to 900 cases in 1890 when a pile was driven through a water conduit in August of that year, exposing the water to contamination from the bay. "One Hundred and Twenty Years of Sewerage: The Provision of Sewers in Toronto 1793–1913" (MA thesis, University of Toronto, Department of Geography, 1993), 132–4. On the history of cholera in Toronto, see Paul S.B. Jackson, "From Liability to Profitability: How Disease, Fear, and Medical Science Cleaned Up the Marshes of Ashbridge's Bay," in *Reshaping Toronto's Waterfront* (Toronto: University of Toronto Press, 2011), 75–96.

27 Between 1874 and 1883, homes with piped water increased from 1,375 to 16,000. J.M.S. Careless, *Toronto to 1918: An Illustrated History* (Toronto: James Lorimer, 1984), 101.

28 See, for example, MacDougall, "Public Health in Toronto's Municipal Politics"; Heather A. MacDougall, "The Genesis of Public Health Reform in Toronto, 1869–1890," *Urban History Review* 10, no. 3 (February 1982): 1–9; Careless, *Toronto to 1918*; Elwood Jones and Douglas McCalla, "Toronto Waterworks, 1840–77: Continuity and Change in Nineteenth-Century Toronto Politics," *Canadian Historical Review* 60, no. 3 (1979): 300–23.

29 Wayne C. Reeves, *Visions for the Metropolitan Toronto Waterfront, 1: Toward Comprehensive Planning, 1852–1935*, Major Report No. 27 (Department of Geography, University of Toronto, December 1992), 36.

30 Careless, *Toronto to 1918*, 144.

31 Ice cutting in these locations was prohibited except for industrial cooling purposes. Norman Allen, *Report on the Sanitary Condition of the City of Toronto*, 1892, pp. 33–4, file 6, series 365, Department of Public Health Reports, CTA; Robert Wilson, *A Retrospect: A Short Review of the Steps Taken in Sanitation to Transform the Town of Muddy York into the Queen City of the West*, 1934, file 46, series 365, Department of Public Health Reports, 1885–1995, Former City of Toronto Fonds, CTA.

32 Careless, *Toronto to 1918*, 145.

33 As Reeves notes, Toronto City Council commissioned and then ignored no less than twelve expert reports on sewage disposal between 1873 and 1909. *Visions*, 1: 37.

34 Joel Tarr, *The Search for the Ultimate Sink: Urban Pollution in Historical Perspective* (Akron, OH: University of Akron Press, 1996), xlii. See also Christopher Hamlin, *A Science of Impurity: Water Analysis in Nineteenth Century Britain* (Bristol: Adam Hilger, 1990), and *Public Health and Social Justice in the Age of Chadwick: Britain, 1800–1854* (Cambridge and New York: Cambridge University Press, 1998).

35 Coverage in the *Toronto World*, for example, portrayed the distillery in generally sympathetic terms, noting with a certain home-town pride Gooderham and Worts's status as "the largest [distillery] in the world" and the "largest concern in the city." With "a capital of $1,600,000," one reporter concluded, the company "pays into the inland revenue of the Dominion $2,000,000 a year, and is one of the best managed businesses in America." "The Smell at the Don," 8 May 1884.

36 Ibid.

37 William Canniff, *Annual Report of the Medical Health Officer*, 15 November 1889, TCCP, Appendix, p. 1765.

38 *Toronto World*, "The Smell at the Don," 8 May 1884.

39 *Toronto World*, "The Don Cattle Byres," 13 May 1884, 3.

40 These industries included, among others, Gooderham and Worts Distillery, Morrison, Taylor and Co. soap works, Bickell and Wickett tannery on Don, Lawrence Foundry Co., Consumers' Gas Co., Don Brewery, and Copland Brewing and Malting Co.

41 For a compelling examination of the historical processes involved in creating landscapes of risk, see Ellen Stroud, "Troubled Waters in Ecotopia: Environmental Racism in Portland, Oregon," *Radical History Review* 74 (1999): 65–95.

42 *Attorney-General v. Gooderham & Worts et al.* (1884), 10 P.R.U.C., 259. Jeffrey Stinson notes that no evidence exists that the terms of the settlement were fulfilled. *The Heritage of the Port Industrial District* (Toronto: Toronto Harbour Commissioners, 1990), 18.

43 *Report of the City Commissioner*, TCCP, 1888, Appendix, pp. 1488–9; Report No. 33 of the Executive Committee, 4 October 1888, TCCP, Appendix, p. 2019.

44 The local Board of Health reported in December 1888 on "the very satisfactory completion of the work of making a cut at the east end of Ashbridge's Bay ... Already a very gratifying improvement in the condition of the water of the said Bay can be perceived, and your Board believe that by the opening of spring, the place and its surroundings will be in a first-class sanitary condition." *Report No. 8 of the Local Board of Health*, 14 December 1888, TCCP, Appendix, p. 1994.

45 Allen, *Report on the Sanitary Condition of the City of Toronto.*

46 Ibid., 17.

47 TCCP, 1892, Minute 676.

48 Desfor, "Planning Urban Waterfront Industrial Districts," 83.

49 *Report No. 10 of the Local Board of Health*, TCCP, 1892, Appendix A, pp. 325–6; Jamie Benidickson, "Ontario Water Quality, Public Health, and the Law, 1880–1930," in *Essays in the History of Canadian Law*, ed. G. Blaine Baker and Jim Phillips (Toronto: University of Toronto Press, 1999), 120.

50 TCCP, 1892, Minute 721, Appendix A, pp. 484, 569; Desfor, "Planning Urban Waterfront Industrial Districts," 83.

51 Message from Mayor Robert J. Fleming, 26 September 1892, TCCP, Appendix C, p. 511. The pending lawsuits that Fleming referred to may have included the Coleman case, a negligence claim against the city for allowing the condition of Ashbridge's Bay to deteriorate (*Coleman v. City of Toronto* [1893], 23 OR 345), and a June 1892 letter from the solicitors of area landowner James Murphy threatening proceedings against the city unless immediate steps were taken to improve the sanitary condition of the bay (TCCP, 1892, Minutes 576, 638, 842).

52 Keating's Plan is the subject of further discussion in chapter 3. See also Desfor, "Planning Urban Waterfront Industrial Districts," 84–5; Stinson, *The Heritage of the Port Industrial District*, 21.

53 *City Engineer's Report*, 12 November 1892, TCCP, 1892, Appendix A, pp. 568–71.

54 *Rickey v. City of Toronto*, 550–3. Progress on the Keating Plan allowed the city to sidestep the terms of the 1892 injunction requiring them to cease depositing sewage into Ashbridge's Bay. At a hearing 5 May 1893, enforcement of the judgment was suspended; a progress report from the city

engineer to trial judge Justice Rose in July 1894 "practically ended ... the suit." Despite Keating's assurances, however, sewage pollution would persist in Ashbridge's Bay until a trunk sewer was finally constructed in the early 1910s.

55 Stinson, *The Heritage of the Port Industrial District*, 57.

56 *Coleman v. City of Toronto.*

57 *Rickey v. City of Toronto.* For a more detailed discussion of the Schofield case, see Benidickson, "Ontario Water Quality," 120–1.

58 The 1908 by-law authorized the city to raise $2,400,000 for the "construction of intercepting sewers and a sewage disposal plant and $750,000 for the construction of a water filtration plant." TCCP, 1918, Minutes 218, 434.

59 Careless, *Toronto to 1918*, 187.

60 Tarr, *The Search for the Ultimate Sink*, xxi. Michèle Dagenais and Caroline Durand, in their examination of the development of urban wastewater systems in late-nineteenth and early-twentieth-century Montreal, point out the striking similarities of the discourse and the solutions adopted in Montreal with those of other Canadian and American centres in the same period. This similarity, they argue, "attests to the extensive circulation of people and ideas in the period, as well as to the international scope of the question of water." "Cleansing, Draining and Sanitizing," 649. See also Sarah S. Elkind, *Bay Cities and Water Politics: The Battle for Resources in Boston and Oakland* (Lawrence: University Press of Kansas, 1998).

3. Taming a "Monster of Ingratitude"

1 *Toronto Mail and Empire*, 13 February 1895, 19–20, folder 2, box 7, SC 26/2, Vaughan Roberts Papers, Special Collections, Toronto Port Authority Archives (hereafter TPAA).

2 ODPD, *Don Valley Conservation Report*, part 4: 3–4.

3 Hugh Richardson, "York Harbour," in Department of Public Works, *Memorandum with Accompanying Plans and Documents Relative to the Past and Present State of the Harbour of Toronto* (Ottawa: Department of Public Works, 1881), Appendix, 3–10.

4 H. Richardson, W. Chisholm, and J.G. Chewett, *Report of the Select Committee on the Improvement of the Harbour of York*, in ibid., 1–3.

5 W. Hamilton Merritt, "Letter to J.G. Bowes," *Toronto Patriot*, 31 March 1853, reprinted in Department of Public Works, *Memorandum* (Ottawa: Department of Public Works, 1881), 92.

6 While Tully stressed the detrimental effects of the eastern gap upon the harbour and recommended efforts to shore up the narrows in the peninsula, Fleming argued that a permanent opening would accommodate

shipping interests and cleanse the harbour of impurities, and Hind argued that sediment action would mend the gap without any necessary intervention. Toronto Harbour Commissioners, "Reports on the Improvement and Preservation of Toronto Harbour," *Supplement to the Canadian Journal* (1854): 37.

7   Ibid., 38.

8   "The Island Hotel Washed Away," *Toronto Globe*, 14 April 1858, 3; Toronto Harbour Commissioners, *Toronto Harbour: The Passing Years* (Toronto: Toronto Harbour Commissioners, 1985), 11. Once formed, the gap continued to widen until it was permanently reinforced with groynes in the early 1890s.

9   *Report of the Harbour Master*, 18 May 1858, cited in Speight and Van Nostrand, "The Old Don Channel," 11, folder 23, box 262, RG 3/3, TPAA.

10   *Report of the Harbour Master, 1862*, reprinted in Department of Public Works, *Memorandum*, 104.

11   These plans are referenced on Wadsworth and Unwin's 1878 map of the city and in the Report of the Harbour Master, 2 January 1871, cited in Speight and Van Nostrand, "The Old Don Channel," 14.

12   Jeffrey Stinson, *The Heritage of the Port Industrial District* (Toronto: Toronto Harbour Commissioners, 1990), 56.

13   James B. Eads, *Report on Toronto Harbour, Ontario, 1882*, 4 March 1882, 13–14, folder 1, box 1, SC 11, Booklet and Pamphlet Collection, Special Collections, TPAA.

14   Stinson, *The Heritage of the Port Industrial District*, 9.

15   James G. Worts, *Report to the Mayor and Council of the City of Toronto*, 25 February 1878, Harbour Trust Papers, 1851–1911, Board of the Toronto Harbour Commissioners, folder 1, box 3, RG 1/4, TPAA.

16   ODPD, *Don Valley Conservation Report*, part 4: 4.

17   Ibid.

18   *York Gazette*, 23 July 1808, cited in John Ross Robertson, *Robertson's Landmarks of Toronto: A Collection of Historical Sketches of the Old Town of York from 1792 until 1833, and of Toronto from 1834 to 1893* (Toronto: J. Ross Robertson, 1894), vol. 6: 357.

19   With the growing availability of provincial and overseas news after 1820, Toronto newspapers included fewer references to local news items "which could be circulated by word of mouth." After 1840 newspapers began to increase in volume and frequency, allowing greater space for regional issues. Reports of local floods became more frequent after 1850, but even still, years reputed as "bad flood years" for the province as a whole often failed to generate reports of flooding in the Toronto area. These

discrepancies may be due more to a lack of interest in local issues than an absence of flooding in the city. ODPD, *Don Valley Conservation Report*, part 4: 7.

20 *Toronto Globe*, 6 April 1850, cited in ODPD, *Don Valley Conservation Report*, part 4: 8–9.
21 *Toronto Globe*, "The Great Rainstorm," 14 September 1878, 8.
22 Ibid.
23 Ibid.
24 *Toronto Globe*, "The Great Rain Storm," 16 September 1878, 1.
25 Ibid.
26 ODPD, *Don Valley Conservation Report*, part 4: 14.
27 As historical geographer James O'Mara has observed, the Harbour Trust, created in 1850 to administer port activities on the waterfront, "[ceased to make] any positive contributions to the improvement of the harbour before the turn of the century." The Trust's lack of capital and borrowing power, combined with chronic internal dissension and the city's reluctance to surrender adequate power, crippled it from the beginning. "Shaping Urban Waterfronts: The Role of Toronto's Harbour Commissioners, 1911–1960," discussion paper, Department of Geography, York University, 1976, 14–17.
28 Mayor's Inaugural Address, TCCP, 1889, Appendix, 14–15.
29 *Toronto Globe*, "The Don River," 10 October 1881, 7.
30 *Report No. 56 of the Committee on Works*, TCCP, 1881, Appendix, 888–90.
31 TCCP, 1881, Minutes 1026, 1043, 1246.
32 Armstrong and Cook, "Choice Building Lots for Sale, Registered Plan No. 709," 1 November 1887, Registered Plans Book "9," Speight, Van Nostrand and Gibson Ltd. Fonds, item 32, file 6, series 343, fonds 79, CTA.
33 Familiar success stories from other jurisdictions included Long Island New York's Newtown Creek and Cleveland's Cuyahoga River, transformed with retaining walls and regular dredging into commercial waterways in the latter half of the nineteenth century.
34 TCCP, 1880, Minutes 11, 116, 189.
35 TCCP, 1881, Appendix, 1–10.
36 *Toronto Globe*, "The Don," 8 January 1881, clipping from Vaughan Roberts Papers.
37 *Toronto Globe*, "Don River Improvement," 19 February 1881, 9.
38 The *Toronto Globe* estimated present land values at five or six dollars a foot, figures that would expand to "$30, $40, or $60 a foot ... by reason of the improvements." "The Don River," 10 October 1881, 7.
39 TCCP, 1881, Minute 362.
40 *Toronto Globe*, "The Don River," 10 October 1881, 7.

41 Ibid.
42 Ibid.
43 TCCP, 1881, Minute 1246.
44 Frances N. Mellen, "The Development of the Toronto Waterfront during the Railway Expansion Era, 1850–1912" (PhD dissertation, University of Toronto, Department of Geography, 1974), 167, 178; TCCP, 1888, Appendix, 4–5. Howland made an agreement with the CPR by which they were to run tracks down the west bank of the improvement and pay an annual rental fee to the city for the privilege.
45 John R. Stilgoe, *Metropolitan Corridor: Railroads and the American Scene* (New Haven and London: Yale University Press, 1983).
46 Council received the approval of the Ontario Legislature on 25 March 1886, in An Act respecting the River Don Improvements (Statutes of Ontario, Act 49 Vic., cap. 66); the act was passed subject to the approval of the eligible electors of the city of Toronto (TCCP, 1886, Minute 927).
47 TCCP, 1886, Minute 927; *Report of the City Engineer*, 17 August 1886, TCCP, Appendix, 547–9.
48 *Report of the City Clerk to the City of Toronto Council*, 21 September 1886, TCCP, Appendix, 809–10.
49 By-Law No. 1767, To authorize the straightening and improvement of the River Don, TCCP, 1886, Minute 1006.
50 TCCP, 1888, Appendix, 4–5.
51 *Toronto Globe*, "A Scene at the Don," 14 July 1887, 5.
52 By-Law 2184, to authorize the City Treasurer to borrow a sum not exceeding $150,000, for the purpose of carrying on the Don Improvements, passed 12 November 1888, TCCP, Appendix, 1756–66.
53 Land purchases were expected to cost more than double the original estimate of $75,000; tenders had run $20,000 over budget and bridge construction $50,000 over budget. Mayor's Inaugural Address, TCCP, 1889, Appendix, 14–15.
54 The CPR's claim to exclusive use contradicted the terms of Don Improvement Act, which "distinctly [stipulated] that the railway reserves on both sides of the Don Improvement shall be used upon equal terms upon all railways in common, and that no company [was] to have the exclusive use of them" (Letter from Mayor E.F. Clarke to Toronto City Council, 25 February 1889, Don Improvement Committee Communications, 1889, file 1, series 907, CTA. Reprinted in TCCP, 1889, Appendix, 168–9). In response, the CPR threatened to exercise its power under the Dominion Railway Act to expropriate lands required for railway purposes along the Improvement. The 1890 Privy Council ruling granted overall control of the timetables and

management of the two tracks to the CPR. Tracks could be used by other railways provided "periodical compensation" were made to the CPR, which would hold responsibility for regular maintenance of the tracks and any associated improvement costs (*Report of the Joint Special Committee re: Esplanade and Don Improvements*, 25 July 1890, TCCP, Appendix, 1497–1504).

55 TCCP, 1885, Appendix, 918.

56 *Report No. 25 of the Committee on Works*, 3 November 1887, TCCP, Appendix, 1311–12; *Report No. 30 of the Committee on Works*, 10 January 1889, TCCP, 1888, Appendix, 2071.

57 *Report of the City Engineer*, 15 August 1888, TCCP, Appendix, 1505–7; Mayor's Inaugural Address, TCCP, 1889, Appendix, 14–15. In an attempt to contain these costs, the city twice amended the original by-law to reduce the amount of land required for the improvement. See By-Law No. 1774, A By-law to take lands required for straightening and improving the River Don, passed 27 September 1886 (TCCP, 1886, Minute 1007); By-Law 1803, To repeal By Law No. 1774, entitled, "A By-Law to take lands for straightening and improving the River Don," and enact a new By-law in lieu thereof, taking a less quantity of land, passed 12 April 1887 (TCCP, 1887, Minute 385); and By-Law No. 2005, A By-law to repeal By-law No.1803, respecting lands taken for straightening and improving the River Don, and to make other provisions in lieu thereof, passed 7 May 1888.

58 These demands were especially frequent through the winter of 1885, when a series of letters from Toronto residents urged council to act expediently in initiating the Don Improvement Project as a method of unemployment relief. TCCP, 1885, Minutes 809, 845, 873, 879.

59 TCCP, 1887, Appendix, 66–8. The *Engineer's Annual Report* for 1887 reported that a total of $3,314.69 was spent on employing the "unemployed poor" to work on the gaol hill cutting in 1887.

60 TCCP, 1887, Minute 484; *Report No. 31 of the Committee on Works*, TCCP, 1887, Appendix, 1090; *Annual Report for the City Engineer*, 1887, TCCP, 1888, Appendix, 1896–8.

61 *Report of the City Engineer*, 15 August 1888, TCCP, Appendix, 1505–6. "Cribbing" referred to the practice of reinforcing the vertical cedar piles with horizontal planks of wood, a more elaborate and consequently more expensive procedure than simply "piling" the channel.

62 Mayor's Inaugural Address, 1889, TCCP, Appendix, 14–15.

63 *Toronto Mail and Empire*, 12 February 1902, reprinted in Vaughan Roberts Papers, p. 22.

64 Kivas Tully, "Toronto Harbour," letter to the editor, *Toronto Patriot*, 10 February 1853.

65 *Toronto Globe*, 8 May 1883, reprinted in Vaughan Roberts Papers, p. 15; TCCP, 1883, Minute 569; "Toronto Harbour Works: Specifications for dredging the proposed cut from the River Don to Ashbridge's Bay," 11 June 1883, "Keating Channel File," Researcher Reference Files, TPAA.
66 *Toronto Mail and Empire*, 13 February 1885, reprinted in Vaughan Roberts Papers, p. 19. For an excellent overview of the negotiations and false starts in pursuing the Don Diversion, see Michael Moir, "Historical Development of Keating Channel," letter to Dennis Lang, Director of Engineering, Toronto Port Authority, 16 March 1990, file No. 570-D-2, "Keating Channel File," TPAA.
67 *City Engineer's Report*, 12 November 1892, TCCP, 1892, Appendix A, 568–71.
68 Stinson, *The Heritage of the Port Industrial District*, 57.
69 *Toronto Globe*, "A Suit Threatened," 3 May 1897, 6.
70 Kivas Tully, "Toronto Harbour Works," 1898, Records Department Inventory, Records Department Fonds, folder 1, box 105, RG 3/3, TPAA.
71 *Annual Report of the Harbour Master, 1904*, Harbour Trust Papers, 1851–1911, Board of the Toronto Harbour Commissioners, vol. 1, box 4, RG 1/4, TPAA.
72 By-law No. 4821 for the Straightening of the River Don, TCCP, 1906, Appendix B, 559. Council passed the by-law 10 December 1906 (TCCP, 1906, Minute 801).
73 *Toronto Evening Telegram*, 1 September 1906, 19 June 1909, 15 July 1909, reprinted in Vaughan Roberts Papers, pp. 26–7.
74 Continuing problems with the Don and Ashbridge's Bay and concerns about the deterioration of port facilities led to the establishment of the Toronto Harbour Commissioners (THC) by a federal act of Parliament in 1911. Unlike the earlier Toronto Harbour Trust, the THC was granted significant power, together with 1,285 acres of marshland in Ashbridge's Bay and a broad mandate to improve the Toronto waterfront (Stinson, *The Heritage of the Port Industrial District*, 22). The agency was governed by a five-member board, three of whom were city councillors.
75 The second alternative, estimated at $626,000, would cost $360,000 more than the first alternative priced at $266,000. E.L. Cousins to Board of the Toronto Harbour Commissioners, 3 September 1912, "Keating Channel File," Researcher Reference Files, TPAA. No minutes exist of the discussion that led to the decision to adopt the second alternative.
76 British American Oil first recorded their objection to the proposed Don alignment in January 1913; by June of that year they had proposed an alternate alignment for the river, and in early July Cousins reported that

a "compromise plan ... had been arrived at as a result of his conference with the representatives of the company." Minutes 401, 673, and 702, 1913, Board of the Toronto Harbour Commissioners, RG 1/1, TPAA.

77 Toronto Harbour Commissioners, *Annual Report of the Toronto Harbor Commissioners for the Years 1915 and 1916* (Toronto: Toronto Harbor Commissioners, 1917); Stinson, *The Heritage of the Port Industrial District*, 57. Backfilling of the former river channel and Keating's 1893 "Cut" from the harbour to Ashbridge's Bay continued into the early 1920s.

78 *Toronto Globe*, "Notes and Comments," 4 February 1897, 6.

79 An agreement on rental rates was reached in 1895. As Mellen shows, however, conflict persisted when the CPR failed to pay the agreed rental rates in the years that followed. Mellen, "The Development of the Toronto Waterfront," 202.

80 Swing bridges were originally planned for the GTR crossing south of Eastern Avenue and the Queen Street crossing. They were abandoned due to the extra costs involved and the unwillingness of the GTR to share expenses.

81 *Toronto Mail and Empire*, 12 February 1902.

82 *Toronto Mail*, 20 March 1894, reprinted in Vaughan Roberts Papers, pp. 18–19.

83 Catherine Brace, "One Hundred and Twenty Years of Sewerage: The Provision of Sewers in Toronto 1793–1913" (MA thesis, University of Toronto, Department of Geography, 1993), 132.

84 *Toronto Mail and Empire*, 1 March 1902.

85 *Toronto Mail and Empire*, 6 April 1912, cited in ODPD, part 4: 15.

86 Significant floods in the valley were also reported in 1914, 1918, 1920, 1927, 1936, 1942, and 1948 (ODPD, part 4: 17).

87 Toronto Waterfront Revitalization Corporation and Toronto and Region Conservation Authority, "Don Mouth Naturalization and Port Lands Flood Protection Project: Revised Terms of Reference," June 2006, 31. Each year, the Toronto Port Authority removes approximately 35,000 cubic metres (59,500 tonnes) of sediment from the Keating Channel, and an additional 400 tonnes of debris. Collected sediments are then deposited in underwater containment cells at Tommy Thompson Park (Leslie Street Spit).

88 George H. Rust-D'Eye, *Cabbagetown Remembered* (Erin, ON: Boston Mills Press, 1984), 91.

89 *Rickey v. City of Toronto*. The case was settled in favour of the defendants, who were ordered to pay the plaintiffs $38,000 to purchase their property and settle their claims, and to grant temporary access to the lake via Coatsworth Cut at the east end of Ashbridge's Bay.

90 For an overview of sewerage developments in Toronto, see Wayne C. Reeves, *Visions for the Metropolitan Toronto Waterfront, 1: Toward Comprehensive Planning, 1852–1935*, Major Report No. 27 (Department of Geography, University of Toronto, December 1992) 36–44.

91 As Catherine Brace has shown, beleaguered budgets, competing expert opinions on disease etiology and sewage management, and a lack of public support all contributed to the city's reluctance to act on the sewage issue in nineteenth-century Toronto. The Toronto electorate turned down trunk sewer proposals three times between 1850 and 1907 before finally approving plans for a trunk sewer and sewage treatment plant in 1908. "One Hundred and Twenty Years of Sewerage," 147, 153; "Public Works in the Canadian City: The Provision of Sewers in Toronto 1870–1913," *Urban History Review* 23, no. 2 (1995): 40–1.

4. Refuge and Subsistence in an Urban Borderland

1 Henry Scadding, *Toronto of Old: Collections and Recollections Illustrative of the Early Settlement and Social Life of the Capital of Ontario* (Toronto: Adam, Stevenson, 1873), 228–9.

2 Isobel K. Ganton, "Development between Parliament Street and the Don River, 1793–1884," unpublished ms, 1974, pp. 49-50, item 347, fonds 92, Papers and Theses Collection, City of Toronto Archives (CTA).

3 Paul Underwood Kellogg, *The Pittsburgh Survey: Findings in Six Volumes* (New York: New York Charities Publication Committee, 1914). References to Skunk Hollow and the Bohemian Flats were obtained from a conversation thread initiated on H-Environment, 21 March 2008.

4 Nancy B. Bouchier and Ken Cruikshank, "The War on the Squatters, 1920–1940: Hamilton's Boathouse Community and the Re-Creation of Recreation on Burlington Bay," *Labour/Le Travail* 51 (2003): 9–46; Ken Cruikshank and Nancy B. Bouchier, "Blighted Areas and Obnoxious Industries: Constructing Environmental Inequality on an Industrial Waterfront, Hamilton, Ontario, 1890–1960," *Environmental History* 9, no. 3 (2004): 464–96.

5 See, for example, Robert Bullard, *Dumping in Dixie: Race, Class and Environmental Quality* (Boulder, CO: Westview Press, 1990); Andrew Hurley, *Environmental Inequalities: Class, Race, and Industrial Pollution in Gary, Indiana, 1945–1980* (Chapel Hill: University of North Carolina Press, 1995); Harold L. Platt, *Shock Cities: The Environmental Transformation and Reform of Manchester and Chicago* (Chicago: University of Chicago Press, 2005).

6 Todd McCallum's work on Depression-era hoboes in Vancouver describes the establishment of a hobo jungle in a derelict area of Vancouver's

waterfront but doesn't explore the connection between marginal space and the marginalized populations that congregated there. "Still Raining, Market Still Rotten: Homeless Men and the Early Years of the Great Depression in Vancouver" (PhD dissertation, Department of History, Queen's University, 2004); "The Great Depression's First History? The Vancouver Archives of Major J.S. Matthews and the Writing of Hobo History," *Canadian Historical Review* 87, no. 1 (2006): 79–107. Similarly, Jill Wade's excellent 1997 article on marginal housing in Vancouver describes squatters living on polluted foreshore lands along Burrard Inlet, False Creek, and the Fraser River but doesn't explore how and why such places were constructed as marginal. "Home or Homelessness? Marginal Housing in Vancouver, 1886–1950," *Urban History Review* 25, no. 2 (1997): 19–29.

7 Valerie L. Kuletz, *The Tainted Desert: Environmental and Social Ruin in the American West* (New York and London: Routledge, 1998), 8, 120.

8 Kay J. Anderson, *Vancouver's Chinatown: Racial Discourse in Canada, 1875–1980* (Montreal and Kingston: McGill-Queen's University Press, 1991). Susan Craddock shows similar dynamics at work in *City Of Plagues: Disease, Poverty, and Deviance in San Francisco* (Minneapolis: University of Minnesota Press, 2000).

9 Felix Driver points to similar associations of marshy low areas with disease and moral depravity in "Moral Geographies: Social Science and the Urban Environment in Mid-Nineteenth Century England," *Transactions of the Institute of British Geographers* 13, no. 3 (1 January 1988): 281, doi:10.2307/622991. On the concept of moral geographies, see also Miles Ogborn and Chris Philo, "Soldiers, Sailors and Moral Locations in Nineteenth-Century Portsmouth," *Area* 26, no. 3 (1 September 1994): 221–31, doi:10.2307/20003452; Teresa Ploszajska, "Moral Landscapes and Manipulated Spaces: Gender, Class and Space in Victorian Reformatory Schools," *Journal of Historical Geography* 20, no. 4 (1994): 413–29.

10 C.K. Clarke, *A History of the Toronto General Hospital: Including an Account of the Medal of the Loyal and Patriotic Society of 1812* (Toronto: William Briggs, 1913), 63. Clarke suggests that the roughly £800 derived annually from the leases fell somewhat short of expectations.

11 Editorial, "Toronto General Hospital," *Upper Canada Journal of Medical, Surgical and Physical Science* 3, no. 2 (1853): 69–70.

12 *Toronto Leader*, 10 August 1853. Reprinted in Clarke, *History of the Toronto General Hospital*, 66–70.

13 In the years that followed, medical schools were constructed near the hospital and Canada's second school of nursing opened on the premises. Toronto Historical Association, *A Glimpse of Toronto's History*, site no. 142.

For a comprehensive history see J.T.H. Connor, *Doing Good: The Life of Toronto's General Hospital* (Toronto: University of Toronto Press, 2000).

14 Communication from Mayor Adam Wilson to City Council, 3 October 1859, TCCP, Appendix no. 1, 459–61. The Magdalens profited from the city's purchase of the Scadding property east of the Don, negotiating a lease of the land immediately north of the proposed jail site for 999 years at a rate of one penny per year. *Report No. 4*, Standing Committee on Police and Prisons, 8 June 1857, TCCP, Minute 396.

15 A considerable literature exists on urban elite assessments of rural places and populations that shares much in common with perceptions of these "in-between" spaces at the city's edge. See, for example, R.W. Sandwell, "Introduction: Finding Rural British Columbia," in *Beyond the City Limits: Rural History in British Columbia*, ed. R.W. Sandwell (Vancouver: UBC Press, 1999), 3–14; Richard White, "Poor Men on Poor Lands: The Back-to-the-Land Movement of the Early Twentieth Century – A Case Study," *Pacific Historical Review* 49 (1980): 105–31; Ian McKay, *The Quest of the Folk: Antimodernism and Cultural Selection in Twentieth-Century Nova Scotia* (Montreal and Kingston: McGill-Queen's University Press, 1994); Raymond Williams, *The Country and the City* (New York and Oxford: Oxford University Press, 1973).

16 *Report of the Select Committee appointed to investigate matters connected with the new Jail and Industrial Farm*, 13 December 1858, TCCP, Minute 471.

17 *Report No. 4, Standing Committee on Police Prisons &c.*, 9 April 1856, TCCP, Minute 229.

18 *Report No. 11, Standing Committee on Police Prisons &c.*, 27 October 1856, TCCP, Minute 683. Negotiations resulted in a final sale of 119 acres of the original 135-acre allotment for the agreed sum of £10,000, funds for which were appropriated from the city's portion of the Clergy Reserve Fund (Minute 826, 12 January 1857).

19 Standing Committee on Finance and Assessment, *Report No. 14*, 5 October 1857, TCCP, Minute 654. The committee report refers to a sum of £9,000 "placed to the credit of the Jail and Industrial Farm account" in 1856, which, they add, "will be altogether insufficient for the purpose specified." By 1857, the Jail account had been completely drained, its funds "appropriated for Sewers and other works already started."

20 *Report of the Select Committee to investigate matters connected with the new Jail and Industrial Farm*, 13 December 1858, TCCP, Minute 471.

21 TCCP, 1859, Appendix 1, 199–200.

22 TCCP, 1859, Appendix 3, 377–80.

23 Riverdale Park was established on the former grounds of the industrial farm, spanning both sides of the valley, in 1880.

24 References to relative land values can be found in Ganton, "Development between Parliament Street and the Don River," 4; and J.M.S. Careless, *Toronto to 1918: An Illustrated History* (Toronto: James Lorimer, 1984), 96.

25 Ogborn and Philo ("Soldiers, Sailors and Moral Locations") document similar tendencies at work in locating social institutions in what were considered to be "moral locations" within nineteenth-century Portsmouth, England. James E. Moran corroborates this in his work on lunatic asylums in Ontario in the same period, arguing that asylums were "strategically located in an area that would promote the health of the patients, with soothing panoramic views and access to fresh water." *Committed to the State Asylum: Insanity and Society in Nineteenth-Century Quebec and Ontario* (Montreal and Kingston: McGill-Queen's University Press, 2001), 84.

26 John Ross Robertson, *Robertson's Landmarks of Toronto: A Collection of Historical Sketches of the Old Town of York from 1792 until 1833, and of Toronto from 1834 to 1893* (Toronto: J. Ross Robertson, 1894), 1: 194–5.

27 The Scadding homestead persisted on the site until much later in the century, but it is unclear to what extent the site was actively farmed after Scadding senior's death in 1824.

28 Williams, *The Country and the City*.

29 For further discussion of prisons and moral reform, see C.J. Taylor, "The Kingston, Ontario Penitentiary and Moral Architecture," *Histoire Sociale / Social History* 12 (1979): 385–407; and Peter Oliver, *"Terror to Evil-Doers": Prisons and Punishments in Nineteenth-Century Ontario* (Toronto: University of Toronto Press, 1998).

30 Williams, *The Country and the City*, 1. See also R.W. Sandwell, *Beyond the City Limits: Rural History in British Columbia* (Vancouver: UBC Press, 1999).

31 *Might's Greater Toronto City Directory, 1900–40* (Toronto: Might Directories). Known as the Swiss Cottage Hospital, it cared for patients with infectious diseases at a location on Winchester Street adjacent to the Don from 1904 to 1930.

32 "Toronto Brick Company, Don Valley, Toronto, Ontario," RG27, vol. 954, files 14–16, LAC.

33 Helen Boritch, "The Making of Toronto the Good: The Organization of Policing and Production of Arrests, 1859 to 1955" (PhD dissertation, University of Toronto, Department of Sociology, 1985), 81–2; Sara Beattie and Amy Mole, *Police Resources in Canada, 2007* (Ottawa: Statistics Canada, 2007), 32.

34 Boritch, "The Making of Toronto the Good," 5–6. Peter Vronsky, doctoral candidate in history, University of Toronto, personal communication, 27 July 2008. John C. Weaver observes similar trends in neighbouring

Hamilton in this period in *Crimes, Constables, and Courts: Order and Transgression in a Canadian City, 1816–1970* (Montreal and Kingston: McGill-Queen's University Press, 1995).

35 George H. Rust-D'Eye, *Cabbagetown Remembered* (Erin, ON: Boston Mills Press, 1984), 58; Toronto Historical Association, *A Glimpse of Toronto's History*, site no. 83.

36 Gaming, or betting for money stakes, would by definition have included blood sports. The Tavern Act of Upper Canada banned in any house "licensed to sell any sorts of liquors … any gaming with cards, dice, draughts, shuffle boards, mississippi or billiard tables, skittles, nine pins, or any other implement of gaming." Statutes of UC, 59 Geo III, C.2, 1818, cited in H. Julia Roberts, "Taverns and Tavern-Goers in Upper Canada, the 1790s to the 1850s" (PhD diss., Department of History, University of Toronto, 1999), 188.

37 Robertson, *Robertson's Landmarks*, 1: 213.

38 Ron Fletcher, *Over the Don* (Toronto: privately printed, 2002), 26. The Butcher's Arms appears as a prominent landmark on Tremaine's 1860 Atlas of the County of York and on an 1868 military map of the area by H.J.W. Gehle. *Sketch Sheets of a Winter Reconnaissance of the Country E. of Toronto between the Don River; & the Township of Scarboro on the E. & the Don & Danforth Rd. on the N. to the Lake Shore*, reprinted in Derek Hayes, *Historical Atlas of Toronto* (Vancouver: Douglas and McIntyre, 2008), 72. Topographical records show a wooded ravine running east-west behind where the tavern was located.

39 Peter DeLottinville, "Joe Beef of Montreal: Working-Class Culture and the Tavern, 1869–1889," *Labour / Le Travailleur* 8/9 (1981): 9–40. See also Julia Roberts, *In Mixed Company: Taverns and Public Life in Upper Canada* (Vancouver: UBC Press, 2009).

40 W. Stewart Wallace, "The Hogan Case: The Story of the Murder That Brought Disaster to the Once Notorious Brooks' Bush Gang of Toronto," *MacLean's Magazine*, 15 August 1931, 46. Several sources on the murder, including Wallace and Charles Sauriol's *Remembering the Don*, refer to Brook's Bush as being "north of the Don Jail." Both the 1860 and 1878 County Atlases for York, however, identify property owned by "Daniel Brook" (D.B. on the 1860 map) *east* of the Jail on Logan Avenue (then Logan's Lane). On the 1860 atlas, a second, smaller lot held by Brook appears further to the north, east of Logan. This placement corroborates statements by local historians that Brook's Bush lay on the site of today's Withrow Park.

41 "Body Found in the Don," *Toronto Daily Globe*, 1 April 1861, 2.

42 "The Late Mr. Hogan," *Toronto Daily Globe*, 2 April 1861, 2.

43 "The Murder of Mr. Hogan," *Toronto Daily Globe*, 9 April 1861, 2.

44 "The Hogan Murder: Trial of Jane Ward and John Sherrick," *Toronto Daily Globe*, 30 April 1861, 2.

45 Wallace, "The Hogan Case," 46.

46 Ibid., 47.

47 "The Convict Jas. Brown: Preparations for the Execution," *Toronto Daily Globe*, 10 March 1862, 2.

48 Robertson, *Robertson's Landmarks*, 1: 271.

49 *Toronto Daily Globe,* 9 April 1861.

50 *Toronto Daily Globe*, 22 April 1861.

51 *Toronto Daily Globe*, 9 April 1861.

52 *Toronto Daily Globe*, 9 October 1861.

53 *Toronto Daily Globe*, 19 October 1861. The *Globe* report of the trial notes that a man was later found guilty of manslaughter and sent to the penitentiary.

54 *Toronto Daily Globe*, 9 April 1861; 22 April 1861.

55 *Toronto Daily Globe*, 22 April 1861.

56 *Toronto Daily Globe*, 19 April 1861.

57 *Toronto Daily Globe*, 22 April 1861.

58 While these women seem to have enjoyed fewer options for employment, they may have benefited from greater access to charity than their male counterparts. Tim Hitchcock finds considerable evidence to support this conclusion in the British context in his *Down and Out in Eighteenth-Century London* (London and New York: Hambledon and London, 2004).

59 *Toronto Daily Globe*, 30 April 1861.

60 *Toronto Daily Globe*, 10 March 1862.

61 *Toronto Daily Globe*, 9 October 1861.

62 Fletcher, *Over the Don*, 20.

63 *Toronto Daily Globe*, 10 March 1862.

64 Catharine Cogan's testimony that John Sherrick loaned a "smock-front and vest" to Robert Wagstaff in order "that he might go to a tavern for some whiskey and some breakfast for us" reflects the expectation among tavern-keepers at the time that patrons present at least a moderately respectable appearance. *Toronto Daily Globe,* 22 April 1861.

65 *Toronto Daily Globe*, 22 April 1861.

66 A fascination with the state's long-established discomfort with transience was the impetus for James C. Scott's 1999 monograph *Seeing Like a State: How Certain Schemes to Improve the Human Condition Have Failed* (New Haven, CT: Yale University Press, 1999). "Gypsies, vagrants, homeless people, itinerants, runaway slaves, and serfs," he observed, "have always

been a thorn in the side of states. Efforts to permanently settle these mobile peoples (sedentarization) seemed to be a perennial state project – perennial, in part, because it so seldom succeeded" (1).

67 James M. Pitsula, "The Treatment of Tramps in Late Nineteenth-Century Toronto," *Canadian Historical Association: Historical Papers* 15, no. 1 (1980): 132.

68 City of Toronto Civic Unemployment Relief Committee, *Report and Recommendations*, May 1931, Pamphlets Relating to Toronto, City of Toronto Archives Collection, file 68, series 607, fonds 2, CTA. See also H.M. Cassidy, *Unemployment and Relief in Ontario, 1929–1932: A Survey and Report* (Toronto: J.M. Dent and Sons, 1932).

69 Toronto historian Carl Benn notes that until police services reforms in the 1850s the city employed only five full-time constables. Over sixty men were employed by the force in the latter half of the nineteenth century. *The History of Toronto: An 11,000 Year Journey* (Toronto: City of Toronto Culture Division, 2006), 31.

70 Bouchier and Cruikshank, "The War on the Squatters," 22.

71 Robert F. Harney and Harold Troper, *Immigrants: A Portrait of the Urban Experience, 1890–1930* (Toronto: Van Nostrand Reinhold, 1975), 38.

72 T.A. Acton, *Gypsy Politics and Traveller Identity* (Hatfield, Hertfordshire: University of Hertfordshire Press, 1997); Marlene Sway, *Familiar Strangers: Gypsy Life in America* (Urbana and Chicago: University of Illinois Press, 1988); John Tylor Lyon, "'A Picturesque Lot': The Gypsies in Peterborough," *Beaver* 78, no. 5 (1998): 25–30.

73 On the connections between authenticity and the myth of the vanishing race, see Paige Raibmon, *Authentic Indians: Episodes of Encounter from the Late-Nineteenth-Century Northwest Coast* (Durham and London: Duke University Press, 2005); McKay, *The Quest of the Folk*.

74 Ian McKay, "The Liberal Order Framework: A Prospectus for a Reconnaissance of Canadian History," *Canadian Historical Review* 81, no. 4 (2000): 626.

75 Sporadic deportations seemed to continue throughout the 1910s. In his annual report to the Toronto Board of Health, for example, medical officer of health Charles Hastings reports the deportation of a group of Roma he viewed as "sleeping and living like animals." *Annual Report to the Toronto Board of Health*, 1914, p. 112, Department of Public Health Reports, 1885–1995, Former City of Toronto Fonds, file 16, series 365, fonds 200, CTA.

76 "Gypsies at York Mills," *Toronto Star*, 2 June 1920.

77 "Gypsy Camp in North Toronto," *Toronto Star*, 25 May 1920.

78 Sway, *Familiar Strangers*, 39, 44, 110.

79 Anne Sutherland, *Gypsies: The Hidden Americans* (London: Tavistock, 1975), 85–94; Sway, *Familiar Strangers*, 110.

80 Sway, *Familiar Strangers*, 101.
81 David Mayall, *Gypsy-Travellers in Nineteenth-Century Society* (Cambridge and New York: Cambridge University Press, 1988), 58.
82 Sutherland, *Gypsies: The Hidden Americans*, 259; Sway, *Familiar Strangers*, 125.
83 "Forty-Two Homeless Men Snoozed on Heated Bricks," *Toronto Daily Star*, 2 December 1930. Plainclothesmen apparently entered the site in the early hours of the morning and shook men awake with offers of work to test their resolve to find employment. All men, the *Star* article reported, readied themselves quickly only to find the offers were a ruse.
84 *Toronto Globe*, 3 October 1931, 4.
85 Card of thanks, 4 August 1931, courtesy of the East York Foundation Collection, Todmorden Mills Heritage Site, City of Toronto.
86 "Don Valley Not Safe for Policeman Soon, Says Range Officer," *Toronto Globe*, 4 August 1931.
87 See, for example, McCallum, "The Great Depression's First History?"; and Wade, "Home or Homelessness."
88 "He Enlisted in Toronto," *Toronto Daily Star*, 9 July 1931.
89 John J. MacArthur, letter to the editor, *Toronto Globe*, 19 September 1931. The project never materialized.
90 "300 Jobless Sleep Nightly Along Don River's Banks," *Toronto Daily Star*, 19 June 1931. Michiel Horn provides some context for both the heavy burden experienced by Canadian municipalities in providing relief, and the attempt to clamp down on assistance to transients in order to force them out of the city and into relief camps. *The Great Depression of the 1930s in Canada* (Ottawa: Canadian Historical Association, 1984), 12.
91 Rev. Peter Bryce, "Jobless in Don Valley 'Jungle' Confident Work Will Be Found," *Toronto Daily Star*, 20 August 1931.
92 True Davidson, *The Golden Years of East York* (Toronto: Borough of East York, 1976), 82.
93 "Police Will Watch Every Freight Train for Jobless Influx," *Toronto Globe*, 26 September 1931; "City Relief Work to Start at Once 'For Own Citizens,'" *Toronto Globe*, 19 September 1931. Until this time, the hobo jungle likely existed with police acquiescence, constables agreeing to turn a blind eye provided transients jumped from trains before they entered the city.
94 "Quota from South in Jobless Draft Estimated at 2,500," *Toronto Globe*, 30 September 1931.
95 "East York Policemen Houseclean 'Jungle,'" *Toronto Globe*, 7 October 1931.
96 "Men of Don Valley Jungle a Healthy and Husky Lot," *Toronto Daily Star*, 30 September 1931.
97 Eric Hobsbawm defined "social bandits" as "peasant outlaws whom the lord and state regard as criminals, but who ... are considered by their

people as heroes … fighters for justice, perhaps even leaders of liberation, and in any case as men to be admired, helped and supported." *Bandits* (New York: Delacorte Press, 1969), 1. See also his *Primitive Rebels: Studies in Archaic Forms of Social Movement in the 19th and 20th Centuries* (New York: Norton, 1965).

5. Charles Sauriol and the Don Valley Conservation Movement

1   Charles Sauriol, *Tales of the Don* (Toronto: Natural Heritage/Natural History, 1984), 19.
2   Charles Sauriol, "Boyhood Memories of South Riverdale," ca 1980, Manuscripts of Charles Sauriol, 194?–1995, Charles Sauriol Fonds, file 6, series 107, fonds 4, City of Toronto Archives (CTA).
3   Ben Jordan outlines the connections between the early-twentieth-century conservation movement and the Scouting movement in the United States in his recent article, "'Conservation of Boyhood': Boy Scouting's Modest Manliness and Natural Resource Conservation, 1910–1930," *Environmental History* 15, no. 4 (October 2010): 612–42.
4   Donald Worster, *A Passion for Nature: The Life of John Muir* (Oxford and New York: Oxford University Press, 2008); Donald Worster, *A River Running West: The Life of John Wesley Powell* (Oxford and New York: Oxford University Press, 2002); Mark Hamilton Lytle, *The Gentle Subversive: Rachel Carson, Silent Spring, and the Rise of the Environmental Movement* (Oxford University Press, 2007); Dyana Z. Furmansky, *Rosalie Edge, Hawk of Mercy: The Activist Who Saved Nature from the Conservationists* (A Wormsloe Foundation Nature Book, 2009); Jack E. Davis, *An Everglades Providence: Marjory Stoneman Douglas and the American Environmental Century* (Athens: University of Georgia Press, 2009). In the Canadian context, see Anthony Robertson, *Above Tide: Reflections on Roderick Haig-Brown* (Madeira Park, BC: Harbour, 1984); James King, *Farley: The Life of Farley Mowat* (Hanover, NH: Steerforth, 2002); Donald B Smith, *From the Land of the Shadows: The Making of Grey Owl* (Vancouver and Toronto: Douglas and McIntyre, 1999).
5   Among very few monograph-length studies is Daniel Nelson's study of Ohio congressman John F. Seiberling, Jr, and his role in the creation of the Cuyahoga Valley National Park (*A Passion for the Land: John F. Seiberling and the Environmental Movement* [Kent, OH: Kent State University Press, 2009]). Other conservationists of regional significance receive coverage in monographs focused on particular places or developments, such as Adam Rome's *The Bulldozer in the Countryside: Suburban Sprawl and the Rise of*

American Environmentalism (Cambridge and New York: Cambridge University Press, 2001), and Richard Walker's *Country in the City: The Greening of the San Francisco Bay Area* (Seattle: University of Washington Press, 2008).

6 David Nasaw, "Historians and Biography," *American Historical Review* 114, no. 3 (June 2009): 576.

7 Alice Kessler-Harris, "Why Biography?" *American Historical Review* 114, no. 3 (June 2009): 626.

8 Jack Davis makes a similar argument in charting the development of core ideas in American environmentalism against the long twentieth-century life of Florida Everglades advocate Marjory Stoneman Douglas (*An Everglades Providence*). For a comparable use of "environmental life-writing" as a biographical approach, see Steven J. Holmes, *The Young John Muir: An Environmental Biography* (Madison: University of Wisconsin Press, 1999).

9 While considerable literature exists on the history of urban sprawl in Canadian centres, very little has been written about grassroots responses to suburban development and their connections to strains of conservationist thought in Canada.

10 Pierre Nora, *Realms of Memory: Rethinking the French Past* (New York: Columbia University Press, 1996), 1: 1.

11 Charles Sauriol, *Remembering the Don: A Rare Record of Earlier Times within the Don River Valley* (Toronto: Consolidated Amethyst Communications, 1981), 19.

12 Charles Sauriol, "The Don Valley as I Knew It," vol. 5, 1938–42, file 38, series 107, fonds 4, Charles Sauriol Fonds, CTA.

13 Sauriol, *Remembering the Don*, 137.

14 Charles Sauriol, "Fourteen Years on Fourteen Acres" (1945), Charles Sauriol Fonds, file 4, series 107, fonds 4, CTA. On "simple-living" movements in American history, see David E. Shi, *The Simple Life: Plain Living and High Thinking in American Culture* (Oxford and New York: Oxford University Press, 1985).

15 Sauriol, *Remembering the Don*, 31.

16 Sauriol, "Fourteen Years."

17 Sauriol, *Remembering the Don*, 136.

18 T.J. Jackson Lears, *No Place of Grace: Antimodernism and the Transformation of American Culture, 1880–1920* (New York: Pantheon, 1981). Ian McKay has documented similar trends in the Canadian context in *The Quest of the Folk: Antimodernism and Cultural Selection in Twentieth-Century Nova Scotia* (Montreal and Kingston: McGill-Queen's University Press, 1994).

19 Alan F.J. Artibise and Gilbert A. Stelter, "Conservation Planning and Urban Planning: The Canadian Commission of Conservation in Historical

Perspective," in *Consuming Canada: Readings in Environmental History*, ed. Chad Gaffield and Pam Gaffield (Toronto: Copp Clark, 1995), 154.

20 The "back-to-nature" movement differed from the "back-to-the-land" movement of the same period, which "sought both to revitalize rural life for those already on the land and to encourage city dwellers to take up homesteading." Back to nature, in contrast, championed short respites in nature as a tonic for city-weary urban dwellers (Shi, *The Simple Life*, 194).

21 Sauriol, "The Don Valley as I Knew It," 2: 194.

22 Sauriol, "Fourteen Years."

23 For a useful review of the history of ideas in English-Canadian conservation, see George Altmeyer, "Three Ideas of Nature in Canada, 1893–1914," in *Consuming Canada: Readings in Environmental History,* ed. Chad Gaffield and Pam Gaffield (Toronto: Copp Clark, 1995), 105. For comparable developments among progressive conservationists in the United States in this period, see David Stradling and William Cronon, *Conservation in the Progressive Era: Classic Texts* (Seattle: University of Washington Press, 2004).

24 Ontario Department of Planning and Development (ODPD), *Don Valley Conservation Report* (Toronto: ODPD, 1950): part 1: 10.

25 Don Valley Conservation Association (DVCA), "Presentation of a Plan for the Protection and Beautification of the Don Valley," 19 October 1953, Publications of Charles Sauriol, ca 1939–1995, Charles Sauriol Fonds, file 8, series 104, fonds 4, CTA.

26 Constructed in the 1920s and 30s, these plants were designed to process sewage from their immediate area and release minimally treated effluent into an adjacent river or stream. Gore and Storrie, Consulting Engineers, *Toronto and York Planning Board Report on Water Supply and Sewage Disposal for the City of Toronto and Related Areas*, 1949, p. 90, Records of the Information Officer for the Metropolitan Toronto Planning Department, Municipality of Metropolitan Toronto Fonds, file 227, series 40, CTA; Richard W. White, *Urban Infrastructure and Urban Growth in the Toronto Region: 1950s to the 1990s* (Toronto: Neptis Foundation, 2003), 11.

27 ODPD, *Don Valley Conservation Report*, part 6: 15.

28 Wayne C. Reeves, "From the Ground Up: Fragments toward an Environmental History of Tkaronto," in *GreenTOpia: Towards a Sustainable Toronto*, ed. Alana Wilcox, Christina Palassio, and Jonny Dovercourt (Toronto: Coach House Books, 2007), 71.

29 Don Watershed Regeneration Council, *Forging a New Deal for the Don* (Toronto: Toronto and Region Conservation Authority, 2006), 5.

30 DVCA, "Presentation of a Plan.

31 DVCA, *The Cardinal* (Fall 1954), Charles Sauriol Fonds, file 14, series 104, fonds 4, CTA.

32 Rome, *Bulldozer in the Countryside*, 119–52; Nelson, *A Passion for the Land*.
33 Sauriol, "Beginnings of the Don Valley Conservation Association," *The Cardinal*, (Spring 1954), and *Trails of the Don* (Orillia, ON: Hemlock Press, 1992), 268–9.
34 On the exclusionary effects of twentieth-century conservation policies in the United States and Canada, see Karl Jacoby, *Crimes against Nature: Squatters, Poachers, Thieves, and the Hidden History of American Conservation* (Berkeley and Los Angeles: University of California Press, 2001); Tina Loo, *States of Nature: Conserving Canada's Wildlife in the Twentieth Century* (Vancouver: UBC Press, 2007); and John Sandlos, *Hunters at the Margin: Native People and Wildlife Conservation in the Northwest Territories* (Vancouver: UBC Press, 2007).
35 DVCA, *The Cardinal* (Spring 1951), Charles Sauriol Fonds, file 14, series 104, fonds 4, CTA.
36 John R. Stilgoe, *Metropolitan Corridor: Railroads and the American Scene* (New Haven and London: Yale University Press, 1983), esp. chapter 13.
37 Sauriol, *Tales of the Don*; Sauriol, "Beginnings of the Don Valley Conservation Association."
38 Sauriol, *Trails of the Don*, 282.
39 Toronto and Region Conservation Authority (TRCA), "Hurricane Hazel 50 Years Later," http://www.hurricanehazel.ca/ (accessed 17 July 2010); Jim Gifford and Mike Filey, *Hurricane Hazel: Canada's Storm of the Century* (Toronto: Dundurn Press, 2004).
40 While Hazel can be credited with tipping the balance toward watershed conservation in southern Ontario, and greatly accelerating plans for the acquisition of valley lands, flood-plain protection had been a subject of discussion among conservation-minded planners and scientists for a number of years before the storm hit. The City Planning Board's 1943 *Master Plan for the City of Toronto and Environs*, for example, proposed (unsuccessfully) to protect the Don and Humber river valleys from "encroachment and vandalism" by incorporating them within a U-shaped green belt linked by a low-speed "drive-way."
41 Metropolitan Toronto and Region Conservation Authority, "Plan for Flood Control and Water Conservation" (Woodbridge, ON: MTRCA, 1959); TRCA, "The History of Flood Control in the TRCA," http://trca.on.ca/flood-monitoring/index.dot (accessed 17 July 2010).
42 Thanks to Toronto historian Richard White for this insight.
43 The use of the term "drive-way" here is unusual. Given the period in which this plan was developed, it was likely meant as a "parkway" or scenic low-speed drive. In any case, planners evidently envisioned a very different kind of road than the expressway that was eventually built through the valley, somewhat ironically named the Don Valley Parkway.

44 ODPD, *Don Valley Conservation Report*, part 6: 22.

45 Wayne C. Reeves, *Visions for the Metropolitan Toronto Waterfront, 2: Forging a Regional Identity, 1913–68* (Major Report No. 28, Department of Geography, University of Toronto, April 1993), 61–4. Cooperation between the MTRCA and the Metropolitan Toronto Parks Department, established in 1955, saw valley lands acquired in the flood-plains protection program transferred to Metro for development as regional parks at Metro's expense. By 1966, the MTRCA had acquired almost 70 per cent of Metro's over 2,000-hectare park system.

46 Joy Parr, *Sensing Changes: Technologies, Environments, and the Everyday, 1953–2003* (Vancouver: UBC Press, 2009).

47 Charles Sauriol, *Green Footsteps: Recollections of a Grassroots Conservationist* (Toronto: Hemlock Press, 1991), 13.

48 Ibid.

49 Sauriol, "Sauriol, Charles, 1932–1995," file 28, series 103, General Subject Files of Charles Sauriol, fonds 4, Charles Sauriol Fonds, CTA.

50 Samuel P. Hays, *Beauty, Health, and Permanence: Environmental Politics in the United States, 1955–1985* (Cambridge: Cambridge University Press, 1987).

51 Rome, *Bulldozer in the Countryside*, 7–8.

52 Thomas Claridge, "Pollution Probe Mourns for Beloved, Dead Don," *Globe and Mail*, 17 November 1969, 1.

53 For more on the history of Pollution Probe and its influence on environmental politics in Ontario, see Ryan O'Connor, *The First Green Wave: Pollution Probe and the Origins of Environmental Activism in Ontario* (Vancouver: UBC Press, 2014).

54 "Mock Rites Mourn Death of Don River Killed by Pollution," *Toronto Daily Star*, 17 November 1969, 21; Claridge, "Pollution Probe."

55 Robert Gottlieb, *Forcing the Spring: The Transformation of the American Environmental Movement* (Washington, DC: Island Press, 2005), 252–3.

56 "America's Sewage System and the Price of Optimism," *Time*, 1 August 1969, http://content.time.com/time/magazine/article/0,9171,901182,00.html. For an insightful analysis of changes in the public perception of fires on the Cuyahoga, see David Stradling and Richard Stradling, "Perceptions of the Burning River: Deindustrialization and Cleveland's Cuyahoga River," *Environmental History* 13, no. 3 (2008): 515–35.

57 Sauriol, *Green Footsteps*, 21.

58 Toronto Area Watershed Management Study and Paul Theil Associates, *Strategy for Improvement of Don River Water Quality: Summary Report* (Toronto: Queen's Printer, 1989), 4.

59 Sauriol, "Diary," 1964–9, Diaries of Charles Sauriol, 1926–1994, file 16, series 292, fonds 4, CTA.

60 Ibid.

61 Sauriol, *Green Footsteps*, 279.

62 Toronto City Council Proceedings, 23 February 1989, cited in Mark J. Wilson (chair of the Task Force to Bring Back the Don 1991–8), "How Did the Task Force to Bring Back the Don Get Started?" http://archive.is/AuInq (accessed 30 January 2014).

63 A number of other citizen-led groups have since formed to address concerns about habitat degradation, access, and pollution in the watershed. See Jennifer Bonnell, "Bringing Back the Don: Sixty Years of Community Action," in *HtO: Toronto's Water from Lake Iroquois to Lost Rivers to Low-Flow Toilets*, ed. Wayne Reeves and Christina Palassio (Toronto: Coach House Books, 2008), 266–83.

64 Sauriol, *Remembering the Don*, 140.

65 Sauriol, *Green Footsteps*, 6.

6. Metro Toronto and the Don Valley Parkway

1 Timothy J. Colton, *Big Daddy: Frederick G. Gardiner and the Building of Metropolitan Toronto* (Toronto: University of Toronto Press, 1980), 62.

2 Gore and Storrie, Consulting Engineers, *Toronto and York Planning Board Report on Water Supply and Sewage Disposal for the City of Toronto and Related Areas*, 1949, file 227, series 40, fonds 220, City of Toronto Archives (CTA). As urban historian Richard White has illustrated, postwar growth exacerbated established patterns of underserviced suburban development and overburdened municipal finances apparent by the 1920s and 30s. *Urban Infrastructure and Urban Growth in the Toronto Region: 1950s to the 1990s* (Toronto: Neptis Foundation, 2003), 11.

3 John Sewell, *The Shape of the Suburbs: Understanding Toronto's Sprawl* (Toronto: University of Toronto Press, 2009), 15.

4 Metropolitan Toronto Planning Board, "A Brief, Prepared by the Planning Board, Heads of Departments, and Officials of the Municipality of Metropolitan Toronto Presented to The Royal Commission on Canada's Economic Prospects by Frederick G. Gardiner, Q.C.," 3 January 1956, 98–9.

5 Frederick Goldwin Gardiner, "The Face of the City Has Changed. An Address to the Inaugural Meeting of the Metropolitan Council," 12 January 1960, p. 4, Frederick G. Gardiner: Clippings and Ephemera, microform, 3 reels, FILM G221 G221, Toronto Reference Library.

6 Colton, *Big Daddy*, 60.

7 Ibid., 63.
8 Timothy Davis, "The Rise and Decline of the American Parkway," in *The World beyond the Windshield: Roads and Landscapes in the United States and Europe*, ed. Christof Mauch and Thomas Zeller (Athens: Ohio University Press, 2008), 38.
9 Matthew Dalbey, *Regional Visionaries and Metropolitan Boosters: Decentralization, Regional Planning, and Parkways during the Interwar Years* (Boston: Kluwer Academic Publishers, 2002), 18–20.
10 Ibid., 25.
11 Ibid., 26.
12 John C. van Nostrand, "The Queen Elizabeth Way: Public Utility versus Public Space," *Urban History Review* 12, no. 2 (1983): 1–23.
13 Davis, "The Rise and Decline of the American Parkway," 56–57.
14 See van Nostrand, "The Queen Elizabeth Way."
15 "Plans of Boulevard System, 1891–1932," file 17, series 724, fonds 200, CTA.
16 "Don Valley Roadway Planned as Relief Work," *Toronto Board of Trade Journal* (November 1932).
17 Bill 61, "An Act to Conserve and Improve the Valley of the Don River," Journals of the Legislative Assembly of Ontario, 1933, 15, 222.
18 Mike Filey, "Parkway with a Past," in *Toronto Sketches 9* (Toronto: Dundurn Group, 2006), 151–3.
19 "Belt Line Traffic Plan Is Laid before Citizens," *Globe and Mail*, 1 January 1938.
20 Stephen Bocking, "Constructing Urban Expertise: Professional and Political Authority in Toronto, 1940–1970," *Journal of Urban History* 33, no. 1 (2006): 51–76.
21 Toronto City Planning Board, *The Master Plan for the City of Toronto and Environs* (Toronto, 31 December 1943).
22 Richard White, "The Growth Plan for the Greater Golden Horseshoe in Historical Perspective" (Neptis Foundation, December 2007), 9, http://www.neptis.org/publications/growth-plan-greater-golden-horseshoe-historical-perspective (accessed 30 January 2014).
23 Comparable to the 1932 "Don Driveways" plan, the 1945 Don Roadway project proposed a traffic artery along the east bank of the Lower Don, cutting northwest along the old Beltline railway to terminate at Mount Pleasant and Merton streets. A proposed extension along the river's east branch to O'Connor Drive would purportedly clear congestion in East York. The Roadway plan was approved by almost 75 per cent of the electorate in a municipal plebiscite on 1 January 1946 – the same ballot that would

grant overwhelming approval to the construction of the Yonge Street subway.

24 Metro assigned the development of the plans to two companies: the Foundation of Canada Engineering Corporation Ltd. (FENCO) in association with Frederic R. Harris of Canada Ltd., a subsidiary of a New York firm experienced in expressway design.

25 *Engaging of Consultants for Don Valley Parkway*, Report No. 2 of the Executive Committee, Appendix A, p. 48, Municipality of Metropolitan Toronto Council Minutes (hereafter Metro Council Minutes), 1955.

26 FENCO-Harris, *Functional Report on the Proposed Don Valley Parkway to the Municipality of Metropolitan Toronto*, October 1955, item 683, series 10, fonds 220, CTA.

27 Joseph Hall, "DVP: The Scenic Highway We Love to Hate Turns 25," *Toronto Star*, 7 March 1992.

28 Appendix A, 102, Metro Council Minutes, 1953.

29 Metropolitan Toronto Planning Board Minutes (hereafter MTPB Minutes), nos. 1–8, 1 December 1953, file 2, subseries 1, series 9, fonds 257, CTA; MTPB Minutes, nos. 9–26, December 1954.

30 MTPB Minutes, nos. 9–26, December 1954.

31 "You'll Just Naturally Like It in Don Mills," *Toronto Daily Star*, 15 September 1955.

32 *Report No. 27 of the Roads and Traffic Committee*, Appendix A, 62, Metro Council Minutes, 1956.

33 *Report No. 24 of Roads and Traffic Committee*, Appendix A, 1851–5, Metro Council Minutes, 13 December 1955.

34 "Experts Advise 'No' But Have to Build Don Road – Gardiner," *Toronto Daily Star*, 19 January 1955. The subway-expressway debate resurfaced two years later in the form of a very public dispute between Gardiner and TTC Chair Allan Lamport. Here again the debate centred on which development to prioritize, the DVP or the construction of an east-west subway line. Although Metro Council had approved plans for the Bloor-Danforth line in 1958, Gardiner insisted that funding could not be allocated until the completion of the DVP. Despite heated protest from the Toronto Transit Commission, the DVP went ahead, and transit advocates had to wait another two years before construction began on the Bloor-Danforth subway. "Gardiner Favors Road to Aid Few, Lamport Charges," *Toronto Daily Star*, 13 March 1957.

35 Metropolitan Toronto Planning Board, Transportation and Services Division, *Don Valley Parkway: Report and Analysis of Study for the Municipality of Metropolitan Toronto*, August 1955, 66–8.

36　Colton, *Big Daddy*, 62.

37　James C. Scott, *Seeing Like a State: How Certain Schemes to Improve the Human Condition Have Failed* (New Haven, CT: Yale University Press, 1999), 57.

38　Colton, *Big Daddy*, 21.

39　Ibid., 120.

40　Gerry Toner, "Sees 70 P.C. Ont. Industry 2,000,000 here by 1973," *Toronto Telegram*, 9 April 1953, in "Frederick G. Gardiner: Clippings and Ephemera," microfilm, Urban Affairs Library (UAL).

41　"Urge Don Valley Parkway to Relieve East Traffic," *Toronto Daily Star*, 18 May 1954; "Woman Raps Mayor for 'Pious Talk,'" *Toronto Daily Star*, 13 February 1957.

42　Lee Belland, "Six-Lane Road in Valley Will Link Expressway with Toronto Arteries," *Toronto Daily Star*, 4 October 1955.

43　Ron Haggart, "Don Route, Too Good, Perhaps Too Cheap," *Globe and Mail*, 9 June 1958.

44　David MacFarlane, "Paved Paradise," *Toronto Life*, May 2006.

45　A report from the Metro Legal Department in December 1955 concluded that Metro lacked the authority to establish parking areas. The Executive Committee recommended that an application be made to the province to enact the enabling legislation. The parking lots were never constructed. Appendix A, 1851–5, Metro Council Minutes, 1955.

46　Dalbey, *Regional Visionaries and Metropolitan Boosters*, 28.

47　Davis, "The Rise and Decline of the American Parkway," 41.

48　Frederick Goldwin Gardiner, "The Face of the City Has Changed. An Address to the Inaugural Meeting of the Metropolitan Council," 12 January 1960, 4.

49　"Progress Report: Toronto 1970: Transportation," *Globe and Mail*, 5 November 1963.

50　Joseph Hall, "DVP: The Scenic Highway We Love to Hate Turns 25," *Toronto Daily Star*, 7 March 1992.

51　Richard T.T. Forman et al., *Road Ecology: Science And Solutions* (Washington, DC: Island Press, 2003), 326–7.

52　Canada, *Canadian Environmental Sustainability Indicators*, 2007, http://www5.statcan.gc.ca/bsolc/olc-cel/olc-cel?catno=16-251-X&lang=eng.

53　Hall, "DVP."

54　Ibid.

55　Ron Haggart, "Ernest Thompson Seton and the New Parkway," *Toronto Daily Star*, 30 August 1961.

56　Michael Smith, "Love It or Hate It, Parkway's 25 Years Old," *Toronto Star*, 13 August 1986.

57　*Agreement with City of Toronto Respecting Use of City Park Lands for Two Metropolitan Road Projects*, Report No. 26 of the Executive Committee,

Appendix A, 895, Metro Council Minutes, 1958; "Park on Lakefront $2,600,000 Project Aims at World Fair," *Toronto Daily Star*, 11 June 1958.

58 Douglas Blanchard, "Can Be Close to Nature Even Driving to Job," *Toronto Daily Star*, 17 July 1958.

59 Fred Hollett, "Parkway Trip Hits Big Jam," *Toronto Daily Star*, 1 September 1961.

60 "Snarls Till '66 on Don Parkway," *Toronto Daily Star*, 5 September 1961; "Parkway Drivers Snarl," *Toronto Daily Star*, 6 September 1961; "Parkway Extension," *Globe and Mail*, 15 September 1961; Hollett, "Parkway Trip Hits Big Jam."

61 Dr Morton Shulman, Chief Coroner, *Metropolitan Toronto Coroner's Office Automobile Fatality Research Project*, part 1: *The Unnecessary Hazards of Toronto's Don Valley Expressway*, 31 August 1965.

62 G.O. Grant, Commissioner of Roads, "Comments on Report by Coroner Dr. Morton Shulman," 31 August 1965, and "Traffic Fatalities on the Don Valley Parkway," 16 September 1965, file 727, series 11, fonds 220, CTA.

63 Hall, "DVP."

64 "Mudslide Closes Northbound Don Parkway," *Globe and Mail*, 19 April 1969.

65 Gabrielle Barnett, "Drive-By Viewing: Visual Consciousness and Forest Preservation in the Automobile Age," *Technology and Culture* 45, no. 1 (January 2004): 30–54. Barnett draws her conceptual apparatus from Wolfgang Schivelbusch, *The Railway Journey: The Industrialization of Time and Space in the 19th Century* (Berkeley: University of California Press, 1986).

66 Barnett, "Drive-By Viewing," 50.

67 Charles Sauriol, "Diary: 1934–1935," n.d., Diaries of Charles Sauriol, 1926–1994, file 16, series 292, fonds 4, CTA.

68 Don Valley Conservation Association, "Presentation of a Plan for the Protection and Beautification of the Don Valley," 19 October 1953, file 8, series 104, fonds 4, CTA.

69 Hall, "DVP."

70 City of Toronto, *Don Valley Corridor Transportation Study Master Plan: Summary Report*, 2005.

71 Hall, "DVP."

7. Remembering the Don

1 See http://ebw.evergreen.ca/ (accessed 24 June 2014).

2 Toronto Waterfront Revitalization Corporation, and Toronto and Region Conservation Authority, "Don Mouth Naturalization and Port Lands Flood

Protection Project: Revised Terms of Reference," June 2006, 1; Michael
Van Valkenburgh Associates, for Waterfront Toronto, "Lower Don Lands
Framework Plan" (Waterfront Toronto, May 2013), 8.

3 Raphael Samuel, *Theatres of Memory* (New York: Verso, 1994), 8.

4 Pierre Nora, *Realms of Memory: Rethinking the French Past* (New York: Columbia University Press, 1996), 1.

5 As Joy Parr has demonstrated, the rapid environmental changes wrought
by major development projects often have a disorienting effect upon local
residents and their embodied understandings of place. Although the processes and projects that have transformed the Lower Don Lands have occurred over a much longer time period and their immediate effects lie well
outside of living memory, the transformation of the landscape has been no
less significant. See Parr, *Sensing Changes: Technologies, Environments, and the
Everyday, 1953–2003* (Vancouver: UBC Press, 2009); and "Notes for a More
Sensuous History of Twentieth-Century Canada: The Timely, the Tacit, and
the Material Body," *Canadian Historical Review* 82, no. 4 (2001): 720–45.

6 See, for example, D.W. Meinig, "The Beholding Eye: Ten Versions of the
Same Scene," in *The Interpretation of Ordinary Landscapes: Geographical Essays*, ed. D.W. Meinig (New York and Oxford: Oxford University Press,
1979), 33–48; and John Brinckerhoff Jackson, *Landscape in Sight: Looking at
America*, ed. Helen Lefkowitz Horowitz (New Haven, CT: Yale University
Press, 1997).

7 Created in 2001 by the government of Canada, the province of Ontario,
and the city of Toronto, with the objective to fund, coordinate, and oversee the revitalization of the Toronto waterfront, the Toronto Waterfront
Revitalization Corporation (TWRC) later changed its name to Waterfront Toronto. For simplicity, I have used the name "Waterfront Toronto"
throughout.

8 Plans to transform the Toronto waterfront are situated within a broader
trend of port lands revitalization initiatives around the world, as cities have
sought to transform problematic industrial harbourfronts into attractive
and profitable spaces for recreation and residential development. Examples
include the Canary Wharf and Isle of Dogs projects in London's Docklands
(http://www.lddc-history.org.uk/), waterfront regeneration initiatives in
Copenhagen (including designated swimming areas at the Copenhagen
Harbour Baths), and the HafenCity Docklands regeneration project in
Hamburg, Germany (http://www.hafencity.com/en/home.html)
(accessed 24 June 2014).

9 Toronto Waterfront Revitalization Corporation, *Lower Don Lands Innovative
Design Competition: Jury Report*, May 2007, 1.

10 Ibid., 5.

11 Michael Van Valkenburgh Associates (MVVA), *Port Lands Estuary*, May 2007, 42. For a video overview of the design, see http://www.youtube.com/watch?v=bEQiNXXgu4g (accessed 24 June 2014).

12 MVVA, *Port Lands Estuary*, 8–9.

13 Ibid., 14, 18. These neighbourhoods would be located on either side of Keating Channel and on the north side of the Ship Channel south of the restored river mouth.

14 MVVA, *Port Lands Estuary*, 10.

15 The Task Force to Bring Back the Don, *Bringing Back the Don* (Toronto: City of Toronto Planning and Development Department, August 1991), 48–9.

16 David Crombie, *Regeneration: Toronto's Waterfront and the Sustainable City. Final Report, Royal Commission on the Future of the Toronto Waterfront* (Ottawa: Minister of Supply and Services Canada, 1992), 252.

17 Toronto Waterfront Revitalization Corporation and Toronto and Region Conservation Authority, "Revised Terms of Reference," 5.

18 Toronto Waterfront Revitalization (TWR) Task Force, *Our Toronto Waterfront: Gateway to the New Canada*, March 2000, 50. In November 1999, the city of Toronto, the province of Ontario, and the federal government formed the TWR Task Force with a mandate to develop a strategic master plan for the development of the Toronto waterfront. In producing their final report, the task force drew upon a substantial body of existing waterfront studies, including the work of the Royal Commission on the Future of the Toronto Waterfront and its successor agency, the Waterfront Regeneration Trust; the Gardiner/Lakeshore Task Force; and the Task Force to Bring Back the Don.

19 The Plan won the 2002 Award of Excellence from the Canadian Institute of Planners and the international 2002 Excellence on the Waterfront Award from the Waterfront Center in Washington, DC. City of Toronto, *Waterfront Revitalization Chronology*, fact sheet, January 2008.

20 City of Toronto, *Making Waves: Principles for Building Toronto's Waterfront, Central Waterfront Part II Plan*, October 2001, 8.

21 Toronto Waterfront Revitalization Corporation, *Building the Foundation: Toronto Waterfront Revitalization Corporation Annual Report 2002/03*, 2003, 6.

22 The Lower Don Lands is currently overlaid with a veritable maze of planning processes. In addition to the individual Don Mouth Naturalization and Port Lands Flood Protection environmental assessment (EA), which harmonizes federal and provincial environmental assessment requirements, a class EA was completed in 2005 for the Lower Don River West Remedial Flood Protection Project, which aims to remove flood risk over 210

hectares of land west of the Don River. Further south in the Port Lands, Waterfront Toronto, the city of Toronto and the Toronto Transit Commission (TTC) have initiated the Lower Don Lands Infrastructure Municipal Class EA, which assesses the transit and servicing infrastructure needs for the area.

23 MVVA, for Waterfront Toronto, "Lower Don Lands Framework Plan," 8.

24 Meinig, "The Beholding Eye," 40.

25 MVVA, *Port Lands Estuary*, 4.

26 David Lowenthal, *The Past Is a Foreign Country* (New York: Cambridge University Press, 1985), xxiv.

27 MVVA, *Port Lands Estuary*, 26. The MVVA proposal identifies only the silos of the Victory Soya Mills (north of the Keating Channel) for potential heritage uses. Subsequent planning documents have added the ESSROC silos (on Cherry Street south of Keating Channel) as another candidate for heritage preservation (MVVA, for Waterfront Toronto, "Lower Don Lands Framework Plan," 15). As Waterfront Toronto and the TRCA note in their 2006 Terms of Reference for the project, "prior to 2004, there were over sixty-one individual built heritage features located within [the Lower Don Lands] … In the intervening time some demolition of structures has occurred. The City of Toronto's current Inventory of Heritage Properties identified a total of 31 designated properties and 21 listed structures or landscapes within this area." TWRC and TRCA, "Revised Terms of Reference," 40.

28 MVVA, *Port Lands Estuary*, 26, 44.

29 David Harvey, "Between Space and Time: Reflections on the Geographical Imagination," *Annals of the Association of American Geographers* 80, no. 3 (September 1990): 418–34. See also Max Page, *The Creative Destruction of Manhattan, 1900–1940* (Chicago: University of Chicago Press, 2001).

30 MVVA, *Port Lands Estuary*, 14.

31 Ibid., 36.

32 *TRCA and Waterfront Toronto, Don Mouth Naturalization and Port Lands Flood Protection Environmental Assessment: Executive Summary* (September 2013): chapter 6, pp. 15–16.

33 Soil-washing treatments such as those employed at the Port Lands facility remove a wide range of contaminants, including metals, gasoline, fuel oils, and by-products of burning. Soils containing hazardous wastes are not accepted for treatment, but disposed of at a hazardous-waste landfill. Waterfront Toronto, "Pilot Soil Recycling Facility Fact Sheet," April 2012, http://www.waterfrontoronto.ca/explore_projects2/port_lands/unwin_avenue_improvements (accessed 9 May 2013).

34 Joseph Bouchette, *Plan of York Harbour*, 12 August 1815, T1815/fold, Toronto Map Collection, Special Collections, Toronto Reference Library.

35 MVVA, *Port Lands Estuary*, 10.

36 This is a common interpretation of ecological restoration. As Eric Higgs writes, restoration in the sense of bringing something back to a previous or original condition works well for paintings and old buildings, where "the ultimate goal is present under layers of grime or soil." Ecosystems, however, "are in constant motion," with no discernible point of origin. Rather than working with "a fixed historical point in time or a suite of specific ecological conditions," ecological restorationists attempt instead to determine the "historical range of variability" for an ecosystem through the use of "reference conditions," historical inferences drawn from records or remnant ecosystems. *Nature by Design: People, Natural Process, and Ecological Restoration* (Cambridge, MA: MIT Press, 2003), 118–19.

37 Kenneth Dion, senior project manager, TRCA, personal communication, 10 July 2008.

38 Mark Woods makes a compelling argument for reconceptualizing ecological restoration as the renewal of "wildness and freedom" rather than "naturalness." See "Ecological Restoration and the Renewal of Wildness and Freedom," in *Recognizing the Autonomy of Nature: Theory and Practice* (New York: Columbia University Press, 2005), 170–88.

39 For case studies in this vein, see Marcus Hall, *Earth Repair: A Transatlantic History of Environmental Restoration* (Charlottesville: University of Virginia Press, 2005).

40 I use the term "postmodern" here with specific reference to its use in architecture and urban design literature. David Harvey elaborates on the use of the term in this context to signify a kind of "architectural bricolage," one that "cultivates ... a conception of the urban fabric as necessarily fragmented, a 'palimpsest' of past forms superimposed upon each other, and a 'collage' of current uses, many of which may be ephemeral." *The Condition of Postmodernity* (Oxford and Cambridge, MA: Blackwell, 1989), 66.

41 MVVA, for Waterfront Toronto, "Lower Don Lands Framework Plan," 4–5.

42 Ibid, 5.

43 These include the Lower Don Lands Municipal Class EA, the Don Mouth Naturalization and Port Lands Flood Protection EA, the Cherry Street Transit EA, the Queens Quay Boulevard Transit EA, the West Don Lands Municipal Class EA, the Gardiner Expressway Individual EA, and the Don and Waterfront Trunk Sewers EA (ibid., 5, 10–11, 29).

44 Christopher Hume, *On the Waterfront: How a Small Agency with Paltry Power and Precarious Funding Changed a City*, StarDispatches (Toronto: Toronto

Star Newspapers, 2013), 33–6; Gabriel Eidelman, "Who's in Charge?
Jurisdictional Gridlock and the Genesis of Waterfront Toronto," in *Reshaping Toronto's Waterfront*, ed. Gene Desfor and Jennefer Laidley (Toronto:
University of Toronto Press, 2011), 263–86.

45 CodeBlueTO, a coalition of individuals, organizations, and groups committed to transparency and public engagement in planning the revitalization of Toronto's waterfront, formed in the fall of 2011 in response to
Councillor Ford's proposals for the Port Lands and succeeded in rallying
significant public support for Waterfront Toronto and "the people's plans"
for the waterfront (http://codeblueto.com/) (accessed 15 May 2013).

46 Under the new phasing, the spillway between Keating Channel and the
Ship Channel would be constructed first, permitting development of city-owned lands west of Cherry Street. Phase 2 includes constructing the sediment management area and raising the Don Roadway to remove the large
area to the south and east in the Port Lands from flood risk. Phase 3 would
construct the new river course, including new parks and naturalization
areas, as far as the existing Polson Slip. Phases 4 and 5 would complete the
mouth of the river into the Inner Harbour, beginning with the construction of the north bank of the river and completing the south bank "if and
when the Lafarge property land use changes." Cost reductions achieved
by these and other adjustments are anticipated at about $130 million. City
of Toronto, Waterfront Toronto, and Toronto and Region Conservation
Authority, "Port Lands Acceleration Initiative, Appendix 1: Summary of
Findings" (2012), 10, 15–17, http://www.portlandsconsultation.ca/; City
of Toronto, Waterfront Toronto, and Toronto and Region Conservation
Authority, "Port Lands Acceleration Initiative, Appendix 10: Port Lands
Planning Summary" (2012), 16, http://www.portlandsconsultation.ca/
(accessed 24 July 2014).

47 William J. Clinton Foundation, "Press Release: Clinton Climate Initiative
to Demonstrate Model for Sustainable Urban Growth with Projects in Ten
Countries on Six Continents," 18 May 2009, http://www.clintonfoundation.org/main/news-and-media/press-releases-and-statements/press-release-clinton-climate-initiative-to-demostrate-model-for-sustainable-urb.
html (accessed 30 January 2014). The MVVA Port Lands Estuary proposal
received the American Society of Landscape Architects 2008 Award of
Honor and the Best Futuristic Design Award at the 2009 Building Exchange Conference in Hamburg, Germany.

48 MVVA, for Waterfront Toronto, "Lower Don Lands Framework Plan," 5, 32.

49 Toronto Harbour Commissioners, "Reports on the Improvement and Preservation of Toronto Harbour," *Supplement to the Canadian Journal* (1854): 1.

50 Hume, *On the Waterfront*.

51 A range of potential in-stream habitat improvements were evaluated for
    their ability to exacerbate flooding, their projected maintenance require-
    ments, and their effects upon existing infrastructure such as the DVP,
    Bayview Avenue, and the Lower Don Trail. In the end, three viable options
    were identified: the replacement of the existing sheet piling along the river
    banks with more naturalized armoured banks; the continued planting of ri-
    parian vegetation; and the strategic placement of boulders and other coarse
    rock material within the river bed to vary flow rates and improve the diver-
    sity of wildlife habitat. Waterfront Toronto and Toronto and Region Conser-
    vation Authority, *Don Mouth Naturalization and Port Lands Flood Protection
    Project: Amended Environmental Assessment Report*, Appendix J, 21–2.
52 Lowenthal, *The Past is a Foreign Country*, xxiv.
53 Very little active industry remains in the Port Lands. Land use is mostly
    commercial/industrial, with limited recreational uses along the waterfront
    (including the Docks Entertainment Complex and the Martin Goodman
    Trail). Rail links to area businesses and industries bisect the area. Other
    active uses include the Don Rail Yard, paper and scrap metal recycling
    plants, City of Toronto recycling facilities, and businesses related to the
    film industry.
54 Officially titled the Outer Harbour East Headland, the peninsula was
    originally intended as a breakwater for harbour expansion in anticipation of
    greater volumes of shipping traffic with the opening of the St Lawrence Sea-
    way in 1959. When heightened shipping volumes failed to materialize, the
    breakwater project was abandoned and the spit took up its main function as
    a dumping site for excavated materials and waste from construction sites.
    The Toronto Harbour Commissioners forwarded several development plans
    over the years, including an "aquatic park" with a hotel, amphitheatre, and
    boating facilities. Citizens' advocacy by the Toronto Field Naturalists and
    the Friends of the Spit, established in 1977, eventually secured the site's
    status as an urban park. The northern half of the spit is open to the public
    as Tommy Thompson Park, managed by the TRCA, while the southern half
    remains an active dumping zone, managed by the Toronto Port Authority.
    The entire peninsula will eventually become parkland. For further details on
    the Spit and its historical role in harbour authorities' visions for the Outer
    Harbour, see Roy Merrens, "Port Authorities as Urban Land Developers:
    The Case of the Toronto Harbour Commissioners and Their Outer Harbour
    Project, 1912–1968," *Urban History Review* 17, no. 2 (October 1988): 92–105.
55 Friends of the Spit, http://www.friendsofthespit.ca/spit_about.htm (ac-
    cessed 5 February 2010).
56 Merrens, "Port Authorities as Urban Land Developers"; Christopher Sand-
    erson and Pierre Filion, "From Harbour Commission to Port Authority:

Institutionalizing the Federal Government's Role in Waterfront Development," in *Reshaping Toronto's Waterfront*, ed. Gene Desfor and Jennefer Laidley (Toronto: University of Toronto Press, 2011), 235.

Conclusion

1 Richard Harris, *Unplanned Suburbs: Toronto's American Tragedy, 1900 to 1950* (Baltimore: John Hopkins University Press, 1996), 13.
2 This work has been initiated in studies such as Judith Fingard, *The Dark Side of Life in Victorian Halifax* (Porters Lake, NS: Pottersfield Press, 1989); Ken Cruikshank and Nancy B. Bouchier, "Blighted Areas and Obnoxious Industries: Constructing Environmental Inequality on an Industrial Waterfront, Hamilton, Ontario, 1890–1960," *Environmental History* 9, no. 3 (2004): 464–96; and Jill Wade, "Home or Homelessness? Marginal Housing in Vancouver, 1886–1950," *Urban History Review* 25, no. 2 (1997): 19–29, but much remains to be done in documenting the intersections between social and environmental history within urban peripheries.
3 David E. Shi, *The Simple Life: Plain Living and High Thinking in American Culture* (Oxford and New York: Oxford University Press, 1985).
4 Jenny Price, "Remaking American Environmentalism: On the Banks of the L.A. River," *Environmental History* 13, no. 3 (2008): 536–55.
5 The Don's score of 34.8 out of 100 makes it the most polluted river in Ontario (Peter Gorrie, "The Dirty Don: Environment Canada's Water Quality Index Puts a Numeric Value to the 'Embarrassment' That Is the River: 34.8 out of 100," *Toronto Star*, 7 December 2007; Canada, *Canadian Environmental Sustainability Indicators*, 2007, http://www5.statcan.gc.ca/bsolc/olc-cel/olc-cel?catno=16-251-X&lang=eng (accessed 24 June 2014).
6 Ibid., xiii.
7 Of the 42 fish species that historically populated the Don, 21 remain, most of which are pollution-tolerant, and most of which inhabit the river's upper reaches. Regular surveys by the TRCA have found only 19 fish species in the lower Don, a low number compared with "the 25–27 species typically found in other river mouths along the north shore of Lake Ontario." Almost 90 per cent of fish collected were white sucker, emerald shiner, and spottail shiner, "all common species with low sensitivity." Toronto Waterfront Revitalization Corporation and Toronto and Region Conservation Authority, "Revised Terms of Reference," 33; Don Watershed Regeneration Council, *Forging a New Deal for the Don* (Toronto: Toronto and Region Conservation Authority, 2006).

8 Don Watershed Regeneration Council, *Forging a New Deal*, 11. In 2002, wetland habitat – those areas covered by marsh, wetland, or open water – constituted less than half of 1 per cent of watershed lands.
9 Ibid., 11.
10 Ibid., 7.
11 In addition to these ecological restoration initiatives, the city has initiated a twenty-five-year Wet Weather Flow Master Plan to reduce the impacts of polluted stormwater run-off within Toronto-area watersheds. The total capital cost for the twenty-five-year plan is approximately $1.047 billion, or $42 million per year. For more information, see https://www1.toronto.ca/wps/portal/contentonly?vgnextoid=972bab501d8ce310VgnVCM10000071d60f89RCRD (accessed 24 June 2014).
12 The Task Force to Bring Back the Don operated from 1989 until 2011, when its staff support from the city was eliminated.

References

Primary Sources

Archival Collections

Archives of Ontario
  F556. Ely Playter Fonds. Ely Playter Diary.
  F 47-11. Simcoe Family Fonds. Elizabeth Simcoe Sketches.
  RG 1-61-0-6. Miscellaneous Records Relating to Land surveys, Land surveyors and Land administration, 1792–1928.
  RG 1-112-1. Conservation Authorities Branch. Conservation Authorities Branch Photograph Albums.

City of Toronto Archives
  Fonds 2. City of Toronto Archives Collection.
    Series 60. City of Toronto Reports Collection.
    Series 112. Ephemera Relating to Toronto, 1854–2008.
    Series 607. Pamphlets Relating to Toronto.
    Series 1243. File 3. Mixed Media Materials Relating to Toronto. Skinner Family Records.
  Fonds 4. Charles Sauriol Fonds.
    Series 80. Photographs of the Don Valley.
    Series 81. Photographs of the Sauriol Cottage.
    Series 101. File 20. Photographs of Charles Sauriol. Historical Photographs of the Don Valley.
    Series 103. General Subject Files of Charles Sauriol, ca 1970–95.
    Series 104. Publications of Charles Sauriol, ca 1939–95.
    Series 107. Manuscripts of Charles Sauriol, 194?–1995.
    Series 292. Diaries of Charles Sauriol, 1926–94.

Fonds 70. Larry Becker Fonds.
Series 330. Larry Becker Postcards, ca 1890–1997.
Series 654. Larry Becker Library and Rare Books.
Fonds 79. Series 343. Speight, Van Nostrand and Gibson Ltd. Fonds. Manuscript Reference Materials of Speight, Van Nostrand and Gibson Ltd.
Fonds 92. Papers and Theses Collection.
Fonds 200. Former City of Toronto Fonds, 1834–1997.
Series 365. Department of Public Health Reports, 1885–1995.
Series 725. City of Toronto Public Works Dept. Maps and Plans, ca 1841–ca 1976
Series 1078. Toronto City Council Proceedings, Printed, 1859–1996.
Fonds 220. Municipality of Metropolitan Toronto Fonds.
Series 3. Road Construction Photographs of the Metropolitan Toronto Roads and Traffic Department, 1954–87.
Series 10. Official reports received by the Metropolitan Toronto Clerk's Department, 1949–90.
Series 40. Records of the Information Officer for the Metropolitan Toronto Planning Department, 1943–84.
Fonds 257. Metropolitan Toronto Planning Board Fonds.
Fonds 1231. James Salmon Collection.
Fonds 1244. William James Family Fonds.
Fonds 1548, Series 393. Alan Howard Fonds. John Boyd Sr Photographs.

Library and Archives Canada
R224-114-8-E. German Prisoner-of-War Labour Project Files, 1943–74.

Thomas Fisher Rare Book Library, University of Toronto
MS COLL 73. De Grassi Papers.

Toronto Port Authority Archives
PC 14. Photograph Collection. Les Baxter Collection.
Researcher Reference Files.
"Don River File."
"Keating Channel File."
RG 1. Board of the Toronto Harbour Commissioners Fonds.
Series 1. Board Minutes, 1911–40.
Series 2. Annual Reports, 1911–40.
Series 4. Harbour Trust Papers, 1851–1911.

RG 3. Records Department Fonds. Series 3. Records Department Inventory (Central Registry).
SC 11. Special Collections. Booklet and Pamphlet Collection.
SC 26. Vaughan Roberts Papers.

Toronto Public Library
 Toronto Reference Library
  Local History Publications.
  Frederick G. Gardiner: Clippings and Ephemera.
  Special Collections. Toronto Map Collection.

University of Toronto Map and Data Library. Digital Map Collection.

Government Documents

Archaeological Services Inc. "The Stage 4 Salvage Excavation of the Baker Site (AkGu-15), Lot 11, Concession 2 (WYS), Block 10, O.P.A. 400, Former Township of Vaughan, City of Vaughan, Regional Municipality of York, Ontario: License Report." Heritage Operations Unit, Ontario Ministry of Culture, June 2006.
Canada. Department of Public Works. *Memorandum with Accompanying Plans and Documents Relative to the Past and Present State of the Harbour of Toronto.* Ottawa: Department of Public Works, 1881.
– Environment Canada, Statistics Canada, and Health Canada. *Canadian Environmental Sustainability Indicators 2007,* n.d. http://www5.statcan.gc.ca/bsolc/olc-cel/olc-cel?catno=16-251-X&lang=eng.
– Indian Claims Commission. *Mississaugas of the New Credit First Nation Inquiry: Toronto Purchase Claim.* Ottawa: Indian Claims Commission, June 2003. http://www.indianclaims.ca/claimsmap/completed_claims_8-en.asp?id=73.
City of Toronto. *Making Waves: Principles for Building Toronto's Waterfront, Central Waterfront Part II Plan,* October 2001.
– *Don Valley Corridor Transportation Study Master Plan: Summary Report,* 2005.
– *Waterfront Revitalization Chronology.* Fact sheet, January 2008.
City of Toronto, Waterfront Toronto, and Toronto and Region Conservation Authority. "Port Lands Acceleration Initiative. Appendix 1: Summary of Findings," 2012. http://www.portlandsconsultation.ca/.
– "Port Lands Acceleration Initiative. Appendix 10: Port Lands Planning Summary," 2012. http://www.portlandsconsultation.ca/.
Don Watershed Regeneration Council. *Forging a New Deal for the Don.* Toronto: Toronto and Region Conservation Authority, 2006.

Metropolitan Toronto and Region Conservation Authority. *Forty Steps to a New Don: The Report of the Don Watershed Task Force.* Toronto: Metropolitan Toronto and Region Conservation Authority, 1994.

– *Plan for Flood Control and Water Conservation.* Woodbridge, Ontario, 1959.

Metropolitan Toronto and Region Remedial Action Plan. *Clean Waters, Clear Choices.* Toronto: Metropolitan Toronto and Region Remedial Action Plan, 1994.

Metropolitan Toronto Planning Board. "A Brief, Prepared by the Planning Board, Heads of Departments, and Officials of the Municipality of Metropolitan Toronto Presented to The Royal Commission on Canada's Economic Prospects by Frederick G. Gardiner, Q.C.," 3 January 1956.

– Transportation and Services Division. *Don Valley Parkway: Report and Analysis of Study for the Municipality of Metropolitan Toronto,* August 1955.

Michael Van Valkenburgh Associates, Inc. (MVVA). *Port Lands Estuary,* May 2007.

– for Waterfront Toronto. "Lower Don Lands Framework Plan." Waterfront Toronto, May 2013.

Ontario Department of Planning and Development. *Don Valley Conservation Report.* Toronto: Ontario Department of Planning and Development, 1950.

Task Force to Bring Back the Don. *Bringing Back the Don.* Toronto: City of Toronto Planning and Development Department, August 1991.

Toronto Harbour Commissioners. *Annual Report of the Toronto Harbor Commissioners for the Years 1915 and 1916.* Toronto: Toronto Harbour Commissioners, 1917.

– "Reports on the Improvement and Preservation of Toronto Harbour." *Supplement to the Canadian Journal* (1854).

– *Toronto Harbour: The Passing Years.* Toronto: Toronto Harbour Commissioners, 1985.

Toronto and Region Conservation Authority and Waterfront Toronto. *Don Mouth Naturalization and Port Lands Flood Protection Environmental Assessment: Executive Summary,* September 2013.

– *Don Mouth Naturalization and Port Lands Flood Protection Project: Amended Environmental Assessment Report,* April 2011.

Toronto and York Planning Board. *Second Report.* Toronto, 1951.

Toronto Area Watershed Management Study, and Paul Theil Associates Ltd. *Strategy for Improvement of Don River Water Quality: Summary Report.* Toronto: Queen's Printer, 1989.

Toronto City Planning Board. *Second Annual Report.* Toronto, 1943.

– *The Master Plan for the City of Toronto and Environs.* Toronto, 31 December 1943.

Toronto Waterfront Revitalization Corporation. *Building the Foundation: Toronto Waterfront Revitalization Corporation Annual Report 2002/03,* 2003.

– *Lower Don Lands Innovative Design Competition: Jury Report,* May 2007.

Toronto Waterfront Revitalization Corporation, and Toronto and Region Conservation Authority. *Don Mouth Naturalization and Port Lands Flood Protection Project: Revised Terms of Reference*. June 2006.

Toronto Waterfront Revitalization Task Force. *Our Toronto Waterfront: Gateway to the New Canada*, March 2000.

Waterfront Toronto. *Waterfront Revitalization Initiative: Proposed Five-Year Forecast / Ten-Year Plan 2007–2016*. Backgrounder Report to City of Toronto Executive Committee. Toronto, June 25, 2007. http://www.toronto.ca/legdocs/mmis/2007/ex/bgrd/backgroundfile-5086.pdf.

Theses and Unpublished Papers

Boritch, Helen. "The Making of Toronto the Good: the Organization of Policing and Production of Arrests, 1859 to 1955." PhD dissertation, University of Toronto, Department of Sociology, 1985.

Brace, Catherine. "One Hundred and Twenty Years of Sewerage: The Provision of Sewers in Toronto 1793–1913." MA thesis, University of Toronto, Department of Geography, 1993.

Clifford, Jim. "Suburban and Industrial Growth in the Lower Lea River Valley: An Environmental History of West Ham from 1855 to 1935." PhD dissertation, Graduate Programme in History, York University.

Ganton, Isobel K. "Development between Parliament Street and the Don River, 1793–1884," 1974. City of Toronto Archives. Fonds 92, Papers and Theses Collection, item 347.

Ingram, Darcy. "Nature's Improvement: Wildlife, Conservation, and Conflict in Quebec, 1850–1914." PhD dissertation, Department of History, McGill University, 2008.

Kheraj, Sean. "Inventing Nature's Past: An Environmental History of Stanley Park." PhD dissertation, York University, Graduate Programme in History, 2007.

McCallum, Todd. "'Still raining, market still rotten': Homeless Men and the Early Years of the Great Depression in Vancouver." PhD dissertation, Department of History, Queen's University, 2004.

McKee, Leila Gay Mitchell. "Voluntary Youth Organizations in Toronto, 1880–1930." PhD dissertation, Department of History, York University, 1983.

Mellen, Frances N. "The Development of the Toronto Waterfront during the Railway Expansion Era, 1850–1912." PhD dissertation, University of Toronto, Department of Geography, 1974.

Roberts, H. Julia. "Taverns and Tavern-Goers in Upper Canada, the 1790s to the 1850s." PhD dissertation, Department of History, University of Toronto, 1999.

Smith, Susan. "Industrial Development along the Banks of the Don River South of the Present Bloor-Danforth Thoroughfare from 1793–1911." Course paper, Department of Geography, University of Toronto, 1994.

Published Primary Sources

Adam, Graeme Mercer, Charles Pelham Mulvany, and Christopher Blackett Robinson. *History of Toronto and County of York*. Toronto: C. Blackett Robinson, 1885.

Attorney-General v. Gooderham & Worts et al. 1884. 10 P.R.U.C. 259.

Bixby, M.G. *Industries of Canada: Historical and Commercial Sketches of Toronto and Environs*. M.G. Bixby and Co., 1866.

Bonnycastle, Sir Richard H. "Report on the Preservation of the Harbour of York, Upper Canada, January 14, 1834." In *Memorandum with Accompanying Plans and Documents Relative to the Past and Present State of the Harbour of Toronto*, Appendix, pp. 10–17. Ottawa: Department of Public Works, 1881.

Bouchette, Joseph. "The British dominions in North America, or, A topographical and statistical description of the provinces of Lower and Upper Canada, New Brunswick, Nova Scotia, the Islands of Newfoundland, Prince Edward, and Cape Breton, including considerations on land-granting and emigration: to which are annexed, statistical tables and tables of distances, &c," 1831. http://eco.canadiana.ca/view/oocihm.42808.

Coleman v. City of Toronto. 1893. 23 OR 345.

Cruikshank, E.A., ed. "Simcoe Papers." *Ontario History* 26: 331.

Editorial. "Toronto General Hospital." *Upper Canada Journal of Medical, Surgical and Physical Science* 3, no. 2 (1853): 69–77.

Firth, Edith G. *The Town of York, 1793–1815: A Collection of Documents of Early Toronto*. Toronto: Champlain Society, 1962.

– *The Town of York, 1815–1834: A Further Collection of Documents of Early Toronto*. Toronto: Champlain Society, 1966.

Fleming, Sandford. "Toronto Harbour – Its Formation and Preservation." *Canadian Journal* 2 (1853): 105–7, 223–30.

Guthrie, Ann. *Don Valley Legacy: A Pioneer History*. Erin, ON: Boston Mills Press, 1986.

Hart, Patricia W. *Pioneering in North York: A History of the Borough*. Toronto: General Publishing, 1968.

Hounsom, Eric. *Toronto in 1810*. Toronto: Ryerson Press, 1970.

Innis, Mary Quayle. *Mrs. Simcoe's Diary*. Toronto: MacMillan, 1965.

Jameson, Anna Brownell. *Winter Studies and Summer Rambles in Canada: Selections*. New Canadian Library. Toronto: McClelland and Stewart, 2008.

Keele, W.C. *The Provincial Justice: Or, Magistrate's Manual, Being a Complete Digest of the Criminal Law and a Compendium and General View of the Provincial Law*. Toronto: Upper Canada Gazette Office, 1835.

Kellogg, Paul Underwood. *The Pittsburgh Survey: Findings in Six Volumes*. New York: New York Charities Publication Committee, 1914.

Kenney, J.F., ed. "Walter Butler's Journal of an Expedition along the North Shore of Lake Ontario, 1779." *Canadian Historical Review* 1 (1920): 381–91.

Might's Greater Toronto City Directory. Toronto: Might Directories, 1900–40.

Report of the Commissioners Appointed to Enquire into the Prison and Reformatory System of Ontario. Toronto: Warwick and Sons, 1891.

Richardson, Hugh. "York Harbour." In *Memorandum with Accompanying Plans and Documents Relative to the Past and Present State of the Harbour of Toronto*, Appendix, pp. 3–10. Ottawa: Department of Public Works, 1881.

Richardson, H., W. Chisholm, and J.G. Chewett. "Report of the Select Committee on the Improvement of the Harbour of York." In *Memorandum with Accompanying Plans and Documents Relative to the Past and Present State of the Harbour of Toronto*, Appendix, pp. 1–3. Ottawa: Department of Public Works, 1881.

Rickey v. City of Toronto, Schofield Holden Machine Co. v. City of Toronto. 1914. 30 OLR 523.

Robertson, John Ross. *Robertson's Landmarks of Toronto: A Collection of Historical Sketches of the Old Town of York from 1792 until 1833, and of Toronto from 1834 to 1893*. 4 vols. Toronto: J. Ross Robertson, 1894.

– *The Diary of Mrs. John Graves Simcoe, Wife of the First Lieutenant-Governor of the Province of Upper Canada, 1792–6*. Toronto: W. Briggs, 1911. https://archive.org/details/diaryofmrsjohngr00simcuoft.

Sauriol, Charles. *A Beeman's Journey*. Toronto: Natural Heritage/Natural History, 1984.

– *Green Footsteps: Recollections of a Grassroots Conservationist*. Toronto: Hemlock Press, 1991.

– *Pioneers of the Don*. Toronto: Charles Sauriol, 1995.

– "The Presence of the de Grassi Family on the Don River." *Italian Canadiana* 12 (1996): 124–8.

– *Remembering the Don: A Rare Record of Earlier Times within the Don River Valley*. Toronto: Consolidated Amethyst Communications, 1981.

– *Tales of the Don*. Toronto: Natural Heritage / Natural History, 1984.

– *Trails of the Don*. Orillia, ON: Hemlock Press, 1992.

Scadding, Henry. *Toronto of Old: Collections and Recollections Illustrative of the Early Settlement and Social Life of the Capital of Ontario*. Toronto: Adam, Stevenson and Co., 1873.

Seton, Ernest Thompson. *Trail of an Artist-Naturalist: The Autobiography of Ernest Thompson Seton*. London: Hodder and Stoughton, 1951.

– *Two Little Savages: Being the Adventures of Two Boys Who Lived as Indians and What They Learned*. New York: Grosset and Dunlap, 1903.

Smith, William Henry. *Canada, Past, Present and Future: Being a Historical Geographical, Geological and Statistical Account of Canada West*. Toronto: Thomas Maclear, 1851.

Timperlake, J. *Illustrated Toronto: past and present, being an historical and descriptive guide-book: comprising its architecture, manufacture, trade; its social, literary, scientific, and charitable institutions: its churches, schools, and colleges: and other principal points of interest to the visitor and resident: together with a key to the publisher's bird's-eye view of the city*. Toronto: P.A. Gross, 1877.

White, Richard W. *Urban Infrastructure and Urban Growth in the Toronto Region: 1950s to the 1990s*. Toronto: Neptis Foundation, 2003.

Magazines, Newspapers, and Periodicals

Canadian Geographic
Canadian Magazine
Canadian Manufacturer
Globe and Mail
Grip
Maclean's
Time
Toronto Board of Trade Journal (November 1932)
Toronto Leader
Toronto Life (May 2006)
Toronto Magazine
Toronto Mail and Empire
Toronto Patriot
Toronto Star
Toronto Telegram
Toronto World
University of Toronto Monthly
York Pioneer

Secondary Sources

Acton, T.A. *Gypsy Politics and Traveller Identity*. Hatfield, Hertfordshire: University of Hertfordshire Press, 1997.

Allardyce, Gilbert. "'The Vexed Question of Sawdust': River Pollution in Nineteenth Century New Brunswick." *Dalhousie Review* 52, no. 2 (1972): 177–90.

Altmeyer, George. "Three Ideas of Nature in Canada, 1893–1914." In *Consuming Canada: Readings in Environmental History*, edited by Chad Gaffield and Pam Gaffield, 96–118. Toronto: Copp Clark, 1995.

Anderson, Kay J. *Vancouver's Chinatown: Racial Discourse in Canada, 1875–1980*. Montreal and Kingston: McGill-Queen's University Press, 1991.

Armstrong, Christopher, Matthew Evenden, and H.V. Nelles. *The River Returns: An Environmental History of the Bow*. Montreal and Kingston: McGill-Queen's University Press, 2009.

Armstrong, Frederick H. *A City in the Making: Progress, People and Perils in Victorian Toronto*. Toronto: Dundurn Press, 1988.

Artibise, Alan F.J., and Gilbert A. Stelter. "Conservation Planning and Urban Planning: The Canadian Commission of Conservation in Historical Perspective." In *Consuming Canada: Readings in Environmental History*, edited by Chad Gaffield and Pam Gaffield, 152–69. Toronto: Copp Clark, 1995.

Barnett, Gabrielle. "Drive-By Viewing: Visual Consciousness and Forest Preservation in the Automobile Age." *Technology and Culture* 45, no. 1 (January 2004): 30–54.

Beattie, Sara, and Amy Mole. *Police Resources in Canada, 2007*. Ottawa: Statistics Canada, 2007.

Benidickson, Jamie. *The Culture of Flushing: A Social and Legal History of Sewage*. Vancouver: UBC Press, 2007.

– "Ontario Water Quality, Public Health, and the Law, 1880–1930." In *Essays in the History of Canadian Law*, edited by G. Blaine Baker and Jim Phillips, 115–41. Toronto: University of Toronto Press, 1999.

Benn, Carl. *The History of Toronto: An 11,000 Year Journey*. Toronto: City of Toronto Culture Division, 2006.

Berger, Carl. "The True North Strong and Free." In *Nationalism in Canada*, edited by Peter Russell, 3–26. Toronto and Montreal: McGraw-Hill Ryerson, 1966.

Bocking, Stephen. "Constructing Urban Expertise: Professional and Political Authority in Toronto, 1940–1970." *Journal of Urban History* 33, no. 1 (2006): 51–76.

Bonnell, Jennifer. "Bringing Back the Don: Sixty Years of Community Action." In *HtO: Toronto's Water from Lake Iroquois to Lost Rivers to Low-Flow Toilets*, edited by Wayne Reeves and Christina Palassio, 266–83. Toronto: Coach House Books, 2008.

Bouchier, Nancy B., and Ken Cruikshank. "The War on the Squatters, 1920–1940: Hamilton's Boathouse Community and the Re-Creation of Recreation on Burlington Bay." *Labour / Le Travail* 51 (2003): 9–46.

Brace, Catherine. "Public Works in the Canadian City; the Provision of Sewers in Toronto 1870–1913." *Urban History Review* 23, no. 2 (1995): 33–43.

Brunvand, Jan Harold. *The Vanishing Hitchhiker: American Urban Legends and Their Meaning*. New York: Norton, 1981.

Bullard, Robert. *Dumping in Dixie: Race, Class and Environmental Quality*. Boulder, CO: Westview Press, 1990.

Bunce, Susannah. "Developing Sustainability: Planning, Policy and Property Development in Toronto's East Bayfront." In *Reshaping Toronto's Waterfront*, edited by Gene Desfor and Jennefer Laidley, 287–304. Toronto: University of Toronto Press, 2011.

Burr, Christina. *Spreading the Light: Work and Labour Reform in Late-Nineteenth Century Toronto*. Toronto: University of Toronto Press, 1999.

Campbell, Joseph. *The Hero with a Thousand Faces*. Princeton, NJ: Princeton University Press.

Careless, J.M.S. *Toronto to 1918: An Illustrated History*. Toronto: James Lorimer, 1984.

Cassidy, H.M. *Unemployment and Relief in Ontario, 1929–1932: A Survey and Report*. Toronto: J.M. Dent and Sons, 1932.

Castonguay, Stéphane. "The Production of Flood as Natural Catastrophe: Extreme Events and the Construction of Vulnerability in the Drainage Basin of the St. Francis River (Quebec), Mid-Nineteenth to Mid-Twentieth Century." *Environmental History* 12, no. 4 (2007): 820–44.

Cioc, Mark. *The Rhine: An Eco-Biography, 1815–2000*. Seattle: University of Washington Press, 2002.

Clarke, C.K. *A History of the Toronto General Hospital: Including an Account of the Medal of the Loyal and Patriotic Society of 1812*. Toronto: William Briggs, 1913.

Coleman, A.P. *The Last Million Years: A History of the Pleistocene in North America*. Toronto: University of Toronto Press, 1941.

Collins, Timothy M., Edward K. Muller, and Joel A. Tarr. "Pittsburgh's Three Rivers: From Industrial Infrastructure to Environmental Asset." In *Rivers in History: Perspectives on Waterways in Europe and North America*, edited by Christof Mauch and Thomas Zeller, 41–62. Pittsburgh, PA: University of Pittsburgh Press, 2008.

Colton, Timothy J. *Big Daddy: Frederick G. Gardiner and the Building of Metropolitan Toronto*. Toronto: University of Toronto Press, 1980.

Connor, J.T.H. *Doing Good: The Life of Toronto's General Hospital*. Toronto: University of Toronto Press, 2000.

Cook, Ramsay. *The Regenerators: Social Criticism in Late Victorian English Canada*. Toronto: University of Toronto Press, 1985.

Craddock, Susan. *City Of Plagues: Disease, Poverty, and Deviance in San Francisco*. Minneapolis: University of Minnesota Press, 2000.

Creighton, Donald. *The Empire of the St. Lawrence: A Study in Commerce and Politics*. Toronto: Macmillan, 1956.

Crombie, David. *Regeneration: Toronto's Waterfront and the Sustainable City. Final Report, Royal Commission on the Future of the Toronto Waterfront*. Ottawa: Minister of Supply and Services Canada, 1992.

Cronon, William. *Changes in the Land: Indians, Colonists, and the Ecology of New England*. New York: Hill and Wang, 1983.

– "Modes of Prophecy and Production: Placing Nature in History." *Journal of American History* 76, no. 4 (1990): 1122–31.

– *Nature's Metropolis: Chicago and the Great West*. New York and London: W.W. Norton, 1991.

– "The Trouble with Wilderness; or, Getting Back to the Wrong Nature." In *Uncommon Ground: Rethinking the Human Place in Nature*, edited by William Cronon, 69–90. New York: W.W. Norton, 1996.

Cruikshank, Ken, and Nancy B. Bouchier. "Blighted Areas and Obnoxious Industries: Constructing Environmental Inequality on an Industrial Waterfront, Hamilton, Ontario, 1890-1960." *Environmental History* 9, no. 3 (2004): 464–96.

Curtin, Philip D. *Death by Migration: Europe's Encounter with the Tropical World in the Nineteenth Century*. Cambridge: Cambridge University Press, 1989.

Dagenais, Michèle, and Caroline Durand. "Cleansing, Draining and Sanitizing the City: Conceptions and Uses of Water in the Montreal Region." *Canadian Historical Review* 87, no. 4 (2006): 621–51.

Dalbey, Matthew. *Regional Visionaries and Metropolitan Boosters: Decentralization, Regional Planning, and Parkways During the Interwar Years*. Boston: Kluwer Academic Publishers, 2002.

Daniels, Stephen, and Catherine Nash. "Lifepaths: Geography and Biography." *Journal of Historical Geography* 30 (2004): 449–58.

Darke, Eleanor. *"A Mill Should Be Built Thereon": An Early History of Todmorden Mills*. Toronto: East York Historical Society, 1995.

Darnton, Robert. *The Great Cat Massacre: And Other Episodes in French Cultural History*. Vintage, 1985.

Davidson, True. *The Golden Years of East York*. Toronto: Borough of East York, 1976.

Davis, Natalie Zemon. *The Return of Martin Guerre*. Cambridge, MA: Harvard University Press, 1984.

Davis, Timothy. "The Rise and Decline of the American Parkway." In *The World beyond the Windshield: Roads and Landscapes in the United States and Europe*, edited by Christof Mauch and Thomas Zeller, 35–58. Athens: Ohio University Press, 2008.

Desfor, Gene. "Planning Urban Waterfront Industrial Districts: Toronto's Ashbridge's Bay, 1889–1910." *Urban History Review* 17, no. 2 (1988): 77–91.

Desfor, Gene, and Jennifer Bonnell. "Socio-ecological Change in the Nineteenth and Twenty-First Centuries: The Lower Don River." In *Reshaping Toronto's Waterfront*, edited by Gene Desfor and Jennefer Laidley, 305–25. Toronto: University of Toronto Press, 2011.

Desfor, Gene, and Roger Keil. "Every River Tells a Story: The Don River (Toronto) and the Los Angeles River (Los Angeles) as Articulating Landscapes." *Journal of Environmental Policy and Planning* 2, no. 1 (2000): 5–23.

– *Nature and the City: Making Environmental Policy in Toronto and Los Angeles.* Tucson: University of Arizona Press, 2004.

Desfor, Gene, and Jennefer Laidley, eds. *Reshaping Toronto's Waterfront.* Toronto: University of Toronto Press, 2011.

Dick, Lyle. *Muskox Land: Ellesmere Island in the Age of Contact.* Calgary: University of Calgary Press, 2001.

Donahue, Brian. *The Great Meadow: Farmers and Land in Colonial Concord.* New Haven, CT: Yale University Press, 2007.

Driver, Felix. "Moral Geographies: Social Science and the Urban Environment in Mid-Nineteenth Century England." *Transactions of the Institute of British Geographers* 13, no. 3 (1 January 1988): 275–87.

Eidelman, Gabriel. "Who's in Charge? Jurisdictional Gridlock and the Genesis of Waterfront Toronto." In *Reshaping Toronto's Waterfront*, edited by Gene Desfor and Jennefer Laidley, 263–86. Toronto: University of Toronto Press, 2011.

Elkind, Sarah S. *Bay Cities and Water Politics: The Battle for Resources in Boston and Oakland.* Lawrence: University Press of Kansas, 1998.

Evenden, Matthew. *Fish versus Power: An Environmental History of the Fraser.* Cambridge: Cambridge University Press, 2004.

Eyles, Nick. *Toronto Rocks: The Geological Legacy of the Toronto Region.* Toronto: Fitzhenry and Whiteside, 2004.

Filey, Mike. "Parkway with a Past." In *Toronto Sketches 9*, 151–3. Toronto: Dundurn Group, 2006.

Fingard, Judith. *The Dark Side of Life in Victorian Halifax.* Porters Lake, NS: Pottersfield Press, 1989.

– *Jack in Port: Sailortowns of Eastern Canada.* Toronto: University of Toronto Press, 1982.

Fischler, Raphael. "Development Controls in Toronto in the Nineteenth Century." *Urban History Review* 36, no. 1 (2007): 16–31.

Fletcher, Ron. *Over the Don.* Toronto: privately printed, 2002.

Forman, Richard T.T., Daniel Sperling, John A. Bissonette, Anthony P. Clevenger, Carol D. Cutshall, Virginia H. Dale, and Lenore Fahrig. *Road Ecology: Science and Solutions*. Washington, DC: Island Press, 2003.

Freeman, Victoria. "'Toronto Has No History!' Indigeneity, Settler Colonialism and Historical Memory in Canada's Largest City." *Urban History Review* 38, no. 2 (Spring 2010): 21–35.

Friesen, Gerald. *Citizens and Nation: An Essay on History, Communication, and Canada*. Toronto: University of Toronto Press, 2000.

– "The Evolving Meanings of Region in Canada." *Canadian Historical Review* 82, no. 3 (2001): 530–45.

Gad, Gunter. "Location Patterns of Manufacturing: Toronto in the Early 1880s." *Urban History Review* 22, no. 2 (1994): 113–38.

Ganton, Isobel K. "Land Subdivision in Toronto, 1851–1883." In *Shaping the Urban Landscape*, edited by Gilbert A. Stelter and Alan F.J. Artibise, 200–31. Ottawa: Carleton University Press, 1982.

Gifford, Jim, and Mike Filey. *Hurricane Hazel: Canada's Storm of the Century*. Toronto: Dundurn Press, 2004.

Gillis, R. Peter. "Rivers of Sawdust: The Battle over Industrial Pollution in Canada, 1865–1903." *Journal of Canadian Studies* 21, no. 1 (1986): 84–103.

Glazebrook, G.P. *The Story of Toronto*. Toronto: University of Toronto Press, 1971.

Goheen, Peter. "The Struggle for Urban Public Space: Disposing of the Toronto Waterfront in the Nineteenth Century." In *Cultural Encounters with the Environment*, edited by Alexander B. Murphy and Douglas L. Johnson, 59–78. Lanham, MD: Rowman and Littlefield, 2000.

Gottlieb, Robert. *Forcing the Spring: The Transformation of the American Environmental Movement*. Washington, DC: Island Press, 2005.

Greer, Kirsten, and Laura Cameron. "'Swee-ee-et Cánada, Cánada, Cánada': Sensuous Landscapes of Birdwatching in the Eastern Provinces, 1900–1939." *Material History Review* 62 (Fall 2005): 35–48.

Gregory, Ian N., and Paul S. Ell. *Historical GIS: Technologies, Methodologies, and Scholarship*. Cambridge and New York: Cambridge University Press, 2008.

Guthrie, Ann. *Don Valley Legacy: A Pioneer History*. Erin, ON: Boston Mills Press, 1986.

Hall, Marcus. *Earth Repair: A Transatlantic History of Environmental Restoration*. Charlottesville: University of Virginia Press, 2005.

Hamlin, Christopher. *Public Health and Social Justice in the Age of Chadwick: Britain, 1800–1854*. Cambridge and New York: Cambridge University Press, 1998.

– *A Science of Impurity: Water Analysis in Nineteenth Century Britain*. Bristol: Adam Hilger, 1990.

Harney, Robert F., and Harold Troper. *Immigrants: A Portrait of the Urban Experience, 1890–1930.* Toronto: Van Nostrand Reinhold, 1975.

Harris, Cole. *Making Native Space: Colonialism, Resistance, and Reserves in British Columbia.* Vancouver: UBC Press, 2002.

Harris, Richard. *Unplanned Suburbs: Toronto's American Tragedy, 1900 to 1950.* Baltimore: John Hopkins University Press, 1996.

Harvey, David. *The Condition of Postmodernity.* Oxford and Cambridge, MA: Blackwell, 1989.

Hayes, Derek. *Historical Atlas of Toronto.* Vancouver: Douglas and McIntyre, 2008.

Hays, Samuel P. *Beauty, Health and Permanence: Environmental Politics in the United States, 1955–1985.* Cambridge: Cambridge University Press, 1987.

Herzberg, Louise, and Helen Juhola. "Don Valley." In *Special Places: The Changing Ecosystems of the Toronto Region,* 283–285. Vancouver: UBC Press, 1999.

Higgs, Eric. *Nature by Design: People, Natural Process, and Ecological Restoration.* Cambridge, MA: MIT Press, 2003.

Hillier, Amy, and Anne Kelly Knowles. *Placing History: How Maps, Spatial Data, and GIS Are Changing Historical Scholarship.* Redlands, CA: ESRI Press, 2008.

Hitchcock, Tim. *Down and Out in Eighteenth-Century London.* London and New York: Hambledon and London, 2004.

Hobsbawm, E.J. *Bandits.* New York: Delacorte Press, 1969.

– *Primitive Rebels: Studies in Archaic Forms of Social Movement in the 19th and 20th Centuries.* New York: Norton, 1965.

Hoffman, Ronald. "Introduction." In *Through a Glass Darkly: Reflections on Personal Identity in Early America,* edited by Ronald Hoffman, Mechal Sobel, and Fredrika J. Teute. Chapel Hill: University of North Carolina Press, 1997.

Holmes, Steven J. *The Young John Muir: An Environmental Biography.* Madison: University of Wisconsin Press, 1999.

Horn, Michiel. *The Great Depression of the 1930s in Canada.* Ottawa: Canadian Historical Association, 1984.

Hume, Christopher. *On the Waterfront: How a Small Agency with Paltry Power and Precarious Funding Changed a City.* StarDispatches. Toronto: Toronto Star Newspapers, 2013.

Hurley, Andrew. "Creating Ecological Wastelands: Oil Pollution in New York City, 1870–1900." *Journal of Urban History* 20, no. 3 (May 1994): 340–64.

– *Environmental Inequalities: Class, Race, and Industrial Pollution in Gary, Indiana, 1945–1980.* Chapel Hill: University of North Carolina Press, 1995.

Ingram, Darcy. "'Au temps et dans les quantités qui lui plaisent': Poachers, Outlaws, and Rural Banditry in Quebec." *Histoire Sociale/Social History* 42/83 (May 2009): 1–34.

Innis, Harold A. *The Fur Trade in Canada: An Introduction to Canadian Economic History*. Toronto: University of Toronto Press, 1930.

– "Settlement and the Mining Frontier." In *Canadian Frontiers of Settlement*. Toronto: Macmillan, 1936.

Isenberg, Andrew C. *The Nature of Cities: Culture, Landscape, and Urban Space*. Toronto: Hushion House, 2006.

Jackson, John Brinckerhoff. *Landscape in Sight: Looking at America*. Edited by Helen Lefkowitz Horowitz. New Haven, CT: Yale University Press, 1997.

Jacoby, Karl. *Crimes against Nature: Squatters, Poachers, Thieves, and the Hidden History of American Conservation*. Berkeley and Los Angeles: University of California Press, 2001.

Jasen, Patricia. *Wild Things: Nature, Culture, and Tourism in Ontario, 1790–1914*. Toronto: University of Toronto Press, 1995.

Johnson, Leo A. "The Mississauga–Lake Ontario Land Surrender of 1805." *Ontario History* 83, no. 3 (1990): 233–53.

Keeling, Arn. "Sink or Swim: Water Pollution and Environmental Politics in Vancouver, 1889–1975." *BC Studies* 142/143 (Summer/Autumn 2004): 69–104.

Kelman, Ari. *A River and Its City: The Nature of Landscape in New Orleans*. Berkeley: University of California Press, 2003.

Kennedy, Betty. *Hurricane Hazel*. Toronto: Macmillan of Canada, 1979.

Kheraj, Sean. "Restoring Nature: Ecology, Memory, and the Storm History of Vancouver's Stanley Park." *Canadian Historical Review* 88, no. 4 (2007): 577–612.

Kuletz, Valerie L. *The Tainted Desert: Environmental and Social Ruin in the American West*. New York and London: Routledge, 1998.

Langston, Nancy. *Forest Dreams, Forest Nightmares: The Paradox of Old Growth in the Inland West*. Seattle: University of Washington Press, 1996.

Lears, T.J. Jackson. *No Place of Grace: Antimodernism and Transformation of American Culture, 1880–1920*. New York: Pantheon, 1981.

Lee, Keekok. "Is Nature Autonomous?" In *Recognizing the Autonomy of Nature: Theory and Practice*, edited by Thomas Heyd, 54–74. New York: Columbia University Press, 2005.

Lefebvre, Henri. *The Production of Space*. London: Wiley-Blackwell, 1991.

Lemon, James. *Toronto since 1918: An Illustrated History*. Toronto: Lorimer, 1985.

Lepore, Jill. "Historians Who Love Too Much: Reflections on Microhistory and Biography." *Journal of American History* 88, no. 1 (2001): 129–44.

Levi, Giovanni. "On Microhistory." In *New Perspectives on Historical Writing*, edited by Peter Burke, 93–113. University Park: Pennsylvania State University Press, 1992.

Lewis, Robert. *Manufacturing Montreal: The Making of an Industrial Landscape, 1850 to 1930*. Baltimore and London: Johns Hopkins University Press, 2000.

Locke, John. *The Second Treatise of Government*. Edited by Thomas P. Peardon. New York: Macmillan, 1952.

Loo, Tina. "Making a Modern Wilderness: Conserving Wildlife in Twentieth-Century Canada." *Canadian Historical Review* 82, no. 1 (2001): 92–120.

– *States of Nature: Conserving Canada's Wildlife in the Twentieth Century*. Vancouver: UBC Press, 2007.

Lowenthal, David. *The Past Is a Foreign Country*. New York: Cambridge University Press, 1985.

Lyon, John Tylor. "'A Picturesque Lot': The Gypsies in Peterborough." *Beaver* 78, no. 5 (1998): 25–30.

MacDonald, Robert I. "Toronto's Natural History." In *Toronto: An Illustrated History of Its First 12,000 Years*, edited by Ronald F. Williamson, 11–24. Toronto: James Lorimer, 2008.

MacDougall, Heather A. "The Genesis of Public Health Reform in Toronto, 1869–1890." *Urban History Review* 10, no. 3 (February 1982): 1–9.

– "Public Health in Toronto's Municipal Politics: The Canniff Years, 1883–1890." *Bulletin of the History of Medicine* 55, no. 2 (1981): 186–202.

MacLennan, Hugh. *Seven Rivers of Canada*. Toronto: MacMillan, 1961.

Magnusson, Sigurdur Gylfi. "What Is Microhistory?" History News Network, 8 August 2006. http://hnn.us/article/23720.

Masters, Donald C. *The Rise of Toronto, 1850–1890*. Toronto: University of Toronto Press, 1947.

Mayall, David. *Gypsy-Travellers in Nineteenth-Century Society*. Cambridge and New York: Cambridge University Press, 1988.

Mayne, Alan. "On the Edge of History." *Journal of Urban History* 26, no. 2 (2000): 249–58.

McCallum, Todd. "The Great Depression's First History? The Vancouver Archives of Major J.S. Matthews and the Writing of Hobo History." *Canadian Historical Review* 87, no. 1 (2006): 79–107.

McKay, Ian. "The Liberal Order Framework: A Prospectus for a Reconnaissance of Canadian History." *Canadian Historical Review* 81, no. 4 (2000): 617–45.

– *The Quest of the Folk: Antimodernism and Cultural Selection in Twentieth-Century Nova Scotia*. Montreal and Kingston: McGill-Queen's University Press, 1994.

Meinig, D.W. "The Beholding Eye: Ten Versions of the Same Scene." In *The Interpretation of Ordinary Landscapes: Geographical Essays*, edited by D.W. Meinig, 33–48. New York and Oxford: Oxford University Press, 1979.

Melosi, Martin V. *Effluent America: Cities, Industry, Energy, and the Environment*. Pittsburgh, PA: University of Pittsburgh Press, 2001.

– *Pollution and Reform in American Cities, 1870–1930*. Austin and London: University of Texas Press, 1980.

– *The Sanitary City: Urban Infrastructure in America from Colonial Times to the Present*. Baltimore: Johns Hopkins University Press, 2000.

Merchant, Carolyn. *Reinventing Eden: The Fate of Nature in Western Culture*. London and New York: Routledge, 2003.

Merrens, Roy. "Port Authorities as Urban Land Developers: The Case of the Toronto Harbour Commissioners and Their Outer Harbour Project, 1912–1968." *Urban History Review* 17, no. 2 (October 1988): 92–105.

Michaels, Anne. *Fugitive Pieces*. Toronto: McClelland and Stewart, 1996.

Miedema, Gary. "When the Rivers Really Ran: Water-powered Industry in Toronto." In *HtO: Toronto's Water from Lake Iroquois to Lost Rivers to Low-Flow Toilets*, edited by Wayne Reeves and Christina Palassio, 66–73. Toronto: Coach House Books, 2008.

Mitchell, Don. *The Lie of the Land: Migrant Workers and the California Landscape*. Minneapolis: University of Minnesota Press, 1996.

Mitman, Gregg. "In Search of Health: Landscape and Disease in American Environmental History." *Environmental History* 10, no. 2 (2005): 184–210.

Mitman, Gregg, Michelle Murphy, and Christopher Sellers. "Introduction: A Cloud over History." *Osiris* 19. Landscapes of Exposure: Knowledge and Illness in Modern Environments (2004): 1–17.

Moir, Michael. "Toronto's Waterfront at War, 1914–1918." *Archivaria* 28 (Summer 1989): 126–40.

Moran, James E. *Committed to the State Asylum: Insanity and Society in Nineteenth-Century Quebec and Ontario*. Montreal and Kingston: McGill-Queen's University Press, 2001.

Mosley, Stephen. "Common Ground: Integrating Social and Environmental History." *Journal of Social History* 39, no. 3 (Spring 2006): 915–33.

Murton, James. *Creating a Modern Countryside: Liberalism and Land Resettlement in British Columbia*. Vancouver: UBC Press, 2007.

Myers, Tamara. *Caught: Montreal's Modern Girls and the Law, 1869–1945*. Toronto: University of Toronto Press, 2006.

Nash, Linda. "The Changing Experience of Nature: Historical Encounters with a Northwest River." *Journal of American History* 86, no. 4 (2000): 1600–29.

– *Inescapable Ecologies: A History of Environment, Disease, and Knowledge*. Berkeley: University of California Press, 2006.

Nelles, H.V. *The Politics of Development: Forests, Mines and Hydro-Electric Power in Ontario, 1849–1941*. Toronto: Macmillan, 1974.

Newell, Dianne, and Ralph Greenhill. *Survivals: Aspects of Industrial Archaeology in Ontario*. Erin, ON: Boston Mills Press, 1989.

Nora, Pierre. *Realms of Memory: Rethinking the French Past*. New York: Columbia University Press, 1996.

Ogborn, Miles, and Chris Philo. "Soldiers, Sailors and Moral Locations in Nineteenth-Century Portsmouth." *Area* 26, no. 3 (September 1, 1994): 221–31.

Oliver, Peter. *"Terror to Evil-Doers": Prisons and Punishments in Nineteenth-Century Ontario*. Toronto: University of Toronto Press, 1998.

O'Mara, James. "Shaping Urban Waterfronts: The Role of Toronto's Harbour Commissioners, 1911–1960." Discussion Paper. Department of Geography, York University, 1976.

Ondaatje, Michael. *In the Skin of a Lion*. Toronto: Vintage Canada, 1996.

Otter, Christopher. "Cleansing and Clarifying: Technology and Perception in Nineteenth-Century London." *Journal of British Studies* 43, no. 1 (2004): 40–64.

Park, Robert. *Human Communities: The City and Human Ecology*. Glencoe, IL: Free Press, 1952.

Park, Robert, Ernest W. Burgess, and Roderick D. McKenzie. *The City*. Chicago: University of Chicago Press, 1925.

Parr, Joy. "Notes for a More Sensuous History of Twentieth-Century Canada: The Timely, the Tacit, and the Material Body." *Canadian Historical Review* 82, no. 4 (2001): 720–45.

– *Sensing Changes: Technologies, Environments, and the Everyday, 1953–2003*. Vancouver: UBC Press, 2009.

– "Smells Like? Sources of Uncertainty in the History of a Great Lakes Environment." *Environmental History* 11, no. 2 (April 2006): 282–312.

Perry, Adele. *On the Edge of Empire: Gender, Race, and the Making of British Columbia, 1849–1871*. Toronto: University of Toronto Press, 2001.

Pitsula, James M. "The Treatment of Tramps in Late Nineteenth-Century Toronto." *Canadian Historical Association: Historical Papers* 15, no. 1 (1980): 116–32.

Platt, Harold L. *Shock Cities: The Environmental Transformation and Reform of Manchester and Chicago*. Chicago: University of Chicago Press, 2005.

Ploszajska, Teresa. "Moral Landscapes and Manipulated Spaces: Gender, Class and Space in Victorian Reformatory Schools." *Journal of Historical Geography* 20, no. 4 (1994): 413–29.

Price, Jenny. "Remaking American Environmentalism: On the Banks of the L.A. River." *Environmental History* 13, no. 3 (2008): 536–55.

Pyne, Stephen J. *Fire in America: A Cultural History of Wildland and Rural Fire*. Seattle: University of Washington Press, 1982.

Quarrington, Paul. *The Ravine*. Toronto: Vintage Canada, 2009.

Raibmon, Paige. *Authentic Indians: Episodes of Encounter from the Late-Nineteenth-Century Northwest Coast.* Durham and London: Duke University Press, 2005.

Rajala, Richard A. *Clearcutting the Pacific Rain Forest: Production, Science, and Regulation.* Vancouver: UBC Press, 1999.

Ratcliffe, Barrie M. "Perceptions and Realities of the Urban Margin: The Rag Pickers of Paris in the First Half of the Nineteenth Century." *Canadian Journal of History* 27, no. 2 (1992): 197–233.

Read, Jennifer. "'Let us heed the voice of youth': Laundry Detergents, Phosphates and the Emergence of the Environmental Movement in Ontario." *Journal of the Canadian Historical Association* 7 (1996): 227–50.

Reeves, Wayne. "From Acquisition to Restoration: A History of Protecting Toronto's Natural Places." In *Special Places: The Changing Ecosystems of the Toronto Region*, 229–41. Vancouver: UBC Press, 1999.

– "From the Ground Up: Fragments toward an Environmental History of Tkaronto." In *GreenTOpia: Towards a Sustainable Toronto*, edited by Alana Wilcox, Christina Palassio, and Jonny Dovercourt, 64–75. Toronto: Coach House Books, 2007.

– "Visions for the Metropolitan Toronto Waterfront, I: Toward Comprehensive Planning, 1852–1935." Major report no. 27. Department of Geography, University of Toronto, December 1992.

– "Visions for the Metropolitan Toronto Waterfront, II: Forging a Regional Identity, 1913–68." Major report no. 28, Department of Geography, University of Toronto, April 1993.

Richardson, Judith. *Possessions: The History and Uses of Haunting in the Hudson Valley.* Cambridge, M: Harvard University Press, 2003.

Riendeau, Roger E. "Servicing the Modern City 1900–30." In *Forging a Consensus: Historical Essays on Toronto*, edited by Victor L. Russell, 157–80. Toronto: University of Toronto Press, 1984.

Robinson, Danielle, and Ken Cruikshank. "Hurricane Hazel: Disaster Relief, Politics, and Society in Canada, 1954–55." *Journal of Canadian Studies* 40, no. 1 (2006): 37–70.

Rogers, Edward S., and Donald B. Smith, eds. *Aboriginal Ontario: Historical Perspectives on the First Nations.* Toronto: Dundurn Press, 1994.

Rome, Adam. *The Bulldozer in the Countryside: Suburban Sprawl and the Rise of American Environmentalism.* Cambridge and New York: Cambridge University Press, 2001.

Roots, Betty I., Donald A. Chant, and Conrad E. Heidenreich. *Special Places: The Changing Ecosystems of the Toronto Region.* Vancouver: UBC Press, 1999.

Rust-D'Eye, George H. *Cabbagetown Remembered*. Erin, ON: The Boston Mills Press, 1984.

Samuel, Raphael. *Theatres of Memory*. New York: Verso, 1994.

Sanderson, Christopher, and Pierre Filion. "From Harbour Commission to Port Authority: Institutionalizing the Federal Government's Role in Waterfront Development." In *Reshaping Toronto's Waterfront*, edited by Gene Desfor and Jennefer Laidley, 224–44. Toronto: University of Toronto Press, 2011.

Sandlos, John. *Hunters at the Margin: Native People and Wildlife Conservation in the Northwest Territories*. Vancouver: UBC Press, 2007.

Sandwell, R.W. *Beyond the City Limits: Rural History in British Columbia*. Vancouver: UBC Press, 1999.

– "History on the Ground: Microhistory and Environmental History." In *Method and Meaning in Canadian Environmental History*, edited by Alan MacEachern and William J. Turkel, 124–38. Toronto: Nelson Education, 2008.

– "Introduction: Finding Rural British Columbia." In *Beyond the City Limits: Rural History in British Columbia*, edited by R.W. Sandwell, 3–14. Vancouver: UBC Press, 1999.

– "Rural Reconstruction: Towards a New Synthesis in Canadian History." *Histoire Sociale / Social History* 27, no. 53 (1994): 1–32.

Schama, Simon. *Landscape and Memory*. New York: Knopf, 1995.

Schivelbusch, Wolfgang. *The Railway Journey: The Industrialization of Time and Space in the 19th Century*. Berkeley: University of California Press, 1986.

Schmitt, Peter J. *Back to Nature: The Arcadian Myth in Urban America*. New York: Oxford University Press, 1969.

Scott, James C. *The Art of Not Being Governed: An Anarchist History of Upland Southeast Asia*. New Haven and London: Yale University Press, 2009.

– *Domination and the Arts of Resistance: Hidden Transcripts*. New Haven and London: Yale University Press, 1992.

– *Seeing Like a State: How Certain Schemes to Improve the Human Condition Have Failed*. New Haven, CT: Yale University Press, 1999.

– *Weapons of the Weak: Everyday Forms of Peasant Resistance*. New Haven, CT: Yale University Press, 1987.

Sellers, Christopher C. *Hazards of the Job: From Industrial Disease to Environmental Health Science*. Chapel Hill: University of North Carolina Press, 1997.

Sewell, John. *The Shape of the Suburbs: Understanding Toronto's Sprawl*. Toronto: University of Toronto Press, 2009.

Shi, David E. *The Simple Life: Plain Living and High Thinking in American Culture*. Oxford and New York: Oxford University Press, 1985.

Shields, Rob. *Places on the Margin: Alternative Geographies of Modernity*. London and New York: Routledge, 1991.

Shore, Marlene. *The Science of Social Redemption: McGill, the Chicago School, and the Origins of Social Research in Canada.* Toronto: University of Toronto Press, 1987.

Smith, Donald B. "The Dispossession of the Mississauga Indians: A Missing Chapter in the Early History of Upper Canada." *Ontario History* 73, no. 2 (1981): 67–87.

– "Who Are the Mississauga?." *Ontario History* 67, no. 4 (1975): 211–22.

Spelt, Jacob, and Donald Kerr. *The Changing Face of Toronto – A Study in Urban Geography.* Toronto: Department of Mines and Technical Surveys, Geographical Branch, 1965.

Steinberg, Theodore. "Down to Earth: Nature, Agency, and Power in History." *American Historical Review* 107, no. 3 (2002): 798–820.

– *Nature Incorporated: Industrialization and the Waters of New England.* Cambridge and New York: Cambridge University Press, 1991.

Stewart, Kathleen. *A Space on the Side of the Road.* Princeton, NJ: Princeton University Press, 1996.

Stilgoe, John R. *Borderland: Origins of the American Suburb, 1820–1939.* New Haven and London: Yale University Press, 1988.

– *Metropolitan Corridor: Railroads and the American Scene.* New Haven and London: Yale University Press, 1983.

Stinson, Jeffery. *The Heritage of the Port Industrial District.* Toronto: Toronto Harbour Commissioners, 1990.

Stradling, David, and William Cronon. *Conservation in the Progressive Era: Classic Texts.* Seattle: University of Washington Press, 2004.

Stradling, David, and Richard Stradling. "Perceptions of the Burning River: Deindustrialization and Cleveland's Cuyahoga River." *Environmental History* 13, no. 3 (2008): 515–35.

Stroud, Ellen. "Troubled Waters in Ecotopia: Environmental Racism in Portland, Oregon." *Radical History Review* 74 (1999): 65–95.

Sutherland, Anne. *Gypsies: The Hidden Americans.* London: Tavistock, 1975.

Sway, Marlene. *Familiar Strangers: Gypsy Life in America.* Urbana and Chicago: University of Illinois Press, 1988.

Tarr, Joel A. *Devastation and Renewal.* Pittsburgh, PA: University of Pittsburgh Press, 2005.

– "The Metabolism of the Industrial City: The Case of Pittsburgh." *Journal of Urban History* 28, no. 5 (2002): 511–45.

– *The Search for the Ultimate Sink: Urban Pollution in Historical Perspective.* Akron, OH: University of Akron Press, 1996.

Taylor, C.J. "The Kingston, Ontario Penitentiary and Moral Architecture." *Histoire Sociale / Social History* 12 (1979): 385–407.

Taylor, Griffith. "Topographic Control in the Toronto Region." *Canadian Journal of Economics and Political Science* 2, no. 4 (1936): 493–511.

Thrush, Coll. *Native Seattle: Histories from the Crossing-Over Place*. Seattle: University of Washington Press, 2008.

Toronto Historical Association. *A Glimpse of Toronto's History: Opportunities for the Commemoration of Lost Historic Sites*. Toronto: Toronto Historical Association, 2002.

Trigger, Bruce G., ed. *Handbook of North American Indians*. Vol. 15. Washington, DC: Smithsonian Institution, 1978.

Turkel, William J. *The Archive of Place: Unearthing the Pasts of the Chilcotin Plateau*. Vancouver: UBC Press, 2007.

Valencius, Conevery Bolton. *The Health of the Country: How American Settlers Understood Themselves and Their Land*. New York: Basic Books, 2002.

Vallée, Brian. *Edwin Alonzo Boyd: The Story of the Notorious Boyd Gang*. Toronto: Doubleday, 1997.

Valverde, Mariana. *The Age of Light, Soap, and Water: Moral Reform in English Canada, 1885–1925*. Toronto: McClelland and Stewart, 1991.

van der Merwe, Nikolaas J, Ronald F Williamson, Susan Pfeiffer, Stephen Cox Thomas, and Kim Oakberg Allegretto. "The Moatfield Ossuary: Isotopic Dietary Analysis of an Iroquoian Community, Using Dental Tissue." *Journal of Anthropological Archaeology* 22, no. 3 (2003): 245–61.

van Nostrand, John C. "The Queen Elizabeth Way: Public Utility versus Public Space." *Urban History Review* 12, no. 2 (1983): 1–23.

Wade, Jill. "Home or Homelessness? Marginal Housing in Vancouver, 1886–1950." *Urban History Review* 25, no. 2 (1997): 19–29.

Wall, Sharon. *The Nurture of Nature: Childhood, Antimodernism, and Ontario Summer Camps, 1920–55*. Vancouver: UBC Press, 2009.

Wallace, W. Stewart. "The Hogan Case: The Story of the Murder that Brought Disaster to the Once Notorious Brooks' Bush Gang of Toronto." *MacLean's Magazine*, 15 August 1931.

Weaver, John C. *Crimes, Constables, and Courts: Order and Transgression in a Canadian City, 1816–1970*. Montreal and Kingston: McGill-Queen's University Press, 1995.

– *The Great Land Rush and the Making of the Modern World, 1650–1900*. Montreal and Kingston: McGill-Queen's University Press, 2003.

Webb, James L.A. Jr. *Humanity's Burden: A Global History of Malaria*. Cambridge and New York: Cambridge University Press, 2009.

White, Richard. "Poor Men on Poor Lands: The Back-to-the-Land Movement of the Early Twentieth Century – A Case Study." *Pacific Historical Review* 49 (1980): 105–31.

– *The Organic Machine: The Remaking of the Columbia River*. New York: Hill and Wang, 1995.

White, Richard W. "The Growth Plan for the Greater Golden Horseshoe in Historical Perspective." Neptis Foundation, December 2007.

– *Urban Infrastructure and Urban Growth in the Toronto Region: 1950s to the 1990s*. Toronto: Neptis Foundation, 2003. http://www.neptis.org/publications/growth-plan-greater-golden-horseshoe-historical-perspective (accessed 24 June 2014).

Williams, Raymond. *Problems in Materialism and Culture: Selected Essays*. London: Verso, 1980.

– *The Country and the City*. New York and Oxford: Oxford University Press, 1973.

Williamson, Ronald F. "Before the Visitors." In *Toronto: An Illustrated History of Its First 12,000 Years*, edited by Ronald F. Williamson, 25–52. Toronto: James Lorimer, 2008.

Wood, J. David. *Making Ontario: Agricultural Colonization and Landscape Re-creation before the Railway*. Montreal and Kingston: McGill-Queen's University Press, 2000.

Woods, Mark. "Ecological Restoration and the Renewal of Wildness and Freedom." In *Recognizing the Autonomy of Nature: Theory and Practice*, 170–88. New York: Columbia University Press, 2005.

Worster, Donald. "Transformations of the Earth: Toward an Agroecological Perspective in History." *Journal of American History* 76, no. 4 (1990): 1087–1106.

Index

224n5; literature by, 116, 120–1. *See also* Sauriol, Charles

Cousins, E.L., 67, 214n76

CPR. *See* Canadian Pacific Railway Co.

currents, Lake Ontario. *See* Ontario, Lake

Cuyahoga River, xxii, 58, 123, 134, 211n33

dams, on Don River, xx, 128, 164; and Don River Improvement Project, 66; and milling, 19, 53–4, 71.

Davies, Thomas, 56, 58–9

Davies, William, 35, 206n21

deforestation, 20–2, 28, 46, 52, 72, 122, 200n48.

deindustrialization, xxv, 136, 178–9, 186–7

disease: and environment, 24–6, 76, 78, 80–1; germ theory of, 43, 204n11; and isolation hospitals, 85–7; miasmatic theory of, 41; mortality rates from, in Toronto, 38, 43; and sewage pollution, 37–8, 41–3, 45, 216n91. *See also* cholera; malaria; typhoid fever

Don Breakwater, ix, 48, 50

Don Improvement project. *See* Don River Improvement Project

Don Jail. *See* Toronto Jail

Don Mills (industrial community), 18–19; (suburb), 121, 155–7, 156(f), 161

Don Narrows, 172, 186

Don River: Aboriginal names for, 11; access to, 132, 136, 192; branches of, xix; and the "Don problem," 43, 45, 55, 73, 185; and Don Valley Parkway route, 152, 153(f), 159; drownings in, 52, 53; flow levels,

19–20, 164; naming of, 11; perfume in, xv–xviii; size of, xxii; tributaries of, xix–xx, 6, 13, 53, 87, 196n10; watershed of, xiv(m), xix–xx, 6, 72, 121, 193, 241n8. *See also entries below*; Don Narrows; Forks of the Don; Taylor-Massey Creek; *specific topics*

Don River Improvement Project, xxviii, 60–1(f), 65(m), 69(m); bills/ by-laws associated with, 59; and Canadian Pacific Railway, 58–9, 70, 72, 212n54; compared to Lower Don Lands project, 180, 186; construction of, 59–61; costs of, 62–3, 72; and Cuyahoga River improvements, 58; and disputes between city and Harbour Trust, 55, 60, 66, 73–4; and Don Diversion, 64, 66–7, 74; and Don Improvement Co., 57–8; environmental effects of, 72–3; expropriations for, 57, 59, 62–3; extent of, 55, 59–60, 60–1(f); failures of, 70–4; and Keating Channel, 67, 69(m), 72; modifications to, 64, 66, 67; rationale for, 55–7; and riverside property values, 56, 57, 70; timing of, 61–2. *See also* flooding; industries/industrialization; sewage; unemployed workers; wastes, disposal of Don River Valley: agricultural potential of, 23, 27, 31, 33, 81, 83, 85; as barrier to eastward expansion, xxiii–xxiv; as corridor for transportation, xxiii–xxiv, xxviii, 9, 59, 129, 139, 154–5, 164, 171, 192; sensory experience of, 170; use of by Aboriginal peoples, xxi, 10–13; as wasteland, 30–1, 76–9, 87, 111–12, 132, 164, 190; as wilderness, xxi, xxv, 115, 119, 123–4, 132,

Forks of the Don, xiv(m), xix, 6, 136;
and river geology, 6; and Sauriol
cottage, 113, 115, 118, 118(f), 130(f)

gangs. *See* Brooks Bush Gang
Gardiner, Frederick: as advocate
for federated municipal council,
142–3, 160–1; as advocate for
urban expressways, 129, 140, 143,
158, 171; as Chair of Metro Council, 140, 143, 160, 171; character
of, 159–61; conflict with planners,
158–9; and Don Valley Parkway,
129, 140, 143, 157–60, 167, 171; and
high modernism, 159–60; perceptions of Don Valley, 129, 164, 166;
as reeve of Forest Hill, 142, 160;
retirement of, 171; and subway-
expressway debate, 158–9, 231n34
Gardiner Expressway, xiv(m), 140,
162, 163, 166, 170, 178
glaciation, xix, 4, 6, 12
Gooderham & Worts Distillery, 34(f),
91, 207n35, 207n40; cattle byres
of, xxviii, 28–30, 31, 34(f), 38–42,
203n3, 204n4; lawsuits against,
40–2, 208n42
government breakwater, 42, 50, 51(f),
66, 185, 269(f)
government "park." *See entry below*
government reserve, 7, 8(f), 14, 23,
26–7, 75, 201n60
Grand Trunk Railway, 31, 33, 34(f), 35,
36(f), 49(f), 66, 71, 215n80; bridge
over Don River, 53, 55, 60, 64
Great Depression, 104–7, 108–9(f),
110–12, 120, 223n90
Great Lakes, xxii–xxiii, 7, 9
greenbelts, xx, 142; and Don Valley
Parkway design, 140, 154, 158,

166–7; and 1943 *Master Plan*, 128,
150, 151(f), 152
grist mills. *See* milling
groundwater, xx, 20, 121, 193
GTR. *See* Grand Trunk Railway
gypsies. *See* Roma

Harbour Trust, the, 211n27, 214n74;
conflict with Toronto City Council,
45, 55, 60, 66, 73–4; and Don
Diversion project, 64, 66, 74. *See
also* Toronto harbour; Toronto
Harbour Commission
hazardous materials, storage of in
Don Valley, 33, 205n16
health. *See* public health
hills, levelling of: for Don River
Improvement, 72; for Don Valley
Parkway, 139, 164, 165(f), 166
"hoboes," xxix, 98, 105–7, 108–9(f),
110–12
Hogan, John Sheridan, 77, 90–4, 96
Hogg's Hollow, xx
Holland Landing, 9
homelessness, 75, 77–9, 94–8, 105,
216n6, 221n66. *See also* Brooks
Bush Gang; "hoboes;" Roma
hospitals, isolation, 76–7, 86–7. *See
also* Toronto General Hospital
Humber River: and Carrying Place
Trail, xxii–xxiii, 7, 9; compared to
Don River, xxii–xxiii; and expressway plans, 143; and
greenbelt plans, 128, 150, 151(f),
152, 227n39; industrialization
of, xxiii, 18; parkland along, 161;
Roma encampments on, 99–101;
use of by Aboriginal peoples,
xxiii, 10; watershed, xiv(m), xxii,
196n13